TERRORISM IN THE LATE VICTORIAN NOVEL

Terrorism in the Late Victorian Novel

BARBARA ARNETT MELCHIORI

CROOM HELM
London ● Sydney ● Dover, New Hampshire

© 1985 Barbara Arnett Melchiori
Croom Helm Ltd, Provident House, Burrell Row,
Beckenham, Kent BR3 1AT
Croom Helm Australia Pty Ltd, Suite 4, 6th Floor,
64–76 Kippax Street, Surry Hills, NSW 2010, Australia

British Library Cataloguing in Publication Data

Melchiori, Barbara Arnett
  Terrorism in the late Victorian novel.
  1. English fiction — 19th century
  2. Terrorism in literature
  I. Title
  823′.8′09355   PR830.T4

  ISBN 0-7099-3583-8

Croom Helm Ltd, 51 Washington Street,
Dover, New Hampshire, 03820 USA

Library of Congress Cataloging in Publication Data

Melchiori, Barbara Arnett, 1926-
  Terrorism in the late Victorian novel.

  Includes index.
  1. English fiction—19th century—History and
criticism. 2. Terrorism in literature. 3. Radicalism
in literature. 4. Social movements in literature.
5. Social problems in literature. 6. Terrorism—
History—19th century. I. Title.
  PR878.T47M45 1985   823′.8′09358   85-14923
  ISBN 0-7099-3583-8

Phototypeset by Sunrise Setting, Torquay, Devon
Printed and bound in Great Britain by
Billing & Sons Limited, Worcester.

CONTENTS

for MURIEL BRADBROOK

FOREWORD

The five great terrorist massacres in Italy in recent years, Piazza Fontana (Milan), Piazza della Loggia (Brescia), the Italicus train explosion, the Bologna Station explosion and, as this book is going to press, the Naples-Milan train explosion in a tunnel under the Apennines, together with day-to-day violence in the schools and universities and in the streets and piazzas, had led me to a reflection concerning the patterns of violence, the forces which manipulate and arm single terrorist groups, and how the panic caused by terrorist activity, intended by the activists themselves to weaken and topple a social system, can be used instead to strengthen it, rallying uncritical support round the existing forces of law and order, and slowing down the processes of change.

It was with amazement that during the same years, dipping into little-known and forgotten novels of the late nineteenth century, I discovered the same patterns of violence, the same massacre of innocent victims, the same channelling of panic to create widespread support for existing governments. I began to see that it was all happening over again, and that the only progress lay in the greater technical efficiency of the means of terrorism. Shelter, in the name of that much abused word – freedom – is still provided by many nations to terrorists who are wreaking havoc in others; arms and financial support are being furnished to idealists blind to the way in which their revolutionary fervour is being manipulated; the secret services of all totalitarian and of many democratic countries are manoeuvring terrorist activists outside the reach of any parliamentary control, and the list of innocent victims mounts yearly higher.

Terrorists are rarely enlisted among the dispossessed: rather they spring up (now as in the nineteenth century) among the young in the educated classes, goaded into disgust by the cynicism, exploitation and corruption of the powers they desire to overthrow, or lashed by religious fervour. The movements created by such idealists also attract the psychologically fragile and megalomaniacs, but it is a common error to see these as prime movers.

Studying contemporary reactions to the dynamitards of one hundred years ago in the press but above all in fiction, has helped me to realise that terrorists are often puppets dangling at the end of very long wires, wires so long that we lose sight of the hands that hold them. It was to one such terrorist *in nuce* that Henry James, a writer highly sensitive to what he called 'feelings about aspects', speaking through Madame Grandoni, made an appeal to which I can only subscribe again today:

> I gathered the other night that you're one of the young men who want everything changed — I believe there are a great many in Italy and also in my own dear old Deutschland, and who even think it useful to throw bombs into innocent crowds and shoot pistols at their rulers or at any one . . . But before you go any further please think a little whether you're right.

What I call dynamite novels constitute a hitherto unnoticed current in late nineteenth century fiction. The isolation of this new genre has led me not only to investigate the social history of the Eighties and Nineties, but has also shown me more clearly how the popular novelist collects and uses his material, and how he is both mirroring the social scene and, by highlighting certain aspects of contemporary events, is contributing to form, as well as to reflect, public opinion. Almost all his material was gathered from the press, not only from the day-to-day reports of dynamite outrages and of the panic which they caused, but from articles in the weeklies, monthlies and quarterlies, which analysed this new phenomenon. Interviews with leading terrorist theoreticians themselves were interspersed with statements by authorities in the State and even in the Church to provide the novelist with his background. With very few exceptions (notably Philip May, Grant Allen and the early George Moore) the novelists put across to their readers in more subtle forms the message which they received from the newspapers, acting as *media* in the way we understand the term today. Most of the forty-odd writers I have been considering here were highly skilled professionals, turning out at least one novel per year, and it is my contention that they contributed in no small measure, through the slant which they gave to public opinion, to reinforce the powers that be, and to breed suspicion of the rapidly spreading movements toward socialism.

This, I should add, was the conclusion but certainly not the starting point of my book, for I set out simply to read as widely as possible, to enjoy, present and examine this fascinating new stream, admittedly a very minor one, in the history of the Victorian novel.

Rome, 24 February 1985

ACKNOWLEDGEMENTS

Cambridge, where almost all the material used for the preparation of this book is housed, has, since 1981 when I started plunging deep into dynamite, been the place where most of my work has been done. I am grateful to the staff and members of Clare Hall where there is time for conversation and where innumerable suggestions were offered, and to members of the English faculty who from their wide reading threw out tempting leads. I am grateful too to the staff of the Cambridge University Library who tirelessly and rapidly at my request disturbed the dust on many forgotten nineteenth century novels, and particularly to Janice Fairholm who has followed my work with constant interest. Darko Suvin, in his frequent visits to the old world, allowed me to delve in the bibliography of his work in progress with the generosity of a true scholar. Giorgio Melchiori as always has brought a critical eye and correcting hand to bear on my writing. The Italian Ministry of Education, the Consiglio Nazionale delle Ricerche and the University of Rome, by partially financing research projects on the Victorian novel, have contributed towards the expenses incurred during long periods of reading in England.

1 INFERNAL MACHINES

The dynamite outrages of the past year cost the country a pretty large sum. The amount, as shown by the recently prepared Civil Service Estimates, is close upon £50,000 . . . In the previous year only £12,000 was expended under this head.

These figures, published in the *Pall Mall Gazette* of 4 March 1886, give us today an idea of the escalation of dynamite terrorism over the preceding two years. A graph of this expenditure rise would show a slope of four in one. This does not mean that the risk of being blown sky high in England, or even in London, was four times greater in 1885 than in 1884: part of the extra expenditure went to reinforce the police, and on other preventive measures. Even the new technology of electricity was enlisted. At a time when street illumination was still by gaslight, measures were taken to light up possible targets more effectively so as to make the work of the dynamitard less easy. Under the title 'Electric Light versus Dynamite' the same newspaper published a report of the precautions taken by the authorities for the protection of the Houses of Parliament which involved a constant watch kept from the river:

> . . . an interesting series of experiments was conducted last night to ascertain the applicability of the electric light generated by the Skrivanow battery to the service required . . . The power developed is very great, for when the battery was attached to an arc lamp of 600 candles nominal a beam of light was thrown from the police steam-launch . . .[1]

Probably this beam of light playing over the Houses of Parliament from a boat in the river was one of the very first searchlights ever to be used.

Much of the expenditure went, however, to the repair of public buildings, of which an unprecedented number had been damaged in 1884-5. There was a fresh wave of explosions, although less dramatic in its results, in the early 1890s, but we have to turn to the 1970s and our own days to find anything comparable to what happened in England, and particularly in London, in what I would call the year of the dynamitards.

The invention by Nobel of dynamite in 1863, and of the fulminate of mercury detonating process in 1867 put a great new power into the hands of civil engineers. Mining and quarrying became more rapid, if more dangerous, blasting cleared the way for new roads and railways, and there was serious talk in the 1880s of both a Channel tunnel linking England and France and a tunnel across the Irish Sea (an Anglo-Irish Channel tunnel figures largely in one of the dynamite novels set in the future: Fred Burnaby's *Our Radicals*).[2]

Dynamite, this new material, was relatively easy and inexpensive to manufacture, and small groups or even individuals could handle the greatest destructive force ever before known in the history of civilisation. While the conspirators of the Gunpowder plot had calculated that they would require 36 barrels of gunpowder to blow up the Houses of Parliament, the conspirators of the late nineteenth century could hope to conceal enough dynamite to achieve the same result in the black (or sometimes brown) bag which was to become so dear to the novelist. It might, as one enterprising journalist suggested, probably to the distress of Scotland Yard, be concealed in a lady's dress-improver or bustle, and a conspirator disguised as a lady could easily pass the vigilance of the guards at the entrance to any public building. No thought that a real lady might perhaps be willing to participate apparently entered the journalist's head, and this in spite of reports from Russia and the Continent that women were taking an active part in such plots.

This new and hitherto unprecedented destructive force could, then, be manufactured and transported with relative ease, though at considerable personal risk, especially as the whole question of timers was at an experimental stage, but total dedication to his task has always been the strong point of the political assassin or dynamitard. When novelists turned their attention, as they very soon did, to this new rich vein of plot material this was perhaps the aspect which most interested them: the psychology of the conspirator. What kind of a man was he? How did he get involved in such diabolical and dastardly (the adjectives are contemporary) enterprises?

The question of involvement linked up very conveniently for the novelists with what was by now familiar material of the Victorian novel: the social question. Before the development of what we today term the media, the novel and the newspaper together satisfied a whole range of requirements which are now dealt with by television:

documentary, interviews, debates. It is true that the novel then was much more immediate in its impact than now, often being serialised during the actual process of writing, the author keeping up with his or her weekly or monthly instalments; and even when first published in book form an established author would be correcting the proofs of Volumes one and two, while finishing off Volume three. Reviews followed immediately upon publication, and the author felt much more in touch with his readers then than is possible today. Many novels incorporate essays on subjects directly linked with the theme or message of the book, and sometimes the reader is obligingly informed that the following chapter may be skipped[3] if he merely wants to get on with the story. Other novels incorporate the complete text of a sermon (this is surprisingly enough the case of an early novel by George Bernard Shaw[4]), while all good Victorian novels contain a formidable stock of accurate information.

To observe, to interpret and to teach, as well as to entertain, were the duties nineteenth-century novelists set themselves. All these, even observation, are selective processes when working for the media. The social question had been central for many of the Victorian novels of the early and middle period: Disraeli's *Sybil or The Two Nations*, Mrs Gaskell's *Mary Barton* and *North and South*, Charlotte Brontë's *Shirley*, Charles Kingsley's *Alton Locke*, Dickens's *Hard Times* and George Eliot's *Felix Holt, the Radical* were all directly concerned (as were many others) with class violence and confrontation. They dealt with conspiracies in plenty, and stress was laid by the novelists on the binding oaths which held the plotters together, deterring defaulters. The struggle in all cases was unequal; the forces of insurrection were armed for the most part with sticks and stones or their wooden clogs, a picturesque detail the novelists were quick to seize on, while the troops called out against them had guns.

The most deadly weapon of the masses was in fact arson, which was used in agricultural riots against the single farmstead with its easily accessible and inflammable haystacks, but which they were afraid to use in the towns, for fire could soon get out of control and spread among their own closely packed dwelling places. In mid-century water supplies were scarce and fire-fighting equipment primitive, so that fire was as often as not the accidental outcome of the violent occupation and defence of buildings rather than a deliberate insurrectionist policy. In *Sybil* we have a good example of how popular leaders were presented as unable to restrain their followers:

looting and drunkenness led to the total destruction of Mowbray Castle by fire.

By the 1880s the pattern of public order, and of public disorder, had changed. Municipal police forces on a full-time basis (the 'peelers') were now responsible for patrolling the streets and protecting alike public buildings and public figures. Mass protest movements were being organised by the socialists, particularly H. M. Hyndman's Social Democratic Federation which grew rapidly with the growth of discontent springing from a fresh wave of unemployment, and from the attempt of employers to decrease wages as the demand abroad for British exports fell. Not all the workers felt like meeting their employers' pleas of reduced profits with the abnegation shown by a group of Sheffield workers on 23 March 1885, widely publicised in the national press, perhaps in the hope that their example would be followed elsewhere:

> The puddlers and millmen in the employ of Messrs. William Cooke & Co. of Sheffield, sent a deputation to the manager to say that, being aware of the difficulties under which the Company laboured in consequence of the stagnation in the iron-trade, they agreed to do a week's work for nothing.[5]

They seem to have been a lone example of such self-sacrifice, for only a week later the *Annual Register* reports that nearly half the colliers in South and West Yorkshire, numbering about 30,000, went out on strike against a ten per cent reduction in wages. Food was cheap at the time, as employers kept pointing out, bread prices had dropped steadily with the policy of free trade and restriction of protectionism, but the living conditions of the miners were not such that a 10 per cent reduction could be accepted as tolerable. Even though the workers of Messrs Cooke & Co. were offering one week's free work to their firm, obviously, with the very limited possibilities that a worker had of saving, their offer would hardly be extended further and there is no report in the press that it was. Very probably it was only a last-ditch effort to avoid a permanent wage reduction.

The core of social unrest in the 1880s lay in the increasing difficulties of British industry in finding export outlets in a world market where there was mounting competition to be faced from other more recently industrialised countries, particularly Germany and America, which were often ahead in technological development where British firms were making do with older machinery. The situation was far from desperate in that Britain enjoyed highly privileged trade relations with the Empire, but still a recession had set in. The growth of unemployment reduced the negotiating power of the unions and class conflict became more and more bitter.

Were these embittered and sometimes desperate people potential dynamitards? History has answered very clearly in the negative: they were not. All the major dynamite outrages in England were traced to the Fenians, many of whom were caught and condemned. What is so interesting to us today is that public opinion, the middle-class public opinion which dominated the existing media of the newspaper and the novel, treated this question so ambiguously.

Chemistry had placed in the hands of a few individuals a destructive force which could threaten both the persons and the places of existing institutions. It is difficult to realise today, when the powers of destruction have advanced so much further, and when any one of us who stops to think knows that we are threatened by nuclear annihilation, how frightened Victorian writers and readers were of the use that could be made of dynamite. Henry James, in *The Princess Casamassima*, sums up this feeling of imminent peril:

> Nothing of it appears above the surface; but there's an immense underworld peopled with a thousand forms of revolutionary passion and devotion. The manner in which it's organised is what astonished me. I knew that, or thought I knew it, in a general way, but the reality was a revelation. And on top of it all society lives. People go and come, and buy and sell, and drink and dance, and make money and make love, and seem to know nothing and suspect nothing and think of nothing; and iniquities flourish, and the misery of half the world is prated about as a 'necessary evil,' and generations rot away and starve in the midst of it, and day follows day, and everything is for the best in the best of possible worlds. All that's one half of it; the other half is that everything's doomed! In silence, in darkness, but under the feet of each one of us, the revolution lives and works. It's a wonderful, immeasurable trap, on the lid of which society performs its antics. When once the machinery is complete there will be a great rehearsal.[6]

Even discounting the fact that this speech is spoken by Hyacinth, the little bookbinder, in order to keep the attention of the Princess firmly focused on the plotters, and upon himself in particular, it is one of the best descriptions to be found of the sense of foreboding and of threat, and of a great upheaval from underneath, which pervaded intellectuals in the dynamite years. *The Princess Casamassima* was in the writing just after the London dynamite outrages of 1885 and during the Hyde Park mass protest meetings and Piccadilly rioting of 1886, so that it reflects perhaps better than any other novel this tendency to confuse the external Fenian threat with internal social protest.

In Europe and America in the second half of the nineteenth century (and indeed until the First World War) there were a number of subversive movements active in different countries, with very specific and clearly distinguished aims, but all working to replace the existing form of government, where necessary by violence. The pattern of their activities is complex, partly because they often operated in small groups relatively free from any central command (so that it was difficult for the governing authorities to destroy their networks: where no network existed, none could be destroyed), and these operational splinter groups were naturally liable to split ideologically from their matrix; and partly because they received outside support, in the forms of fund-raising and political asylum, from countries which had a political interest in causing embarrassment to their neighbours.

The biggest, most active and most strongly motivated group was that of the Russian Nihilists. Living under an autocracy which had only recently emerged from the feudal system, they were in rebellion not only against the Czar of all the Russias but against the cruel bureaucracy of a host of minor officials who could impose civil exile without even the privilege of a court trial, and civil exile in Russia meant Siberia. Many thousands whose only crime was to be the relative or friend of a political exile were banished yearly in this way, often for life, although such life sentences were usually of extremely brief duration. The Nihilists, when identified by the Czar's police, often took refuge abroad, and were welcomed in France and Britain, both of which countries were alarmed by the advance of the Czar in Afghanistan (dangerously near British India) and who were only too happy that he should be harassed at home, even when this harassment took the form of political assassination, as in the case of Alexander II on 13 March 1880. Nihilist writers such as Prince Kropotkin and 'Stepniak', the cover name of S. M. Kravchinsky, were welcomed as contributors to such respectable

British journals as the *Nineteenth Century*, the *Fortnightly Review*, the *Pall Mall Gazette*, the *Contemporary Review*, and did much to build up international support for their movement by revealing the total suppression of human rights in Russia, under which their fellow countrymen were living, and, all too often, dying.

The second subversive group was the Fenians. It is interesting that they came from one of the smallest, while the Nihilists came from the largest of European countries, but their motivation was none the less strong. They were fighting for the political independence of their country, and had also a long history of oppression behind them. Certainly they lived under British rule and could always appeal to a court of law, which court could neither condemn them to the knout or to a term of exile in Siberia: the judges were, however, drawn from the land-owning classes, and as for the most part appeals were appeals against evictions it was extremely unlikely that the appeal would be upheld, so that the legal guarantee of civil rights often failed to include a guarantee of the elementary human right of freedom from starvation. Although from a small country they had the tacit support of a big one. Fenian aggressions in England in the 1880s were planned and financed by Irish immigrants in the United States through two militant organisations, O'Donovan Rossa's Skirmishers and the *Clan na Gael*. Despite appeals from Britain for the extradition of dynamite criminals, the government of the United States turned a deaf ear, just as Britain was doing to the Czar. Bartholdi's Statue of Liberty arrived in New York on 19 June 1885 where it was received with a great display of enthusiasm: it was officially inaugurated on 28 October of the following year. It was no moment to be requesting extraditions, although official deploration of the dynamite outrages in London was not lacking. The Irish were one of the most powerful political groups in the United States, and the idea of an independent Ireland friendly to the States was not unattractive, close to the shores of a major rival in trade. In this way political and economic considerations cut across class considerations which might have encouraged governments to stick together in suppressing subversives. A government agreement to this end had in fact been signed between Russia and Germany, and after the dynamite outrages in London the Czar made a further unsuccessful attempt to draw Britain into an extradition pact of this kind.

The third and more ubiquitous and elusive group were the anarchists. They worked side by side with the Nihilists in Russia, although remaining ideologically distinct, and with the French Communards, and were active besides in Germany, Belgium, Italy, Spain, Portugal and Switzerland during the last 20 years of the nineteenth century.

While the Nihilists were directing their violence predominantly against public figures (Alexander II himself had been attacked in 1866, 1867 and 1879 before the final successful attempt in 1880, and governors of provinces, generals and high government officials were a constant target), the Fenians' main objectives were public buildings symbolising the authority of the state which they were repudiating. In both cases members of the public were involved, but were presumably not the intended targets. When visitors to the Tower of London were injured a great outcry was made because the bomb had been placed there on a Saturday afternoon when sightseers were plentiful. Yet it is doubtful whether the moment was not chosen rather because it was easier to avoid the vigilance of the beefeaters by placing the explosive at a time when the Tower was swarming with visitors.

The anarchists, instead, were more ruthless: bombs were thrown into crowded cafés, into restaurants, into opera houses. Naturally enough none of the subversives had any tenderness for the forces of order — police and soldiers, seen as actively supporting the hated institutions, were both natural enemies and natural victims, and a large number fell in the pursuit of duty.

What was the impact of this new material on the novel? Some of the answers to this question are surprising. The writers did not all succeed in keeping the various historical strands of subversion disentangled. A bomb is a bomb, it explodes or it does not, and either way it can often make a good story. The divergence between fact and fiction is most obvious in the attribution of attempts within the British Isles. These, in so far as they were organised at all (some of them were the work of individualists, for even the dynamite faction had its lunatic fringe), were organised by the Fenians. Yet the dynamite novelists of the 1880s and 1890s for the most part were inclined to attribute their fictional attempts to rather vaguely defined anarchists or, occasionally, Nihilists and socialists. Very different is the stand taken by Irish writers who, however pacifist and anti-violence the declarations of the narrator may be, are willing and even eager to shoulder their national responsibility.

The reason can, I believe, only be the wish, conscious or otherwise, to keep the condition of Ireland question out of the novel *qua* media. Whereas Irish writers, whether supporters of Union, Home

Rule or Separation were anxious to bring the question to public debate, the English novelist fought shy of the whole Irish problem and tried to keep it in the background. The real fear of the middle-class writers was, as Henry James so clearly shows, a fear of what was felt to be an inevitable and impending class struggle. The Irish question was only one aspect of this, confused by religious issues and conveniently isolated across the Irish Sea. What the novelist was tending to do was to take the popular fear of explosions, with their threat to life and property, and to canalise this fear so as to build up resistance to the whole socialist movement, which was rapidly growing just at this time. The fact that the socialists were using the traditional and legitimate method of mass demonstrations, and the less legitimate though equally traditional aggression of stone throwing and window breaking, was overlooked.

This tendency by English novelists to identify and confuse socialists and anarchists was largely due to biased press reporting. Every effort was made, not only by the conservative *The Times* but even by the radical *Pall Mall Gazette*, to publicise contacts between socialists and anarchists. The meetings held from time to time in Paris and Zurich, attended by delegations of anarchists, Nihilists, Fenians and socialists were given wide coverage, increasing the reader's sense of an international conspiracy for the overthrow of the Establishment. The fact that the various groups spent much of their time quarrelling even violently among themselves and that such meetings almost always led to the forcible ejection of at least one party, made much less impression on contemporary readers than the feeling that they were being plotted against, that their lives were at risk, their values at stake and their property in imminent danger of confiscation or destruction.

The Victorians were deeply shocked by the dynamite outrages in London. Wilful damage to life and property has no longer the power to shock a post-Hiroshima generation in the same way: we have to remember how long London had been safe, that two hundred years had passed since even the Great Fire, and that the dynamite explosions directed against their most cherished institutions seemed to give the whole of the existing structure of society a premonitory shake. It takes an effort to understand why the whole question of social reform, hopefully leading to social justice, must have seemed so threatening. It was after all to lead, in its best moments, to the creation many years later of the Welfare State. If in the nineteenth century things were not for the best in the best of all possible worlds, yet for the Victorian upper and middle classes who were the opinion makers, they might easily have been a good deal worse. Every gentleman knew something at least of the working conditions enjoyed by his dependents; every lady had some idea of the working hours of her housemaids. What they were afraid of was a reversal of the situation — they were unable to imagine a revolution in which the exploited would not become the exploiters, and the press of the Establishment did much to foster this fear. Every possible connection between socialists and anarchists was therefore given maximum publicity, and the novelists were ready to give a helping hand. The Fenian bombs of fact became the anarchist bombs of fiction — there were plenty of such outrages in Europe at the time to give verisimilitude to such an attribution; the newspapers were full of alarming reports.

A brief survey of the press and of the *Annual Register* for the crucial years should help to give an idea of how it was the novelists of the 1880s and 1890s were encouraged to deal with these new acts of social violence, sometimes as part of their plot structure, sometimes as material for debate. I should add that it is impossible to draw a rigid distinction between those novels which use the new material of dynamite and those which use the old-fashioned gunpowder or revolver of the political assassin. Dynamitards themselves were no purists — they used the material which came most readily to hand. The assassination of the Czar, Alexander II, for instance, was planned by mining the route along which his carriage was expected to pass, but when the carriage took a different direction as it frequently did (only a few months had passed since an attempt to blow up the Czar on the Moscow railway had been foiled because the train with his luggage went over the line first[7]) the Nihilist activists were ready with an alternative plan. A woman conspirator gave the sign of the change of route, and as his carriage passed along the banks of the Catherine Canal a dynamite bomb, thrown by a man named Ryssakoff, burst beneath the carriage, wounding a cossack and some onlookers. The Emperor was unhurt, but had no sooner got down from his carriage than another bomb was thrown which killed both the Czar and the student who threw it. This assassination, on 13 March 1880, of one of the most powerful autocrats in the contemporary world, really touched off the first great wave of European political assassinations.

Queen Victoria herself was not exempt from such attempts. The first on 29 February 1872 in fact involved her in no danger. Her assailant was a 17-year-old Irishman who, as she was about to alight from her carriage at Buckingham Palace, raised a pistol as he presented a petition to the Queen. She was greatly frightened as she was rather ashamed to admit afterwards, crying 'Help, Save me!' The extract from her journal of the same day reports the motive of the petition:

> When I was standing in the hall, General Hardinge came in, bringing an extraordinary document which this boy had intended making me sign! It was in connection with the Fenian prisoners . . . The pistol had not been loaded, but it easily might have been![8]

One curious detail emerges later from the Queen's journal, where she records Mr Bruce's report on the trial of her assailant, Arthur O'Connor:

> As yet there is no evidence either of his connection with the Fenians, or of his being employed as the instrument of others. But further enquiry may possibly throw some light on the origin of his daring and abominable design.[9]

The petition for the imprisoned Fenians seems to have disappeared from the evidence, yet the Queen had seen it with her own eyes. The youth was given an exemplary sentence.

A later attempt was much more dangerous, but the Queen was proud to discover that she was much less frightened than she had been on the previous occasion, ten years earlier. A shot was fired by a certain Maclean on 2 March 1882, as she was driving off from Windsor station. He was caught and sent after his trial to an asylum. The Queen's journal entry for this day records her taking tea and telegraphing 'to all my children and near relations'.[10] She then took a walk to the Mausoleum, in an attempt, it may be supposed, to communicate in some more direct way with Albert. This second attack on Queen Victoria, harmless as it proved in the issue, was yet unsettling, coming as it did only two years after the assassination of the Czar and one year after that of President Garfield of the United States. He was shot on 2 July 1881 in Washington as he was about to take the train for New York, and mortally wounded, though he did not die for 17 days, and seemed for some time to be on the road to recovery. As in the case of the attempts on Queen Victoria, the assassination was the act of a loner and had nothing to do with anarchist activity.

These top-level outrages took place in 1880, 1881 and 1882. In the same years news came through of Nihilist assassinations in Russia: General Stretnikoff at Odessa in 1882 and Colonel Soudaikin the chief of the secret police in 1883. Soudaikin's assassination offered promising material for fiction: the head of the Society for Active Resistance against Terrorists was killed by Degayeff, a former Nihilist who had become a tool of the police. Degayeff was used as a decoy to bring Nihilists to his house where their meetings could be watched by the police, but whether his role as informer got too hot for him, or whether he had all along been playing a double game and only made a pretence of collaborating with the secret police, he lured Soudaikin to his house and shot both him and his nephew while they were drinking tea. This assassination may well have been behind the plot structure of Arthur and Mary Ropes's *On Peter's Island*[11] written much later in 1901. The general feeling in England seems to have been at the time that these were distant events (with the exception of the shooting at Queen Victoria when nobody was hurt) and as there was trade and territorial friction with both Russia and America they gave no great cause for concern.

Explosions were to come nearer home in 1881 with an attack in March on Mansion House, the residence of the Lord Mayor, an attack repeated again in May 1882, and three dynamite attacks in Glasgow on January 1883, followed by more serious attacks in London, both on Whitehall and the offices of *The Times* in March 1883. The damage caused by these explosions was limited in extent, although public alarm was aroused, particularly among the police and the Home Office which was responsible for security, and counter-measures were set on foot. The vulnerability of Londoners was brought home to them even more forcibly in two dynamite explosions which took place in the London Underground, at Praed Street between the stations of Charing Cross and Westminster, on 30 October 1883. The *Pall Mall Gazette* of 31 October commented drily: 'The explosions on the Underground Railway last evening, though fortunately attended with no loss of life, were very alarming and will add a new horror to an already disagreeable mode of locomotion.'

Then came the year of the dynamitards, 1884-5.[12] This began with a great explosion on 25 February 1884, at Victoria Station, and two days later it was revealed that the damage had been intended to be much greater, for similar infernal machines were found by the police to have been placed in Charing Cross, Paddington and Ludgate Hill stations with clockwork detonators set to explode simultaneously. The choice of objectives seems to have been guided by practical considerations. The large quantities of dynamite required could best be transported in the form of luggage, and could also most conveniently be placed in the left-luggage office, without exciting any suspicion. The explosion was heard for miles around, and reporters were soon on the spot to fill the newspapers next morning with details which were to prove invaluable to the next generation of novelists. Under the revealing title: 'Dynamite Destruction at Victoria. Great Destruction of Property' the *Pall Mall Gazette* of 26 February 1884 carried a long account of which only extracts can be given here.

> A terrible explosion occurred at Victoria station this morning, shortly after one o'clock, in one of the cloak-rooms, and there is reason to believe that another dynamite outrage has been committed. The scene of the explosion was the main line department of the London, Brighton, and South Coast Railway situate in the centre of the station yard, and to that section of the station fortunately its destructive effects were confined . . .
>
> The clock in the booking-office having stopped, shows that it was four minutes past one o'clock when the explosion took place . . . Suddenly, the night inspector and his hands, while standing at a distance of from twenty to thirty yards from the cloak-room, experienced a severe shock, and were alarmed by a sound similar to that emitted from a small cannon, 'a red sort of flash,' to use the words of Mr Manning, the night inspector, assisting to vivify this impression. 'It was,' Mr Manning states, 'as if a small cannon had been fired out of the window of the cloak-room up the platform. Everything fell in an instant and it was as quiet as possible afterwards.' . . . 'For the moment,' said Mr Manning 'I was shook up and regular stupefied, and my two men were the same.'

We note the stopped clock, and realism fostered by verbatim accounts in faulty grammar, and then on the following days more details of the luggage in which the dynamite was stored: the package brown in colour and a canvas-covered portmanteau of foreign make:

A cloak-room porter on the main line side named Thomas has described the luggage which came into the cloak-room on the previous night. It included a package very heavy for its size, and handled with great care by the person who left it. The package, brown in colour, must have been about fifteen inches in length, a foot broad, and a foot deep. Moreover, the man gave in a canvas-covered portmanteau of what Thomas thought was a foreign make. This was larger and longer than the one first mentioned, but was relatively lighter in weight. The other articles deposited by this man, the witness thought, were two boxes. On taking up the heavy small bag he was told by the man to be very careful about it. The witness put the other parcels on the top of it. The passenger, or presumed passenger, requested him not to do so, but to put them on the floor separately but close together.[13]

Certainly, reading this report today, we realise how far the porter was from expecting dynamite — how very suspicious the presumed passenger's behaviour would now seem. In the following days, with the discovery of unexploded infernal machines in the left-luggage offices of three other stations there is a more scientific description of how the time bombs were constructed together with reflections on the origin of the aggression:

As reported by us yesterday, infernal machines were discovered at Charing-cross and Paddington Stations under circumstances which clearly prove that the explosion at Victoria Station was only part of a diabolical plan to destroy property and probably life. The two which failed to explode have been found substantially intact. The one at Charing-cross Station was found in an American cloth black bag, and consisted of an American clock with the spring of the alarum so arranged as to pull the trigger of a pistol. Close to this, tightly packed together in a tin case, and with a quick match and several detonators in connection with them, were forty cakes of dynamite. The spring of the alarum had acted and the trigger had been duly pulled, but a long percussion fuse, charged with fulminate of mercury, which was intended to let off the dynamite, had been placed a little out of position, and the hammer of the pistol had struck just to the side of it. It is to this, and to this alone, that the failure of the plot has been, [*sic*] and that the Charing-cross cloak-room, with the hotel above it, has escaped being wrecked. The spring of the alarum is of the same make as a spring found among the débris at Victoria. The cakes of dynamite found at Charing-cross are marked 'Atlas Powder'. They consist, therefore, of a material not manufactured in this country, but well known in America, and of exclusively American make. The discovery at Paddington was made yesterday afternoon. A brown leather bag, studded with brass nails, which had been left in the cloak-room, was opened on suspicion, and was found to contain much the same machinery and explosive stuff as those in the Charing-cross bag. The failure at Paddington had come at a somewhat earlier point in the course of the plan. The clockwork had not been strong enough to pull the trigger of the pistol. The dynamite was of the same sort as that at Charing-cross. It was 'Atlas Powder' but the descriptive title had been effaced. It deserves notice, as possibly affording some clue to the persons engaged in this plot, that inside the Paddington box was found a copy of the *New York Sun* bearing date Feb. 6, 1884. The whole thing is clearly of Irish American origin.[14]

On the same day, 29 February, the mechanism of the unexploded bombs was also described in *The Times* in rather different terms. The reporters were obviously struggling to understand the terminology used by Scotland Yard's scientific squad who seem, by the way, to have given away considerable information by which the dynamitards could later rectify their technical errors:

> The determination with which the authors of the outrage had set about their diabolical work may be illustrated by a description of one of the cakes of dynamite – the one placed opposite to the muzzle of the pistol. This particular cake, which was so arranged as to explode the contents of the cashbox, was studded with detonators, all charged with fulminate of mercury, and all connected by a wire, so as to give a shock to each and all on one being struck.

The language of the journalists is relevant in that they were the medium through which the findings of the police investigators were filtered through to the novelists.

The question of the source of the outrages is likewise taken up by *The Times* of 27 February 1884, and the article ends with a veiled threat of the possibility of reprisals being taken against the Irish working in England whose presence, it states, is 'tolerated' at present:

Having reached the conclusion that dynamite or some similar compound was used at Victoria, it is mere affectation to pretend to doubt that it was used maliciously. It is pretty clear that we have to deal with one of the cowardly outrages by which Irishmen appear to imagine that they further the cause of Irish independence. There is no other class of men among us who have any end to serve by depositing infernal machines in places of public resort, while we know that Irishmen have gloried in similar outrages, and maintain a fund for the avowed object of repeating them.

So much for the actual reporting. Leader writers and commentators joined in the general deploration of the cowardly nature of such attempts which with one accord were defined as dastardly. The copy of the *New York Sun* found in one of the unexploded portmanteaux gave rise to much outcry against the collection of funds in America in support of the dynamitards, and against the right of asylum they were afforded there. Nobody, however, was hurt, and the actual damage done was much less than must have been intended.

Worse was to come. Only one of the four mainline stations where the explosives had been placed was actually damaged, and even there, owing to the fact that the left-luggage office was along a platform and not in the main block, the damage was not so serious. But in the next attempt at simultaneous explosions in London, on 30 May 1884, three of the five powerful charges which had been placed to explode together blew up in the same area within a very short time gap. The dynamitards had profited, we may presume, from all the technical details released to the press by an as-yet-inexperienced Scotland Yard. The fourth 'machine', a bomb at the foot of the Nelson Column in Trafalgar Square, was found unexploded. The other objectives of the attack were Scotland Yard (a bomb was placed in a public urinal adjoining the main building), and the Junior Carlton Club near which two explosions occurred. Most of the injured were in the Rising Sun, a public house opposite Scotland Yard which received the full force of the blast. Twenty-seven people were said to have been taken to hospital. Londoners began to be badly frightened as they realised their vulnerability. Ordinary people were hurt, including two servants of Sir Watkin Wynn who lived at 18 St James's Square, near the club. They rushed to the front door when they heard the first explosion, just in time to receive the full force of the second. The scene in the Rising Sun is dramatically described in the *Pall Mall Gazette* for 31 May 1884:

At the time mentioned the occupants of the tavern, which included a cabman and coachman whose vehicles were at the door, heard a report at first a slight hissing noise, and then another one like the firing of a parl of artillery in their midst, and in an instant all the lights in the tavern were extinguished, and the large plate-glass windows were shattered into thousands of pieces. For some seconds they were stunned by the explosion and the noise caused by the falling of immense quantities of brickwork from the end of the police building opposite. Rushing into the road they found the cab partially covered by a heap of bricks, and the horse struggling to extricate itself from the ruins. Close by was a horse and brougham, nearly covered with bricks and rubbish. The inmates of the tavern, who had been cut and injured more or less by broken glass, were in the darkness screaming loudly for help. On examination it was found that the end of the police building had been blown down exposing the floors and their iron bindings to view. The entire roadway was inches deep in broken glass, which glittered and sparkled in the moonlight.

The sense of insecurity of the readers of this newspaper report was heightened by the information that the public convenience attached to Scotland Yard was actually under police supervision at the time of the explosion. Police Constable Clarke, the officer on duty, saw no-one suspicious in the neighbourhood yet he was near enough at the moment of the explosion to be taken to the Westminster Hospital in a state of collapse. It is not beyond the bounds of possibility that he had popped into the Rising Sun and that the dynamitard had seized the opportunity offered by this momentary absence: it is recorded that upon reaching hospital he was in need of further stimulants which were duly administered. A map of the locality with the sites of the explosions was published, encouraging reader participation of the kind often met with in detective stories: how was the bomb placed in the convenience eluding the surveillance of the constable on guard, and which was the likeliest escape route? The British police needed all the information they could get because they had not yet perfected the infiltration technique used so widely in Russia and on the Continent by which police agents became active members of terrorist groups. Such a network takes time to build up, and all that they could do in 1884 was to offer larger and larger rewards for post-factum information after each explosion had occurred.

The unexploded bomb in Trafalgar Square, at the foot of the Nelson Monument, was seen by some boys who noticed a carpet bag at the base of the pedestal. Scotland Yard was alerted and the bag was found to contain 'seven and a half cakes of what is believed to be dynamite, and a double fuse, having attached to it another cake of the same deadly explosive. The cakes were wrapped in paper, and were about four inches in length and two in depth.'[15] Further exploration revealed a considerable quantity of unexploded material in the stables at Scotland Yard. Clearly the dynamitards were becoming more efficient, although the failure to explode of the bomb at the base of the Nelson Column, the most symbolic of the sites chosen on this occasion, must have somewhat disappointed its constructor. Robert Louis Stevenson and his wife, in their tales collected under the title *More New Arabian Nights*[16], exploited this aspect of the delusions of an experimental chemist whose bombs never went off where or how they were intended to, and the site chosen in 'The Bomb', the best of the tales, was a reminder of this fiasco, in that the authors substituted the effigy of Shakespeare in Leicester Square as the objective.

Six months then passed before the apprehensive Londoners were again startled by a dynamite explosion in the heart of their city, in what *Harper's Magazine* defined as a 'Dastardly Attempt to Destroy London Bridge'. The mechanics of the explosion were not clear, and for some weeks experts discussed whether the dynamite charge had been placed at the support of the bridge from a boat on the river or had been lowered from above. The southern pier was badly damaged, but the bridge remained standing. The explosion took place at six o'clock on a Saturday evening, 13 December 1884. As in the case of the Scotland Yard explosion the precautions taken by the authorities proved inadequate, a fact that must have alarmed the population: 'At the very moment of the explosion an inspector and two constables of the Thames police were in a boat watching the bridge from the river.'[17] The bridge was crowded with Saturday evening traffic of vehicles and pedestrians when suddenly 'a sheet of flame shot up from the southern side of the river'.[18] A few people were thrown down and slightly injured, but once again the damage was presumably less than had been intended. Very probably it was this explosion which furnished the idea for the holocaust in some of the futuristic novels of the bombardment of London. *The Times* of 15 December 1884 drew attention to the risk to life and limb that the dynamitards, it would seem, had deliberately planned:

The fact that the destruction of the bridge would have occasioned the slaughter of a great many working men and poor women must be noted in evidence of the purely mischievous and senseless nature of the outrage.[19]

Once more there was no doubt as to the origin of the explosion. The *Pall Mall Gazette* noted the date as being the seventeenth anniversary of an abortive attempt to release Fenian prisoners from the Clerkenwell jail by an explosion against the surrounding wall, while *The Times* pontificated:

> The miscreants who perpetrated this outrage are still at large; but from various circumstances one may presume that they belong to the same Fenian gang who have planned many similar crimes, with a diabolical cunning which seemed always to ensure success, but also with a skulking cowardice which has invariably caused their murderous work to be ill-done . . . But there is little doubt that if the explosives used be now of English make the orders for their employment still come from America, where alone money for such a nefarious purpose can be raised . . . There is nothing connected in the remotest fashion with politics in these repeated endeavours to destroy public property or to kill or maim harmless people. No sane person could imagine that political ends of any sort could be served by such methods.[20]

It must have been a nervous Christmas for Londoners. The *Annual Register* reported that on 17 December a shipment of 2 cwt of dynamite, labelled 'tin', had been discovered at Dover, while the *Pall Mall Gazette* carried such alarmist titles as: 'Supposed Attempt to Blow up Glasgow Bridge' on 22 December, and again for 29 December 'London Bridge Explosion'. This latter misleading title covers a very confused story of how a man left a mysterious parcel at the Black Horse in Deptford. In the parcel was a box containing four glass bottles:

> One of these, on being examined was found to contain glycerine, two were filled with nitric acid, and the other contained a dark liquor, which is said to be acid. In the box was an ornamental card, on which was writing in French.

There is an attractive air of mystery about this brief report. We are never told, either that day or on the days following, what was written on the card, presumably the clue to the whole problem: this typical mystery, set in Deptford where seamen come and go, with the foreign touch of writing in French (could nobody be found to translate it?) and even the slightly sinister name of the bar where the box was discovered offered food for thought to those novelists who were readers of the *Gazette*. It also kept alive a feeling of apprehension in the general public, an apprehension which was strengthened by reports on 2 January 1885 that there had been a further explosion on the underground railway between Gower Street and Kings Cross stations. Again it was found that dynamite had been used, and that it had been thrown apparently out of the window while the train was in a tunnel, at considerable risk to the dynamiter himself. Windows were broken but the train was not derailed. Conflicting evidence was given by other passengers of the man or men who were believed to have been responsible.

In the 22 days which elapsed between the underground railway explosion and the great London explosions of 24 January 1885, explosions which were designed to carry the attack into the heart of the British Empire, investigators and journalists turned their attention to the United States. Shipping lists were scanned and it seemed increasingly clear that the Fenian dynamiters came over to do their job, probably carrying their dynamite with them in the form of luggage, and then returned to prepare themselves for fresh attacks. The name of O'Donovan Rossa, the head of the New York branch of the Skirmishers, became familiar to English readers, and reports came through that on 9 January Phelan, a member of the Fenian organisation, had been stabbed in their New York offices as a suspected informer. Phelan survived but Carey, who had earlier revealed the identity of the Dublin Phoenix Park murderers, was followed on board ship and assassinated just as he seemed to be making good his escape. Phelan was reported to be one of the party deputed to kill Carey.

This aspect of terrorism, the watch the terrorists had to keep on each other, the impossibility of a change of heart once a man had become involved in an illegal organisation, was one of the characteristics which most attracted the novelists who were to work in the genre; in both fact and fiction it proved to be extremely dangerous to become possessed even inadvertently of secret information. Terrorism was seen to be a dangerous business, not least for the terrorists themselves. They had to be constantly on their guard against the police, against members of the public all of whom were potential witnesses, against the explosive devices they were handling (often of a highly experimental kind) and against each other.

Meanwhile on 14 January 1885 an attempt, defined in the press as an 'extraordinary outrage', was made to blow up the town hall at Warminster:

An infernal machine had apparently been placed on the steps at the entrance, and besides breaking all the windows in the neighbourhood, it is feared that the foundations of the building are damaged. No personal casualties are reported.[21]

One wonders, at this distance in time, whether it was not a rehearsal, testing some new type of detonator or timer, for the great explosions of 24 January. Obviously it was desirable that such a test should be at a good distance from the metropolis so that vigilance, already considerable, should not be further increased, and Warminster is at no great distance from Bristol where the dynamite could easily have been landed.

The great day of the dynamitards, a day which spread panic through London, through England and to a lesser degree through Europe, was a Saturday, 24 January 1885. On this day the Fenians struck a blow at British institutions with three successful and well-timed explosions taking place almost simultaneously at Westminster Hall, in the Houses of Parliament and at the Tower of London. Many people were injured, both in the Hall and in the Tower, for it was a peak visiting time, while the historic buildings suffered serious damage. The shock and panic were tremendous. Only the heroic constables Cox and Cole (one of whom had his hearing permanently impaired, while the other was for a time blinded) behaved, if we are to trust the report in the *Pall Mall Gazette* of 27 January 1885, with truly British phlegm, coping courageously in the face of disaster. The scene is Westminster Hall, and Cole is in the act of removing the smoking bundle which contains the as yet unexploded infernal machine from the spot at the entrance to the crypt where it has been observed by a lady visitor. Cole, according to the reporter, said to his colleague: 'This is dynamite, I believe' and Cox replied: 'It looks like it.'[22] At this moment his burden became literally too hot to hold and he dropped it with the devastating effects which have been recorded. He received the Albert medal for gallantry. The survival of the two policemen was regarded as little short of miraculous and a survey of the damage done to the Hall, as portrayed by many contemporary illustrators in the days succeeding the outrage, strengthens the suspicion already aroused by their conversation that there was something superhuman about the two men who stood nearest to the bomb at the moment of explosion.

Contemporary press reports of the events of 24 January are worth reading in some detail in that they give the measure not only of the damage the dynamite had effected, but also of the panic it provoked. *The Times* of Monday 26 January 1885 dedicates an unprecedented 120,000 words to a description and deploration of the explosions. The first explosion occurred in Westminster Hall, a few minutes after two o'clock, and is reported as follows:

> It was clearly intended that this explosion should occur in the Crypt itself, and the fact that it did not was owing to a remarkable circumstance. Some visitors were passing through the passage of the Crypt when one noticed a parcel on the ground. It is described as the usual 'black bag', and it is important to add, it was surrounded by a woman's or child's dress; and the visitor called her brother's attention to it, remarking, too, that 'it smoked'. Her brother at once seemed to surmise that the parcel contained explosive, for he uttered the word 'Dynamite!' and hurried his sister away, calling the attention of the policeman on duty to the fact that a parcel was in the place. The nearest police constable, Cole by name, picked up the smoking parcel, and brought it to the entrance of the Crypt, where from its heat, or from some other cause, he dropped it. It was fortunate for him that he did so, for in an instant a terrific explosion burst from the parcel.[23]

Mr Green, the man who had uttered the ominous word 'Dynamite!' was very seriously injured, as were the two policemen. A hole some six feet in diameter was blown in the floor, and another in the roof.

Shortly afterwards a second explosion took place in the House of Commons. No-one was injured because the House was not sitting and the visitors present (the public was admitted on Saturdays) had all run out towards the scene of the earlier explosion. This second infernal machine did great structural damage, however, tearing the doors off their hinges, bringing down the strangers' and peers' galleries and doing incalculable damage to panelling and glass.

The third explosion occurred at almost the same time in the Tower of London, in the middle storey of the White Tower, used as a storeroom of ancient arms. The chief damage was done to the Banqueting Hall and the passage to St John's Chapel. The armoury caught fire, and one of the best contemporary reports, admirable for its official terseness amid the spate of adjectives produced by the journalists, was drawn up by Captain Shaw of the Metropolitan Fire Brigade who was called out to extinguish the flames:

> Called at 2.3 p.m. [*sic*], to the Tower of London; Constable and Chief Governor General, Sir Richard James Dacres, GCB; supposed cause of fire, explosion; neither contents nor building insured; called by fire-alarm and military; extinguished by military and firemen with seven private hydrants and three private manuals; damage, south end of first floor (known as a banqueting room) of White Tower and used as stores for ancient arms and armour, and contents severely damaged by explosion, fire, and water; rest of White Tower and the contents by explosion and water. Elizabeth Vellum, aged 20 years, lacerated on the right side of the face; Ann Mann, aged 19 years, severely burnt on head and neck; Ernest Stratton, aged 12 years, severely cut on side of head; Herbert George, aged 11 years, lacerated finger and wound on thigh — all taken to military hospital. A man, name unknown, injured on the head.[24]

The Times leader of 26 January 1885 is interesting in that it registers the first reaction. There is no doubt whatever concerning the Fenian matrix, but the leader writer in his horror and indignation almost nobilitates the actions of the Nihilists and anarchists on the Continent in comparison with those of 'the gang of cowardly murderers' who have placed the London bombs. Does this, I wonder, help to explain why it is that when fiction writers subsequently fell upon these facts as promising plot material they so often uprooted the terrorists from their Irish background? While in fact politicians were increasingly being forced to examine the condition of Ireland, and Gladstone's tardy and somewhat unwilling proposals for a Home Rule Bill were to be the main issue of the general election at the end of the year, novelists (always with the exception of the Irish themselves) put aside the Irish question and dealt instead with anarchists and Nihilists who could more easily take on heroic dimensions and be linked back to the chivalric quest theme of knights setting out to right wrongs and injustices, threatened by forces considerably greater than themselves. The press in England, and not only the Conservative press, with the whole slant it gave in reporting the Irish question, made it impossible for an English writer to think of the Fenians as forming part of that stream of fighters they were willing, even though cautiously, to admire when their objectives were a foreign and not too friendly power. The distinction stands out very clearly when we compare it with the attitude of an Irish writer, the declared pacifist Tom Greer.[25]

For this reason some passages from the leader in *The Times* are worth considering, because they are the first reactions, and would be very widely read. Even today, when we can follow events from hour to hour on the radio, and see them on television screens while they are happening, the sale of newspapers still goes up as soon as there is a major terrorist attack or assassination. The London dynamite attack occurred on a Saturday afternoon, so that the leader writer had Sunday in which to collect information and meditate on the points he wanted to make and this is what he produced for his Monday morning readers:

> There is, indeed, a difference between even the Nihilists and Anarchists of the Continent and the gang of cowardly murderers whose spokesman is O'Donovan Rossa. To compass the assassination of a Sovereign or a Minister, or even the destruction *en masse* of a legislative body, must be, without doubt, condemned and pursued to punishment as crimes inconsistent with the elementary forms of civilization. But such designs are at least intelligible; they go straight to their mark, and they are subject to limits of their own. The Irish-American 'dynamite fiend' chooses, by preference, for the scene of his operations crowds of the labouring classes, of holiday-makers, of ordinary travellers, and sweeps them at random into the meshes of his murderous plot with as little concern for their personal merits or demerits as the Thug feels for those of the victims of his deadly cult . . .
> . . . To strike terror into the souls of Englishmen, whether by the indiscriminate slaughter of holiday-makers and working people, or by the destruction of precious historical monuments, is the avowed object of the dynamite party in the United States. For this money is collected and organizations are established, and to the meaning of it all American opinion has hitherto been curiously blind.[26]

The passage ends with advice as to what the British reaction should be:

> . . . Their traditional and inbred spirit will save them from submission to the insolent dictation of murderers, and their common sense will warn them that if they begin to pay black-mail to one gang of terrorists they will have to go on paying it to others.[27]

The conclusion of *The Times* is that no concessions should be made.

The big questions which were debated in the press on the following days, and indeed in the following weeks, were concerned with security measures and with repression. The foreign press, which gave considerable space to the whole issue, was directly interested in this aspect, as the London explosions (the most serious that had occurred anywhere outside Russia at the time) could well signal an escalation of endemic European terrorism on a similar scale. The reaction of the dynamite faction in New York, as communicated by cable from Philadelphia, was as follows:

> Rossa's crew assembled in the Chambers-street office expressed delight when Rossa exhibited the following translation of a cipher telegram which he says was sent from London on Saturday to a merchant in New York for him: —
> 'House of Commons shattered. Terrible consternation in London. Some say it is well to stop work for a while to see if enemy will give Ireland native Parliament — Number One.'
> Other Irishmen declared the telegram bogus. Phelan, in the hospital, says that Rossa invented it.[28]

Phelan, that is to say, the ex-Fenian and British spy who was still recovering from stab wounds at the hands of O'Donovan Rossa's confederates, gave it as his opinion that the telegram was a fake, an invention of Rossa himself. Whether this be so or not, and whether Rossa might not have been using this mysterious personage to give authority to his own opinion that it would be wiser for the Fenians to lay doggo for a while after achieving such an outstanding success and world publicity on an unprecedented scale, is irrelevant here. What matters is his reference, reported in *The Times*, to a mysterious 'Number One'. This all-powerful but unidentified figure, whose decisions are to be accepted without question, was seized upon by

the novelists as a gift from heaven. And why stop at number one —
why not, as in *On Peter's Island* (or Chesterton's later variant in *The
Man Who was Thursday*), give all the conspirators numbers,
together with cloaks and masks concealing their identity? The idea
was not new; in all ages plotters have had the best reasons for putting
a high price on anonymity, but it was brought to the fore at a moment
of great public sensitivity concerning the behavioural habits of
conspirators.

Reports from abroad in the week immediately following the
London outrages included further evidence of the funding of the
terrorists in the States, evidence which emerged at the trial of an
editor named Patrick Ford, who admitted in the witness box (i.e.
under oath) that the funds collected by him through the *Irish World*
were used for dynamite purposes. The *Pall Mall Gazette* claims that
there is good reason for supposing that most of the dynamite explosions were partly directed from Paris, and that some of the most
notorious Fenians were still lurking in the French capital, crossing
and recrossing from France to England with the greatest impunity.

A number of foreign papers, the *Univers* in France, the *Rassegna*
in Italy and the *Warsaw Official Gazette*, all pleaded for a general
European law for the suppression of dynamiters. The latter puts the
case most strongly:

> The recent Anarchist orgies prove beyond all doubt that the
> separate efforts of the different Governments are not sufficient to
> repress Anarchism . . . Anarchism is an international organiza-
> tion. To that league of destruction a league of defence must be
> opposed. As soon as all the European Governments shall have
> joined hands for that purpose they will certainly prove stronger
> than the murderers' alliance.[29]

A number of English papers took the same stance, that habeas
corpus and the liberty of the subject would have to give way: in the
words of the *Morning Post* 'the rights of repression will for some
time to come outweigh other considerations'.[30]

A cable from St Petersburg of 27 January stated:

> The explosions in the House of Commons and the Tower, coming
> immediately after the publication of the Russo-Prussian
> agreement for political extradition, has naturally raised hopes
> here that England may now be induced to join in the new league

of the two Monarchies against the Anarchists . . . England will, in the end, be compelled to associate her efforts with those of the Continental Powers in exterminating the whole band of dynamitards, without distinction of nationality.[31]

The same cable quoted a passage from the *Moscow Gazette* which rubbed in the same point in a distinctly serve-you-right tone: 'At last she [England] is herself experiencing the evil which she has always maintained for others with her sacred right of asylum!'[32]

It was left for the *Allgemeine Zeitung* of Austria to uphold the opposite view:

Modern civilization is not to be frightened into fits because at the outset a thousand madmen wage war against it. Nor will two entire continents place themselves under martial law and dictatorship because a few insane persons have succeeded in ruining some stonework and perhaps causing the death of one or two innocent persons.[33]

This was very much the line taken in England by the radical *Pall Mall Gazette* which expressed great concern lest the panic which followed the explosions should lead to hurried and mistaken legislative measures, and tried from the very first day to redimension the extent of the outrage. Under a leader very appropriately entitled 'The Scare' it argued:

On the whole, £20,000 represents the outside damage done by the three carefully planned explosions about which all the world is talking this morning. No one was killed; about a score of men, women, and children were slightly injured; two policemen have lost their hearing; and that is all. A wretched twopenny halfpenny affair it is to be sure, and one which ought to be most reassuring and even comforting to all those who have watched the progress of the struggle between society and the demons of dynamite.[34]

On the same day the same paper also published, as a follow-up to its leader, two interviews, one with a Nihilist, 'Stepniak' and one with a Fenian, Michael Davitt.

'Mere baby work', said 'Stepniak', the well-known Nihilist author of 'Subterranean Russia', to one of our representatives this morning; 'these explosions are mere baby work; any child could do as much. Stupid, objectless, directed against no particular individual, furthering no great cause.'

It was a noteworthy journalistic scoop to interview a supporter of one terrorist movement on the results achieved by another, and the pooh-poohing tone adopted smacks more than a little of professional jealousy. While this interview with 'Stepniak' was useful in playing down the panic before it could lead to harmful repressive legislation, the interview with Davitt put the whole question from the Irish point of view and helped the *Gazette* to use the occasion to stress that the only way to eliminate dynamite protests was to eliminate the causes. Davitt's analysis includes the passage:

> The dynamiters are made up of two classes: — (1) Those who convince themselves that the English statesmen can never be persuaded of the reality of an Irish grievance, or the justice of an Irish demand, by ordinary political methods. So long as Ireland is quiet England generally supposes that Ireland's grievances are exhausted . . . (2) Men who have taken part in Irish movements, and suffered in consequence; and the friends and relatives of such persons.[35]

The *Pall Mall Gazette* put forward a convincing case for Home Rule and the general election at the end of 1885 was largely fought on the Irish question, but, regrettably for the subsequent history of Anglo-Irish relations, Gladstone's 1886 Home Rule Bill was defeated.

The Fenians were, however, for the time being played out. Alarm was kept up, there were threats only a week later to blow up the Post Office, the British Museum and the Inland Revenue, and a fortnight later the Law Courts. Dynamite was seized at 69 Harrow Road on 10 February and the press report of this seizure shows how the figure of the dynamitard was evolving in the public mind, and taking the shape we so often meet in fiction:

> A few weeks before Christmas the premises were let to a dark-whiskered man and opened as a second-hand bookshop. Little, however, was seen of the man, and the place was almost invariably left in charge of another person, who is described by his neighbours as having 'a Yankee look' and speaking with a

decided American twang . . . the son on Tuesday night forced an entrance at the shop, and there discovered a considerable quantity of dynamite, as well as material for its manufacture.[36]

On 20 April there was a report of an explosion in Glasgow, and on 23 April there was a dynamite explosion at the Admiralty, Whitehall, severely injuring the Assistant Under-Secretary. This explosion at first renewed all the alarm caused by the January outrages, but on further investigation it appeared impossible that a bomb could have been lobbed over a high wall from the nearby park and in at the window, as at first supposed, under the eye of an imposing array of security forces: 'The explosion occurred while the sun was shining brightly, and while the whole neighbourhood was literally bustling with soldiers and police.'[37]

Another theory that the explosion was the result of an accident in handling specimen war material was soon ruled out: this simply was not done on the desk of the Under-Secretary, or indeed anywhere in the office block. Finally the police authorities gave credit to a suspicion that the outrage was the work of a subordinate engaged in the office, and that it had been specifically directed against the injured official by a junior disappointed in a looked-for promotion. By 2 May this seems to have been the accepted theory because *Punch* of that date came out with a cartoon entitled 'Guy Fawkes Tennyson blowing up the Authorities at the Admiralty' and a comic article: 'How to Utilize Explosions', exploiting the private application of dynamite, another idea which novelists were not slow to take up. By 1 May 1885 London dynamiting had subsided to an 'attempt to blow up a pillar-box' though there were various reports, more or less substantiated, of dynamite plots which either were foiled or fizzled out in other parts of the kingdom.

The whole dynamite question remained very much to the fore in the press for the rest of the year, and may have considerably influenced the outcome of the November elections. First and foremost were the reports of the progress of the injured, particularly of Constables Cole and Cox. Then there were reports of the progress of repairs to the damaged buildings, and estimates of the cost. There was also a long debate in the press, backed up by innumerable readers' letters, on the efficacy or inadequacy of the detective police force. A typical contribution is to be found in *All the Year Round*, 25 April 1885, under the title 'Detectives and their Work':

Since dynamite outrages, and threats and rumours of dynamite outrages, have become a sort of institution in the land, our detective force and its organisation have been subjected to a good deal of adverse criticism . . . But it [dynamiting] is not an ordinary crime, and it is a new one. Assassination of individual rulers, or ministers, we have had from of old, but the modern dynamiter, the wholesale indiscriminate assassin, in comparison with whom the Thug was an embodiment of sweetness and light — this monstrosity, until it sprang into existence, was a creature that the ordinary mind was incapable even of imagining.

This debate on the home front overlapped with the wider international debate regarding the advisability of adopting repressive measures, and particularly of co-ordinating such measures on an international basis, but the more democratic countries, England and America, were unwilling to allow their sovereignty to be curtailed even by so much as the extradition of a man accused of terrorism would entail. England remained in the ironic position of claiming her right to shelter the enemies of the Czar, while accusing America of sheltering in the same way the enemies of the Queen.

When two men, Cunningham alias Dalton and Burton were accused at Bow Street police station on 9 February 1885 of being concerned in causing the explosion at the Tower, it was stated that evidence would be produced to show that they had arrived in England shortly before the explosion in St James Square, that they then left the country, and reappeared again previously to that at London Bridge, and that they could be identified as two of the three men who travelled in the guard's brake on the Metropolitan Railway on 2 January, when an explosion occurred there. This constant coming and going of terrorist activists was one of the features which appears regularly in contemporary reports — their nomadic nature being the only means by which they could hope to enjoy even temporary survival: this was one of the characteristics most immediately picked up by novelists working in the genre. Their dynamitards turn up now here now there, stopping only long enough for the curious landlady or cabman to observe the number of brown boxes and black bags of which their luggage consists. During the various stages of the trial of Cunningham and Burton, pronounced guilty on 18 May after proceedings lasting an entire week and sentenced to penal servitude for life, newspaper readers had ample opportunity to become familiar with the details of their trade, and with those of their fellow conspirators. With 24 of these now under lock and key Londoners must have felt that they could breathe freely again, but on 22 August 1885 the *Pall Mall Gazette* came out with a big title: 'The Dynamite Conspiracy. Explosions to begin again':

> A well-informed correspondent states that the following extraordinary letter has been received by O'Donovan Rossa's European agents, one of whom is now stationed at Havre and another at Antwerp: . . . 'Now, I summon you, in the name of our Brotherhood, and by the solemn oath you have taken, to recommence field operations forthwith'. The names of the places where Rossa orders outrages are written in cypher, the key to which is changed periodically. As an explanation of the dynamite chief's reasons for issuing this circular, I am credibly informed that the apathy referred to was caused by internal wrangling among the dynamiters.

Two things are worthy of note in this report. The reference to solemn oaths is a further reinforcement of the legendary, semi-mythical dynamitard figure who was already finding his way into fiction in just these terms. On the other hand there was nothing mythical about the quarrels among the American dynamite faction. After the worldwide press coverage they had achieved in January things had gone from bad to worse, some of the more experienced agents had been captured, and there was wrangling about the funds collected, as it was stated, from the savings of Irish servant girls. Rossa's personal charisma probably suffered at the hands of the resolute Mrs Yseult Dudley who, possibly inspired by Charlotte Corday, had shot the Fenian leader single-handed on 2 February 1885, but who when he fell wounded at her feet and begged for mercy decided to spare him. The lady was tried and acquitted on the grounds of insanity, but she may have inflicted more damage to Rossa's image than the 'severe flesh wound' caused by her revolver.

By September 1885 the breakdown of the American branch of the Fenian organisation was becoming more apparent, and on 26 September the New York correspondent of the *Daily News* said that the growing indifference on the part of the American Irish to the subject of Irish agitation was strikingly illustrated by the appearance of the last issue of the *Irish World*: 'all the various funds are abandoned . . . The quality of the paper on which the *World* is printed is, moreover, inferior to that used hitherto, which is a significant sign of distress.'[38] Rossa remained at the head of the organisation for a further year, but the wrangling went on and in the end, on 29 November 1886, he was excommunicated and Dr Williams of Chicago took his place as treasurer of the Revolutionary Directory of the Fenian Brotherhood, Rossa having been found guilty of 'fraud, treachery, treason, persistent violation of the constitution in financial matters, and gross indiscretion'.[39]

England could live in peace, at least so far as the Fenians were concerned; London, however, in 1886 was being badly frightened once more, but the enemy this time was within the gates. The unemployed, in unprecedented numbers, led by members of the Social Democratic Federation, were holding huge mass demonstrations and protest marches, some of which got beyond the control of both the organisers and of the police. These marchers did not use dynamite, they resorted to the traditional missiles of bricks and stones, but in the public mind they were identified with the dynamitards and anarchists of the Continent. As this identification was frequently carried over into the novels of the period, it is of direct interest and concern to us.

Notes

1. *Pall Mall Gazette*, 11 Feb. 1885 (henceforth *PMG*).
2. Fred Burnaby, *Our Radicals: A Tale of Love and Politics*, two vols. (London, 1886).
3. This is the case in Anthony Trollope, *The Landleaguers*, three vols. (London, 1883), Vol. 3, p. 142.
4. George Bernard Shaw, *The Irrational Knot*, (London, 1905). First published in *Our Corner*, 1885-7.
5. *Annual Register*, entry for 23 March 1885.
6. Henry James, *The Princess Casamassima*, three vols. (London, 1886). Quotation from Chiltern Library edition (London, 1950), p. 276.
7. This attempt on the life of the Czar may well lie behind the reference made by the anarchist Souvarine in Emile Zola, *Germinal* (Paris, 1885), which is another literary example of a peccant engine: 'Nous étions restés quatorze jours au fond d'un trou, a miner la voie du chemin de fer; et ce n'est pas le train impérial, c'est un train de voyageurs qui a sauté . . .' (Paris, 1968), p. 437.
8. *The Letters of Queen Victoria. A Selection from Her Majesty's Correspondence and Journals*, second series George Earle Buckle (ed.); Vols. 1 and 2, 1862-78 (London, 1926); Vol. 3, 1879-85 (London, 1928); entry for 29 Feb. 1872.
9. Ibid., entry for 1 March 1872.
10. Ibid., entry for 2 March 1882.
11. Arthur R. and Mary E. Ropes, *On Peter's Island* (London, 1901).
12. K. R. M. Short, *The Dynamite War: Irish-American Bombers in Victorian Britain* (Dublin, 1979), which was pointed out to me by Steve Durno when I had

already written the historical chapters of the present book, is an accurate study of police records and the press, and tells the story of the Irish dynamiters from the viewpoint of Scotland Yard, showing how, by trial and error, methods for dealing with this new form of terrorism were evolved.

The same ground, reflecting the same clash of personalities within the police, is covered in fictional form by the detective story of Peter Lovesey, *Invitation to a Dynamite Party* (London, 1974), published before Short's study. As in all his Sergeant Cribb stories, which were turned into a popular TV series, the documentation is excellent and the book, though very entertaining reading, is in fact a serious study and historical re-creation of a period.

13. *PMG*, 27 Feb. 1884.
14. *PMG*, 29 Feb. 1884.
15. *PMG*, 31 May 1884.
16. Robert Louis Stevenson and Fanny Van de Grift Stevenson, *More New Arabian Nights. The Dynamiter* (London, 1885).
17. *PMG*, 15 Dec. 1884.
18. Ibid.
19. *The Times*, 15 Dec. 1884.
20. Ibid.
21. *PMG*, 15 Jan. 1885.
22. *PMG*, 27 Jan. 1885.
23. *The Times*, 26 Jan. 1885.
24. Ibid.
25. Tom Greer, *A Modern Daedalus* (London, 1886).
26. *The Times*, 26 Jan. 1885.
27. Ibid.
28. Ibid.
29. *PMG*, under title 'Reception of News Abroad', 26 Jan. 1885.
30. Ibid.
31. *The Times*, 27 Jan. 1885.
32. Ibid.
33. *PMG*, 26 Jan. 1885.
34. Ibid.
35. Ibid.
36. *PMG*, 12 Feb. 1885.
37. *PMG*, 23 April 1885.
38. *PMG*, under title 'Decline of the Irish Agitation in America', 26 Sept. 1885.
39. *Annual Register*, 29 Nov. 1885.

Ten days after the major London explosions in 1885 a correspondent from the United States sent an extremely interesting article to the *Pall Mall Gazette*. In a moment when the attention of everyone was focused on the activities and pronouncements of O'Donovan Rossa, this correspondent obtained an interview with a 'far more dangerous man', the chemist who was engaged in designing and assembling the explosive devices. It is interesting to note the use of two words in this context, the more modern 'device' in place of the popular 'infernal machine', and the specialised term 'chemist' which we meet so often in dynamite novels. Henry James makes a particularly subtle use of 'chemist' in his *The Princess Casamassima* which, though it is concerned with anarchists, is not directly dealing with dynamite but with that traditional form of political assassination: a revolver shot at a public figure. Paul Muniment, the future leader of the people, is given in this novel the ideas of a dedicated Marxist and the characteristics not of a fanatic but of a single-minded and extremely competent man; James makes him, by trade, an industrial chemist. Muniment is not politically a dynamiter; he explains painstakingly that the purpose behind his movement is not to destroy existing institutions but to turn them to different ends. James puts across Muniment's arguments with considerable fairness but, by the simple fact of making him an industrial chemist, and by drawing attention to the stains on his hands, contrives to throw suspicion on his activities in the eyes of the contemporary reader and to invite the chemist-dynamiter connection which, inevitably, discredits the ideas of a man who might otherwise appear to attack the established order all too convincingly, and even to have a workable alternative to offer.

The above-mentioned correspondent from New York, under the title 'Rossa's Weapons of War', published the following interview with Mezzeroff, which was directly useful to all those novelists who wished to lift their infernal machines out of the world of romance — such as the 'Story of the Destroying Angel' in the Stevensons' *More New Arabian Nights* — and to place them firmly in the nitro-glycerine setting of the late-nineteenth century. The same article may also have proved useful to do-it-yourself anarchists, and the

Scotland Yard Detective Force were probably less than enthusiastic on seeing the technical details of explosives and detonators set out so plainly in sectional diagrams.

> Some time ago, while in New York, I was introduced by an Irish acquaintance to O'Donovan Rossa, Major Horgan, Mezzeroff, and other chiefs of the dynamite party . . . Mezzeroff seemed to me to be a far more dangerous man. He was then at the head of the Irish Dynamite School in Brooklyn, and he was said to be a chemist of no mean attainments . . . He allowed me to look through a notebook in which he had jotted down a number of rough pen-and-ink sketches of devices for utilizing the explosive force of dynamite. Immediately after quitting him I reproduced a few of these sketches in my own pocket-book, and thus I am able to send you sectional drawings of some of the weapons with which the dynamite party hope to terrify England into granting Ireland her independence. Mezzeroff himself informed me, as I left New York, that machines in accordance with several of his designs had been manufactured, and were being sent to Europe as opportunity offered.[1]

The six devices examined are the following: 'Fig. 1, an explosive cigar; fig 2, an 'infernal' walking stick; fig. 3, a percussion bomb; fig. 4, a dynamite flask; fig. 5, a detonator; fig. 6, a flexible flask for sulphuric acid.'[2] Each of these figures is described in considerable detail. It is difficult to take seriously today the proposal for an explosive cigar, but it seems to have inspired an incident in one contemporary novel, Grant Allen's *For Maimie's Sake*,[3] where it is used precisely as its inventor suggested, to get rid of a defecting conspirator:

> Fig. 1 represents a device for an explosive cigar, to be offered, say, to a treacherous accomplice or an inconvenient detective . . . The charge of dynamite in this case is very small, perhaps not more than a drachm; yet Mezzeroff declared that it would certainly destroy the sight of the smoker, and would probably kill him.[4]

Nor should we overlook the fact that it was a real-life dynamiter who listed the explosive cigar device as number one in the table of his inventions. The overriding impression given by novels of this period

is that authors exaggerate those themes of betrayal, of mutual suspicion, of the infiltration of informers within terrorist groups, themes
which offered exciting plot material; Mezzeroff's invention is a
reminder that such fantasies have at least a foundation in fact.

The general public was daily reminded of the reality of dynamite
outrages by cablegrams pouring in to the press from all parts of the
world. The newspapers, well aware of the story value of any such
report, gave considerable space to dynamite plots wherever they
were taking place, thereby both satisfying their readers' curiosity
and creating a feeling of panic which nourished itself feverishly on
fresh accounts of outrages. News poured in from all sides: Canada,
for example, was going through a dynamite scare at the same time as
London. Dynamite charges were place in Toronto, Montreal,
Ottowa and Quebec. On 13 October 1884 *The Times* reported that
two explosions had partially destroyed the new Parliament building
in Quebec. At the end of January 1885, just after the big London
explosions, a telegram from Montreal stated that the chief of the
detective department in that city had notified the Grand Trunk
Railway of a plot to destroy Victoria Bridge.

Now only one of these Canadian dynamite attempts was in fact
successful: the uncompleted Quebec Parliament was really
damaged by two explosions. The Toronto attempt was foiled, as so
often happened, by the charge being discovered and defused, and
the Victoria Bridge attempt was a mere rumour. But the cumulative
effect on an English reader, whose eye caught the title words as it ran
down the newspaper headlines, was a feeling that in Canada, as in
London, people were walking on dynamite. Furthermore a report
came through on 21 January 1885, only three days before the big
London explosions, of an attempt to murder the President of Chile
by an infernal machine. News of this kind, coming from both the
North and South American continents, must have strengthened the
feeling of insecurity — that since the invention of dynamite nowhere
and nobody in the world was safe.

The news from Europe in this period was even more unsettling.
We have to remember that each dynamite incident spread over a
period of months in terms of newspace because the explosion was
often followed at a certain distance in time by reports of the capture
of the terrorists, their trial (as much as a year later), sentence,
execution or, occasionally, escape, recapture and retrial. This news
processing functioned whether the original dynamite attempt had
been successful or not, so that there was no lack of material pouring

daily into the newspapers and titillating their readers. Setting aside for the moment Russia and Ireland, both of which countries had been living for many years in a state of suppressed revolution, the news from the rest of Europe was sufficiently alarming. The success of the Fenian outrages in London did much to encourage terrorists elsewhere, so that this was a peak period for dynamitards; British journalists, well aware of their readers' interest in the whole subject, overlooked no item from however far afield that might meet the demand for dynamite sensation.

The most interesting attempt, from a literary point of view, was yet another non-explosion: the attempt to blow up the German Emperor, William I, at Niederwald on 28 September 1883. Full details of this outrage reached the British public with the report of the trial of the accused in December 1884 and, on account of the great interest of newspaper readers in questions of dynamite around this time, the press coverage was very thorough. Tilley[5] has already convincingly argued that Rupsch and Reinsdorf were the figures behind Hyacinth and Hoffendahl in Henry James's *The Princess Casamassima*, but other minor novelists were also impressed. Edward Jenkins, in his *A Week of Passion*, specifically refers to one of his characters, a hired assassin, as having been formerly engaged in this plot:

> This very German, Dr Schultz, whom we are now seeking, is a distinguished chemist, a professed Anarchist, who tried to kill the Emperor of Germany, and who has slipped over from political to private murders. He is mixed up with all the secret societies, and, I doubt not, with the most dangerous clubs of London and Continental criminals.[6]

Some extracts from reports of the Rupsch-Reinsdorf trial may serve to show the kind of details which caught the attention of the novelists. The *Pall Mall Gazette* gives the following account, under the title 'The Niederwald Plot — Trial of German Anarchists', on 16 December 1884:

> The trial of the men charged with attempting to blow up the Emperor William and his suite with dynamite at the unveiling of the Niederwald Monument, on the 28th of September, 1883, commenced yesterday before the Supreme Court of Leipzig, constituted as a court of High Treason. The discovery of this plot

was concealed at the time, and the public is still ignorant of the details, but it is known that a mine was laid in the path which the Emperor, the King of Saxony, and other dignitaries followed on their way to the Monument, and that it was solely owing to the hesitation of a man told off to ignite the fuse that a catastrophe was averted. One of the accused, Rupsch, aged twenty-one, has made a confession, in which he states that he and his accomplice, Küchler, received orders from one Reinsdorf, a compositor, to carry out the plot. After examining the ground they found that a drain crossed the road not far from the Monument, and they decided that this was the best place for laying the dynamite. On the 27th of September they fetched the stone jar containing the dynamite, charged the fuse, and pushed it into the mouth of the drain as far down as possible, finally covering everything up with grass and leaves. They returned to the spot the next morning and lay concealed till the procession approached, the plan being to let the Emperor approach within fifty paces, and then to light the fuse with a burning cigar. According to Rupsch's story he did not want to kill the Emperor, and so touched the fuse with an unlighted cigar. When the procession had passed Rupsch told Küchler that the fuse would not burn. The latter was much annoyed, and told him to try again as the Emperor returned. Rupsch went back, and this time cut the fuse with his pocket-knife about six feet from the stone jar. He then lighted it, but, naturally, no explosion followed. Both men then went to Rudesheim with the explosives in order to blow up the Grand Concert Hall, in which they were successful, afterwards returning to Elberfeld, where they met their accomplices. Rupsch asserts that he intended all along to frustrate the explosion, but the Public Prosecutor considers this false . . . Reinsdorf is charged with having incited various persons to commit the above crimes, and four others are charged with participation.

The hesitation of Rupsch was the detail which attracted Henry James to this particular conspiracy and which led him to create the figure of Hyacinth with so much sympathy. Here was a young man hiding a change of heart from his fellow conspirators, just as Rupsch had to pretend to set fire to the fuse, and therefore did so with an unlighted cigar, running considerable risk of observation by the security forces surrounding the Emperor, but preferring this risk to the simpler expedient of declaring to his fellow conspirators that he no longer wished to go through with his part in the plot, thereby incurring the punishment meted out to all those who broke their oaths. The trial continued, and the entry for 18 December examines the motivation of the leader, Reinsdorf:

> As to the motives which actuated him, he repudiated, with impassioned gestures, the idea that German workpeople were any happier since the so-called glorious war of 1870, which in his opinion was a dynastic war of conquest. He held that every workman who was not a craven should do his best to end the present state of things. The use of the suffrage was not enough; more active measures must be taken. The main object was to show the deep-rooted discontent of the masses by organized demonstrations. It was a thing of quite secondary importance whether a few princes should be sacrificed or not; but a mere sentimentality about human life should not be allowed to stand in the way of a great idea. The end sanctified the means.[7]

And on 23 December the Berlin correspondent of *The Times*, who had been following the trial, tried to analyse for the paper's English readers the underlying causes and the reasons for the success of the Anarchist movement:

> The whole course of the trial has made me feel very vividly what a huge amount of festering discontent there is below the surface of German society. It affords a new proof, if one were needed, that the Germans have outgrown their political institutions, and that the theoretical freedom of their paper Constitution is not enough for them. The disclosures of the trial make it quite evident that these Anarchist principles are widely disseminated.

The Niederwald trial was held in December, just before the big London explosions, but the end of the story came on 7 February, when Reinsdorf and Küchler were beheaded, so that the attempt on the life of the German Emperor, although it had taken place more than a year earlier, was present in the minds of newspaper readers as interwoven with their own experiences of terrorism, helping, I believe, to engender the confusion between anarchists and Fenians which is carried over into fiction.

Trouble was brewing also in other European countries, taking the form either of political assassination or dynamite. Interesting revelations came from a trial of 23 anarchists held in Vienna in June 1884. The prosecution relied heavily on the evidence of a man called Podboy who had earlier been convicted of high treason and who attempted to improve his own position by turning informer. Reading over reports of these old court cases one is struck repeatedly by the situation in which informers like Podboy found themselves. Once having taken the step of betraying the secrets of their fellow conspirators they had no allies but the police, and were willing to swear to anything the police wished them to say: having lost all sense of personal integrity in their own eyes they had morally nothing further to lose by swearing to false statements which could serve to incriminate or otherwise involve innocent suspects, and the incitement to say what was expected of them was considerable. So that, although these informers were certainly the most useful tools by which existing institutions could defend themselves against the violence of terrorism, their statements do not necessarily provide reliable historical evidence, even in those cases when, under the pressure of the times, they were considered sufficient to secure convictions.

For the contemporary novelist, however, who read the reports of such trials in his or her morning newspaper, they all provided material with which to work. When in the Vienna trial the informer Podboy stated that the anarchists at that time were entirely under the command of a committee in New York, it strengthened the sense of an international plot closing in. The Fenians were unquestionably based in New York where they published the *United Irishman*; if, as Podboy claimed, the anarchists at work on the Continent were likewise being manipulated from a New York base, then the Fenian-anarchist equation could be accepted as proven. According to Podboy the anarchists, like the Fenians, organised clubs and took collections for various purposes connected with the organisation, including the purchase of arms; they had also held secret meetings where the decision was taken to assassinate the Emperor during his visit to Gratz. These meetings were presided over by a Michael Kappauf, who read a letter from New York signed Justus Schwab, announcing that the bombs were already on their way, and urging those present to draw lots in order to fix upon the persons who were to carry out the attempt. The project was foiled by the police and a number of arrests were made.

Some of the lists of suspect material annexed by the police make strange reading. In July 1884 a young man was arrested in Austria on suspicion of connection with the dynamitards and was found to be in possession of a large dynamite bomb, two awls with their points poisoned with prussic acid, and a revolver. These awls escaped the attention of novelists and the tale where they are turned to nefarious use remains to be written. Their potential usefulness to a spy is beyond question, but why the prussic acid? While a writer of fiction must attempt at least to obtain a suspension of disbelief, no such onus beset the chronicler of the *Annual Register* where these curious weapons are recorded.[8]

Meanwhile French dynamiters were experimenting with an early form of the letter bomb on 7 March 1884, soon after the explosion at Victoria station in London: 'An infernal machine, consisting of a box in which were dynamite and other explosives, and addressed to the Comte de Paris, handed into the railway parcels office at Lyons station.'[9] A group of anarchists were tried at Pesth in Hungary, charged with having received some of the valuables stolen from the money-changer Eisert at Vienna on 9 December 1884, which suggests a certain freedom of movement across European frontiers, and that a policy of the organisation of terrorists into auto-sufficient independent nuclei had been adopted in Austria at the time.

On 16 December 1884 three anarchists were expelled from Switzerland, as part of the plan generally adopted in Europe of sending undesirable elements back to where they came from. This practice was distinct from the granting of extradition, which meant that the return of suspected terrorists was requested by a foreign government — a practice which ran counter both to liberal ideas of human rights and to conservative ideas of national prestige. Notwithstanding the question of principle involved, as the threat to life and property increased, more and more terrorists and suspected terrorists were returned to their homelands, always excepting Russia which throughout Europe was regarded as a special case on humanitarian grounds, for reports continued to reach the West of the violation of the most elementary human rights under the regime of the Czar. Germany was the first country in Western Europe to close her borders and to refuse the right of asylum to Russian anarchists and Nihilists, on the basis of a treaty of reciprocity with the Emperor of all the Russias.

Austrian police were continuing their hunt for anarchists at the time and after a three-day house-to-house search in Wiener Neustadt they discovered seditious pamphlets and explosives. A report from Linz on 15 December 1884 lists four anarchists arrested at Urfahr, together with the discovery of a secret printing press and a number of seditious pamphlets. On 20 December the French police caught three men at Mayenne who had arrived with dynamite from America.

A news story from Hungary on 23 December shows how easy it was for the general public to confuse the purposes of the methods of anarchists with other dissident groups:

> A Socialist printing-press was discovered and seized yesterday by the police in an apartment occupied by a woman in a house at Neu Pest. Numerous Socialist papers and manuscripts were also seized on the premises. A compositor named Franz Spielmann and the woman who had let the apartment were arrested.[10]

How were English readers to distinguish the activities of propagandists from the activities of terrorists when they read of them being subjected to the same kind of search, trial and imprisonment?

Another example of press confusion between genres of dissident activity occurred in a report in the *Pall Mall Gazette* on 24 January 1885. It ran under two titles: 'Sentence of French Anarchists' was followed by 'Attempted Assassination of Russian Police Officials' and a rather extraordinary comment arbitrarily linking these events: 'There is no doubt that the attempt was an act of vengeance on the part of the Nihilists'.[11] A thinking reader might have taken pause to consider that Russian Nihilists had plenty of reasons to assassinate their own police without waiting for a sentence against anarchists, *not* Nihilists, in a French court.

On 15 January 1885 an anarchist plot was reported as being discovered at Lyons where, it was stated, the conspirators intended to seize arms and ammunition belonging to the Rifle Society during the night, and then to proclaim a revolution, while on 30 January a report from Berne in Switzerland stated that the police had been especially ordered to keep a vigilant watch at the entrance of the Federal Palace and in its vicinity. This precautionary measure was taken because of rumours of an anarchist plot to blow up the palace. In neither of these cases was any actual harm done, yet the effect of reading about anarchist plots in France and Switzerland, just before and just after the big London explosions of 24 January, was almost as alarming to an English reader as if the conspirators had succeeded. The sense of imminent danger, both at home and abroad, of what Henry James, thinking of London, termed society dancing on the lid of a gigantic trapdoor, must have been very powerful. It is curious to note that Elizabeth Braddon uses almost the same image in *Under the Red Flag*, her book about Paris published in 1885, although she is referring to open, not secret warfare:

> But assuredly, of all who ever danced upon this earth, none ever danced on the edge of a more terrible volcano than that which trembled and throbbed under the feet of these light-hearted revellers tonight — happy, unforseeing, rejoicing in the balmy breath of summer, the starlit sky, the warmth and the flowers, with no thought that this fair Paris, whitely beautiful in the sheen of starlight and moonlight, was like a phantasmal or fairy city — a city of palaces which were soon to sink in dust and ashes, beauty that was to be changed for burning while joy and love fled shrieking from a carnival of blood and fire.

Mrs Braddon is describing Paris faced by destruction at the hands of Bismarck, but the similarity of concept of her passage with that quoted earlier from Henry James may well mean that it was the actuality of the threat to London which touched off her awareness of the threat to Paris about which she was writing.

One piece of deliberate scaremongering at this time was a report from the St Louis *Daily News*, taken up also in the British press, purporting to retail the plans of Cunningham alias Byrne alias Gilbert (the man held for the London explosions) for what should have been a holocaust:

> Byrne had it all planned, and I have a map of London at home that is all marked with red ink, where Byrne wrote in the location of the buildings he wanted to destroy. The one hundred young men were to get into London, and carry their materials with them as best they could, or they might manufacture machines or explosive packages in London. A certain day and a certain hour were to be designated for the destruction. The signal was to be the mid-air explosion of a dynamite bomb dropped from a balloon over the English capital. The explosion was to be of sufficient force to startle all London, and while the city was in excitement machines, timed for three or four minutes, were to be placed under the walls of all the public buildings. Just imagine the ruin and terror that could be wrought in that way in a few minutes.[12]

There was no evidence whatsoever for the existence of any plan on this scale, but this dynamitard's pipe-dream caught the attention of newspaper readers, and of novelists such as George Griffith and E. Douglas Fawcett, who drew pictures, set in the near future, of the destruction of London. The signal for the commencement of hostilities, to be given by a bomb dropped from a balloon, was the touch which particularly fascinated these early science fiction writers whose imagination had been caught by Verne's *Mathias Sandorf* of which the first translation appeared most opportunely in London in 1886. Twenty-two years before H. G. Wells wrote *The War in the Air*, the awful possibility of balloons or other flying machines being used to drop explosives from the sky entered the minds of a number of writers, and was explored in the form of boys' adventure stories. In books such as Tom Greer's *A Modern Daedalus* the ethics of a war of destruction as opposed to the earlier concept of a war of territorial conquest is examined, as the end of Victorian faith in indefinite scientific progress comes into sight. More and more scientific nightmares were written in the last two decades of the century, as a sense that the end of the century might mark the end of the world crept in (William Minto's *The Crack of Doom*,[13] the story of a comet on a collision course toward the earth, belongs to this genre).

Then came the First World War and the destructive powers of science were given greater scope than ever before, while H. G. Wells in 1914 in *The World Set Free* was already foretelling the use of nuclear fission. Hiroshima in the Second World War put a full stop to the long enduring belief in human progress, but reading the novels of the late nineteenth century we find a foreshadowing of history, a growing fear of the direction in which man was moving. Applied science had recently produced both dynamite and airborne vehicles, so the corespondent of the St Louis *Daily News* was only one of the first to link the two together in a new vision of destruction. This kind of scaremongering could be both commercially and politically motivated. The desire to boost newspaper sales often went hand in hand with the wish to discredit genuine labour movements. Only a week after the report of the 'balloon' plot, *The Times* chronicled Paris disturbances of unemployed demanding work and relief under the title 'The French Anarchists', and reported in the following terms:

While a strong force of police was concentrated in front of the

Opera last night some bands of Anarchists took the opportunity of committing excesses in other parts of the city. About 150 young men, headed by one bearing a red handkerchief tied to the end of a stick, went down the Rue Lafayette cheering for the Commune and the social revolution . . .

A second band . . . smashed some china outside a café and threw one of them at a jeweller's shop window, but no pillage was attempted. A third band halted before a baker's shop in the rue d'Allemagne and asked for bread. The baker gave them some loaves, but most of the recipients handed him money for them. Altogether 15 arrests were made.[14]

Whether there were really anarchists present is doubtful — the only flag mentioned is an improvisation, a red (not black) handkerchief tied to a stick. The behaviour of these protest marchers seemed to offer no very serious threat to society, but by publishing under the title 'The French Anarchists' *The Times* is keeping alive the sense of danger threatening. The *Pall Mall Gazette* reports the same event without any mention of anarchists:

There was a riotous demonstration of the unemployed in Paris yesterday. They had been invited to come in their thousands, and to flaunt their rags in the faces of the rich, not to move their compassion, but to excite their fears.[15]

What was clearly a social protest, convened at the Place de l' Opéra to accentuate the contrast between rich and poor, is viewed by the Conservative press as a continuation of anarchist activity on the Continent, and sympathy is denied to the unemployed by confusing two very different kinds of protest by biased reporting.

Meanwhile, the real attempts were continuing. On 11 February 1885 a dynamite cartridge was found in an outhouse connected with the building of the Main Guard at Frankfort-on-the-Main (the scene of a recent anarchist murder of a police inspector), but the bomb did not explode owing to a defective fuse. On 13 February two anarchists were arrested in a house at Labokue in the Reichenberg district in Austria. A secret printing press, several revolutionary publications and some dynamite were found on the premises. On 20 February the *Pall Mall Gazette* reported, under the title 'Outrage at the Italian Parliament House': 'A bottle filled with gunpowder was exploded last night by some persons unknown near the senators' and deputies' entrance to the Italian Parliament House. The explosion however, caused no damage.'

France, Austria and Italy were all close enough to England to make such news alarming, but the threat was to come nearer home. On 18 February 1885 the Dynamite Revolutionary Section of the Irish Revolutionary Party issued a warning which the *Pall Mall Gazette* published under the title: 'Fenian Manifesto to the British Cabinet':

> We, representatives of the extreme section of the revolutionary party assembled in council, give notice that should the British Parliament, in the course of the present session, vote the renewal of the Crimes Act, a measure which we regard as unjustifiable, we are firmly resolved to assert the *lex talionis*, by availing ourselves of the resources of civilization.[16]

'The resources of civilisation' is a memorable euphemism for dynamite which for a time became common coin. *Figaro* at the end of February published an account of an alleged conversation with Flannerty, the secretary of the Fenian dynamiters, who declared that a reign of terror would shortly commence in England. Flannerty was referring to the outcome of a conclave of dynamite conspirators which had been held in Paris on 23 February. The report of this congress, which was attended by Irish revolutionaries from both England and the United States and by Russian Nihilists is worth quoting at some length as given by a Reuter correspondent who claims to have obtained an eyewitness account:

> Round the table were seated eleven delegates, two of whom represented the Irish Revolutionists in Great Britain, and three others the Extremists in the United States. There were also two representatives for Ireland, two for the Continent, and two who declared themselves to be delegates from the Invincibles. Thirteen Fenians were also present, who sat behind against the wall of the room, and were not allowed to take part in the discussions.
>
> A Russian Nihilist stood in one corner with a manufacturer of dynamite who had come to arrange for the sale of a quantity of that explosive. Every person present carried a revolver with which to shoot any English detective who might appear . . . the president addressed the meeting. He spoke of the past and future

of dynamite, and invited the delegates to discuss the best means for putting an end to the evil administration of England in Ireland. (Cries of 'Down with England', and 'Long Live Dynamite'.)

Patrick Corcoran then detailed at considerable length the 'crimes and tyrannies' committed by England in Ireland, and proposed the following resolution:—

'That this Congress, considering that England has thrown down the glove, accepts the challenge and defies her, taking all the risks which may follow. It resolves to punish England for her odious crimes by pursuing the war as in the past, but on a more extended scale, by employing more vigorous means and by causing explosions not only in London, but in all the towns and villages in England.'

Corcoran spoke warmly in support of the resolution. Several of those present pleaded the cause of the innocent women and children who would perish in the explosions, declaring that the dynamitards would thus lose the sympathy of mankind. They were not making war against the English people, but against the British Government. It would, therefore, be better to attack only the British navy, barracks and arsenals. These counsels, however, did not prevail.

It was then proposed to effect a fusion between the Invincibles and the Dynamite party, but the plan was prevented by a telegram received from 'Number One'.

The Congress rejected a proposal for an alliance with the Russian Nihilists, on the ground that Russia was the enemy of England, and therefore indirectly the friend of Ireland.

James Macdermott, the informer, was again condemned to death. It was also decided to despatch two dynamitards acquainted with military tactics to the Mahdi in order to instruct him in the mode of using dynamite cannons, a new invention of the dynamite manufacturer who was present at the meeting, and who is expecting to receive a large order for the weapons in question.[17]

This account of the February 1885 international dynamite congress was extremely useful to novelists who wanted to write topical novels on the subject. The themes touched on here include: the international nature of the gathering; the proposal to increase the scale and extend the range of dynamite outrages; the defeat of the moderates who argued that the attacks should be aimed at military targets to avoid the shedding of innocent blood; the telegram from a mysterious 'number one'; the proposed alliance between Irish revolutionaries and Nihilists; a death sentence passed on an informer. All these themes were to find a place in the plots of the dynamite novels, some of which were already in the process of being written at the time when the report of this congress appeared in the press.

An original idea launched at the Paris meeting was that of furnishing the Mahdi (England's enemy number one) with aid in the form of a contingent of military experts on dynamite. England was at this time engaged in a somewhat inglorious war in the Soudan; the news of the fall of Khartoum and the death of General Gordon (26 January 1885) almost coincided with the big London dynamite explosions — in fact Queen Victoria's journals were so full of mourning for Gordon that she made no remark on disasters nearer home.[18] The proposal made at the dynamite congress to assist the enemy in time of war was therefore open treachery on the part of the British (which included the Irish) delegates.

It is more surprising to find the Workmen's Peace Association following suit on 25 February, a few days later, when they voted a rider to their motion against the war to the effect that 'it was prompted by the capitalist class and that the Soudanese deserved to be triumphant in their endeavour to obtain their rights'. The *Saturday Review* of 28 February 1885 reports a resolution proposed on this occasion by anarchists to pledge the meeting to 'fight against all tyrants, abolish all national frontiers, and sweep away all exploiters' who, as the *Review* adds 'are apparently the same with employers of labour'.

In all probability the reason why the British press gave news space to these extreme proposals was to discredit the whole Peace Association movement and with it the more moderate proposals mooted, which are not even reported. It was wartime; news from the front was anything but reassuring; this absence of national loyalty served to dispel any lingering doubts as to the obnoxious nature of all opinions held by such a movement. In such a moment of national solidarity it is sufficiently surprising to find dissident voices raised at all, yet only a week earlier Arnold White in an article 'A Day's Work at the Docks. By One Who Has Done it' in the *Pall Mall Gazette* reported:

One young gentleman, who had seen better days in the coster-monger's line, avowed himself an ardent admirer of O'Donovan Rossa. As far as I could gather, he was of opinion that Mr Rossa's political achievements were likely to lead to Government doing something for the unemployed in London . . .[19]

White, who had done his stint on the docks in order to get copy to document his plea for better working conditions for casual labourers, reports the docker's logic with a supercilious air, yet the 'young gentleman' was in fact voicing somewhat inarticulately a growing feeling that class loyalty had deeper roots than national loyalty — a feeling that the power of the press was to be increasingly called upon to combat in the years that followed.

A few weeks later the *Saturday Review* of 18 April 1885 returned to the charge of unpatriotic behaviour on the part, this time, of the socialists of the Social Democratic Federation, and implied that foreign capital was being used to undermine the morale of the British worker, from whose ranks Tommy Atkins was also drawn. As war seemed to be impending with Russia over the question of Afghanistan, the theory was that roubles were about to pass from the Czar's coffers into the hands of British socialists (which the press was equating with Nihilists and anarchists). The innate unlikeliness of this did nothing to detract from its usefulness as a means of discrediting the whole socialist movement in Britain.

> If the present complications result in war, the promoters of future Hyde Park meetings may not impossibly be subsidized by pay-masters who would willingly limit the activity of Woolwich [military and naval establishments]. Patriotism is as little in favour by Socialist demagogues as freedom or respect for property. Unemployed workers may well be excused for misun-derstanding the causes and proper remedies of the Commercial depression from which they suffer. It is a misfortune that their natural discontent furnishes materials for political adventurers.
>
> If Mr Hyndman's speech is accurately reported, he ought to be criminally prosecuted. An educated man is not to be excused for telling an ignorant crowd, of whom some may be in actual distress, that, instead of professing patriotism, if they wanted to fight they should fight the 'landowners'; and if they wanted to slaughter anybody, though he did not want to slaughter anybody,

they should slaughter the landowners, and not those who had done them no harm.

This kind of internationalism was combated in the press by intense patriotism (jingoism was the term soon to be used) and it is worthwhile to remember that Rudyard Kipling, a poet of the Empire who would almost certainly have become poet laureate had he not unwisely referred to Queen Victoria as 'the weeping widow at Windsor', was just beginning to write — his patriotic *Departmental Ditties* came out in 1886.

It was not only the Establishment in England that was becoming alarmed by this new trend of international socialism. In Paris in March 1885 not only were Fenian leaders arrested and expelled but the Prefect of Police drew up a decree absolutely prohibiting the display of red banners, and this in a country with a Republican government. At the funeral of Victor Hugo, at which a record 40,000 people were present, the police intervened and took away both socialist and anarchist banners. As so often, British press reports mixed the two movements inextricably together and the *Pall Mall Gazette* on 2 June 1885 reports: 'The knots of Communists who appeared on the scene early with their red and black flags, had their revolutionary emblems taken from them by the Police, and there was no disturbance.' Only a few days earlier, at the funeral of a leader of the Commune at the Père La Chaise cemetery there had been considerably more trouble over the flags (red this time) and the number injured by the police is given by the *Pall Mall Gazette* as 'more than a dozen' and by *Harper's Monthly Magazine* as 'over a hundred', figures in which the contradiction is only apparent.

Dynamiting proper, as distinct from mass movements of social protest, continued throughout Europe for the rest of 1885. In March a post office was blown up at Temesvar in Hungary, the whole of the furniture destroyed, and the three officials on duty were seriously injured. This may merely have been caused by dynamite in transit, and it is not clear where the explosion was intended to take place, because it was attributed to three small bags described as clover seed, received from Mannheim, known to be a resort of German anarchists, which was afterwards thought to be dynamite in a granulated form. On 6 June a report came from Madrid that a bomb supposed to have contained dynamite exploded outside the residence of a Catalan senator at Villanueva: one man was seriously and a woman slightly injured. On 24 June a telegram from Vienna carried the following report:

At Fünfkirchen, in Hungary, a terrible explosion has just occurred, in which the inventor of a new sort of dynamite has fallen a victim to his own invention. The man, a German named Lisch, resided with his aged mother in an isolated house, in which he was accustomed to carry on his dangerous trade. He had sold the patents for his new explosive in America and elsewhere. Just prior to the explosion he was engaged in nailing up a box containing a consignment of the material, when suddenly the whole blew up, unroofing the house and burying the inventor and his mother under the falling ruins.[20]

Robert Louis Stevenson and his wife who had just published their *More New Arabian Nights* when this Hungarian explosion occurred must have read this account of an inventor blown up with his own dynamite with the greatest interest as it was the kind of situation they so often envisaged in their tales.

In July 1885 the dynamite victim was a dog, who picked up an experimental cartridge and was only kept at a distance by a shower of stones until the poor animal sat down to gnaw its explosive bone and was blown to smithereens. On the same day, 28 July, an attempt was made to blow up the church at Sanvignes, near Montceau-les Mines, and three men were arrested and charged with the crime.

On 16 October 1885 at Leghorn a dynamite bomb was thrown into the barracks of the local police, but no-one was injured. Still in October another dynamite attempt against a church, this time at Brives, Carrège, was made in France, similar to the attack in July against the church at Sanvignes. On 27 November a bomb was placed under the windows of a café in Madrid. The explosion injured a waiter and two officers, and a number of arrests were made. The following day dynamite was used in an attempt to wreck a train in Switzerland on the Winterthur-Zurich line. The explosion seriously injured one of the passengers, although the train was only slightly damaged. On 17 November *The Times* reported an explosion at Sternberg, near Olmütz, while the *Pall Mall Gazette* of 9 December carried news of the arrest of the group responsible:

Four Anarchists, including one woman, were arrested yesterday in the manufacturing town of Sternberg, in Moravia. In the garden of one of the prisoners eight kilogrammes of dynamite were discovered. It has been ascertained that two robberies had been planned by the prisoners, the proceeds of which were intended to be employed in furthering the objects of their party.

That is to say this group, one of the members of which was a woman (as often happened in Russia but was less common in Europe at the time), was self-sufficient and not relying on external financial support.

After the end of 1885 dynamite activity diminished for a time, particularly in England, and government attention turned to that new threat to the Establishment, the mass protest movement of the unemployed. Since the Chartist demonstrations of the 1840s nothing had been seen in London like the Hyde Park meetings of the winter and early spring of 1886, and these too found their way into novels, particularly Mallock's *The Old Order Changes* and James's *The Princess Casamassima*. Much of the press attempted to establish links between terrorism and these movements of spontaneous social protest against unemployment and decreasing wages (spontaneous in the sense that many of the hunger marchers were not politicised although their organisation was in the hands of Hyndman and the Social Democratic Federation) and the stones thrown through the windows of the London clubs were seen as so many dynamite bombs *in nuce*.

In 1892-4 there was a fresh wave all over the Continent of political assassinations and dynamite activity (which had never wholly died down in Russia and Ireland), particularly in France and Spain. These outrages were by no means so violent in England as the 1885 outbreaks, but on 15 February 1892 Bourdin, a French anarchist, contrived to blow himself up in Greenwich Park, thereby furnishing Conrad with the basic plot material for the most widely read of all British dynamite novels: *The Secret Agent*. This attempt caused nothing like the panic of the 1884-5 London explosions, but the newspapers began once again to carry reports of the dynamitings and interest was reawakened so that the stream of dynamite novels which began in 1884 continued through to the end of the century and beyond.

When on 25 April 1892 a Paris wineshop was dynamited on the Boulevard Magenta, killing the proprietor and severely injuring five other inmates of the buildings, it was seen as the old story of an act of revenge against a suspected informer, for it was the very wineshop where the anarchist Ravachol had been arrested. Ravachol was held responsible for the resumption of bomb outrages in France, when in March 1892, at a fortnight's distance from each other, he blew up the houses of a judge and the prosecuting attorney in the trial of some anarchists arrested for promoting violent workers' demonstrations in Clichy on May Day 1891.

The theme of dynamite was also blended with women's liberation, and at the conference of the Women's Emancipation Union held at Birmingham in October 1892 one of the speakers suggested the use of dynamite to enforce the rights of her sex; adding that if they had a regiment of women who could shoot straight they would have the franchise in a week.

On 8 November 1892 further news came from Paris: a bomb placed in the offices of the Carmaux mining company was foolishly removed to the nearby police station where it shortly afterwards exploded, killing six people and destroying much of the building. As far as I have discovered nobody has written a novel around this particular bomb, yet the simplicity with which the problem of introducing dynamite into a guarded police station was overcome with the collaboration of the police themselves promises well for ironic treatment — possibly the fiction writers were afraid that their readers would find such a tale altogether beyond the bounds of credibility.

On the day after Christmas 1892 there was a renewed alarm in England, and steps were taken to protect public buildings both in London and in the provinces. Rules regarding public safety which in the last few years had been relaxed were ordered to be stringently enforced in view of the revival of the dynamite campaign, because on Christmas Eve a violent explosion, attributed to dynamite, had wrecked a large portion of the Dublin detective office which stood close to the Castle and the municipal buildings. Tension was kept alive by revolver shots in Downing Street on 26 April 1893 and a bomb in Dublin on 6 May.

On 20 June 1893 news came through of a peccant engine in Madrid which killed the anarchist who was placing it and seriously injured his accomplice. On 24 September an anarchist named Pallas threw a bomb in Barcelona during a review of troops. The bomb killed the horse on which Marshal Martinez Campos was riding and injured the Marshal together with 13 other officers and men, besides a large number of spectators. The thrower of the bomb was taken alive.

On 25 September 1893 we find yet another example of the risks run by informers, even by potential informers. At Pittsburgh, Pennsylvania, a Mr and Mrs Reese, who had become acquainted with some of the secrets of an anarchist organisation, were brutally murdered, and on the same day in San Francisco a labour union employed anarchist techniques, placing a dynamite bomb against a boarding house frequented by non-union sailors. Six were seriously injured, three of whom subsequently died. Meanwhile things were getting worse in Barcelona. On 7 November at the Lyceo theatre, during a performance of *William Tell*, two bombs were thrown from an upper gallery into the stalls. Only one exploded, but it killed 23 people, and others were killed and injured in the ensuing panic. The police at once arrested all known anarchists, and on 10 November the government of Spain suspended the constitution in Barcelona in so far as it concerned the liberties of the subject to allow the rounding up and arrest of all suspected persons. Furthermore an anarchist club was raided by police at Barcelona, and apparatus for the manufacture of bombs was found, besides papers proving that the club was the headquarters of a revolutionary movement. Later in the month, on 23 November, at Cajar near Granada, the home of the Secretary of the Agricultural Committee was blown to pieces by a bomb.

On 13 November 1893 the assassination by anarchists of the Serbian minister in Paris was a forewarning of that most fatal of all terrorist attacks when 21 years later the bomb thrown and shots fired at Sarajevo on 28 June 1914, assassinating the Archduke Francis Ferdinand of Austria and his wife, touched off the fuse of the First World War.

On 16 November 1893 a bomb exploded in an army barracks at Marseilles, wrecking part of the general's quarters and the guard house, and on 20 November a dynamite conspiracy in Montreal to blow up the Nelson Monument there came to the ears of the authorities and three young men were arrested on the spot, one carrying the incriminating dynamite bomb. This attempt caused a considerable stir in that one of the youths in question was the son of the ex-premier of Quebec, Hon. Honoré Mercier, which suggests that recruitment to the ranks of the dynamiters in the West, as well as in Russia, came not so much from the down-and-outs as from intellectuals.

In 25 November 1893 infernal machines were sent by post from Orleans in France to the German Emperor and German Chancellor, disguised as seeds for planting, but the devices were discovered in time. On 27 November a tin box containing dynamite, but with the fuse extinguished, was thrown into a yard adjoining barracks in Dublin. Two men were arrested but one was at once discharged. In the evening of the same day he was found shot in a lane near the quays, the kind of summary justice meted out to a suspected informer which played such a central part in the dynamite novels. A similar case occurred in Prague less than a month later when on 23 December a young man called Rudolph Mrva, a police spy who under the name of Rigoletto di Toscana had acted as chief investigator of the Omladina party, was found stabbed and there is little doubt that his assassination was the work of the confederates whom he had betrayed to the police.

Meanwhile one of the biggest dynamite outrages in Europe took place in Paris on 9 December 1893. During the sitting of the French Chamber of Deputies an explosive bomb was thrown from an upper gallery — but, striking against the balustrade, it exploded in the air instead of upon the floor of the House. About 80 persons were hurt, including 30 members. The thrower of the bomb, the well-known anarchist named Vaillant, was himself among the injured. The French anarchists continued their activities even after the capture of Vaillant. On 12 February 1894, in protest against Vaillant's execution on 5 February, a bomb was thrown into the midst of the people assembled in a café attached to the Terminus Hotel, Rue St Lazare in Paris, and a dozen persons were more or less injured. The man who threw the bomb had been seated in the gallery and tried to escape in the confusion, wounding several people with revolver shots when an attempt was made to capture him. When finally overpowered it was ascertained that his real name was Emile Henri, born at Barcelona of French parents. Some of the details of this man may have suggested to Conrad the idea he develops in his short story 'The Anarchist', published in *A Set of Six* in 1908.

On 20 February 1894, still in Paris, a dynamiter prepared a booby trap for the police, fixing a bomb on a shelf over the door in a house where he was lodging in such a way that it would fall and explode when the door opened. He then wrote to the commisary of police for the district to say that he had committed suicide. Three people were wounded as a result of his device, and one, the landlady, died. On 25 February the Italian anarchists made an attempt to emulate the Spanish, and a bomb was thrown in the Pisa opera house during a performance, but unlike the Madrid outrage, nobody was injured. On 8 March the Italian anarchists tried instead to emulate the French, and a bomb was thrown not inside but outside the Parliament in Piazza Montecitorio. One person was killed and seven were injured.

On 15 March 1894 the church of the Madeleine in Paris was the setting for a peccant engine explosion. A man, subsequently identified as the well-known Belgian anarchist named Jean Pauwels, let fall a bomb which presumably he had intended to throw among the congregation. It exploded at the door, killing Pauwels instantly and horribly mutilating him.

After the Greenwich Park explosion in 1892 England was relatively quiet. Foreign anarchists took refuge in London from time to time. One, François Polti, was arrested in London with a bomb in his possession (did this suggest the idea of the 'Professor' to Conrad?) and his rooms, on being searched, were found to contain a large stock of explosive materials, Another anarchist named Farnara, but who was said to be the Carnot who employed Polti, took refuge further afield, and was arrested in Stratford.

On 1 May 1894 the London anarchists, or rather the foreign anarchists based in London, considered the date propitious to come out into the open and attempted to speak in Hyde Park, but had to be protected by the police from the angry crowds. On 3 May a doctor and his wife were seriously injured at Liège in Belgium by the explosion of a bomb on the doorstep of their house, while on the same day in York Town in Western Australia the presbytery attached to the Roman Catholic church was wrecked. On 8 May a bomb exploded, injuring three persons, at the entrance of the Odescalchi palace in Rome, while at Algiers a small hotel kept by an Italian named Tosti was blown up by dynamite. This was clearly a vendetta of the kind so popular with the novelists, because Tosti had given evidence at Toulon which led to the conviction of two anarchists, so he had been hunted down to his home in another continent. On 11 May there was a dynamite explosion in a fashionable quarter of Paris, the Avenue Kléber, and on 25 May a plot was discovered at Buenos Aires to blow up the Parliament and exchange.

In the following month, June 1894, there were two assassination attempts, one in Italy and one in France: an anarchist named Paolo Lega tried to shoot the Italian Prime Minister, Francesco Crispi, on his way to Parliament, but the Premier escaped unhurt. The President of the French Republic instead was stabbed and mortally wounded on 24 June by an Italian named Santo Caserio during his visit to Lyons, as he was driving from the Palais de Commerce to attend a gala performance at the Great Theatre.

In 1895 there was notably less anarchist activity, partly due to the number of arrests made in 1894, particularly in Spain, France and Germany. The sporadic attempts which did occur seem to have been the work of individuals and their objectives of local rather than national importance: the editor of a Hungarian newspaper, the manager of a French mining company, a leading manufacturer at Mulhousen. A bomb was thrown in Paris into the doorway of Rothchild's bank in the Rue Lafitte, but not only did it fail to explode, but the youth who threw it was at once captured. The great wave of dynamiting was over.

The foregoing paragraphs list, for the most part, the successful attempts, those in which the dynamite in fact exploded. There were also many unsuccessful attempts reported in the press, together with police searches and the discovery of dynamite caches in the houses of terrorists. Added to this were the reports of arrests and trials of men, and sometimes women, charged with perpetrating these crimes, or of printing and distributing anarchist propaganda, so that those novelists who after the London explosions had set to work on dynamite novels found plenty of material in the British press to furnish them with realistic details, fresh episodes coming to hand even as they were writing. It is not so important, I believe, to trace specific 'sources in single newspaper reports. It is rather that all newspapers at the time were carrying these and similar accounts so that the effect was cumulative. I have taken most, though not all, of the material quoted from the *Annual Register* and from two newspapers of different political tendencies: *The Times* and the *Pall Mall Gazette*. Both were papers catering for 'top people'; both are referred to in journals and letters for these years by such eminent writers as George Gissing and Henry James. Both carried ample and well-written book reviews. It therefore seems reasonable to suppose that other writers of the period also saw the same papers, either at home or in their clubs. One thing at least is certain: whatever paper the novelist in the mid-1880s and early 1890s propped up on his breakfast table, it would speak to him of dynamite outrages, infernal machines, and most intriguing of all, of peccant engines.

Notes

1. *PMG*, 4 Feb. 1885.
2. Ibid.
3. Grant Allen, *For Maimie's Sake: A Tale of Love and Dynamite* (London, 1886), p. 24.
4. *PMG*, 4 Feb. 1885.
5. W. H. Tilley, *The Background of 'The Princess Casamassima'* (University of Florida Monographs, 1961).
6. Edward Jenkins, *A Week of Passion* (London, 1884), Vol. 2, p. 135.
7. *PMG*, 18 Dec. 1884.

8. *Annual Register*, July 1884.
9. *Annual Register*, 7 March 1884.
10. *PMG*, 23 Dec. 1884.
11. *PMG*, 24 Jan. 1885.
12. *PMG*, 31 Jan. 1885.
13. William Minto, *The Crack of Doom*, three vols. (London, 1886).
14. *The Times*, 11 Feb. 1885.
15. *PMG*, 10 Feb. 1885.
16. *PMG*, 20 Feb. 1885.
17. Reuter correspondent's report, as published in *PMG*, 24 Feb. 1885.
18. This is so far as we can judge from Buckle's edition of the *Letters* which gives an ample selection from the Queen's journals and correspondence.
19. *PMG*, 17 Feb. 1885.
20. *PMG*, 24 June, 1885.

3 PECCANT ENGINES

Robert Louis Stevenson and his wife, Fanny Van de Grift, were the first writers to exploit the bomb which goes off not with a bang but a whimper in their *More New Arabian Nights: The Dynamiter*, 1885. This deliberately humorous treatment of what was becoming a tragic theme almost backfired on the authors themselves. The plots of all but one of the stories in this collection of tales date back to 1883, when dynamite was not yet felt to be a threat to be taken very seriously in England. They were not, in the first place, intended for publication at all: the story of their inception is narrated by Gosse in his preface to the 1907 edition of Stevenson's *Works*:

> During the later part of his stay at Hyères, in the winter of 1883, R.L.S. was reduced to temporary blindness by a distressing attack of ophthalmic conjunctivitis. Mrs Stevenson states that, for her husband's amusement through this dreary time, a scheme was set on foot. 'I was to go out,' she said, 'for an hour's walk every afternoon, if it were only back and forth in front of our door, and invent a story to repeat when I came in — a sort of Arabian Night's entertainment where I was to take the part of Scheherazade and he the Sultan. There had been several dynamite outrages in London about this time, the most of them turning out fiascos. It occurred to me to take an impotent dynamite intrigue as the thread to string my stories on. I began with the Mormon tale, and followed it with innumerable others, one for each afternoon. As time passed, my husband gradually regained his health to a degree, became again absorbed in his work, and the stories of Scheherazade were thought of no more.'[1]

It was only in the following year that the Stevensons, finding themselves very short of money, decided to put these tales together and publish them. They had never been written out before, but were quickly jotted down, and as the result was rather a slim volume Stevenson added another: 'The Explosive Bomb', the story of a man running round London unable to get rid of an infernal machine timed to explode within the hour. Every time he manages to deposit it somebody more or less politely returns it to him. The comedy was

of the simplest possible sort, and was intended to counteract the
scaremongering of the press after the early London explosions by
showing the terrorists to be hopelessly inefficient and dangerous to
no one but themselves. Comedy has always been an excellent way of
relaxing tension and the aim of the joint authors was admirable.
Unfortunately, when the book was already in preparation, the big
London explosions of January 1885 took place and the Stevensons
felt that this was hardly the moment to expect people to laugh at
Zero and his exploits.

So they hit on the idea of dedicating their work to 'Messrs Cole
and Cox, Police Officers', the two policemen who had been injured
in the Westminster Hall explosion. The preface deserves to be
reprinted in its entirety as an example of writing one's way out of a
very embarrassing situation. The Stevensons are seen here trying
very hard indeed to get into line with public opinion, praising the
police for their defence of 'the child' and 'the breeding woman'.
They join in the attack on Mr Parnell, the member for Ireland who
refused to rise in the British Parliament and condemn the actions of
the dynamiters. They even, for good measure, drag in General
Gordon, setting forth upon his tragic enterprise, implying perhaps
that it was a particularly ungenerous moment to attack England at
home when she was undergoing defeat abroad. Their central
argument, that they have not treated the subject seriously because
dynamite terrorism is a crime which preserves none of the features
of nobility, hardly stands up to close examination, but they so
appealed to public sympathy by dedicating the book to the heroes of
the hour and touching on all the themes that filled the leaders in the
popular press, that their book raised no outcry and may even have
sold all the better just because of its topicality. The preface reads:

Gentlemen,
    In the volume now in your hands, the authors have touched
upon that ugly devil of crime, with which it is your glory to have
contended. It were a waste of ink to do so in a serious spirit. Let us
dedicate our horror to acts of a more mingled strain, where crime
preserves some features of nobility, and where reason and
humanity can still relish the temptation. Horror, in this case, is
due to Mr Parnell: he sits before posterity silent, Mr Forster's
appeal echoing down the ages. Horror is due to ourselves, in that
we have so long coquetted with political crime; not seriously
weighing, not acutely following it from cause to consequence; but

with a generous unfounded heat of sentiment, like the schoolboy with the penny tale, applauding what was specious. When it touched ourselves (truly in a vile shape), we proved false to these imaginations; discovered, in a clap, that crime was no less cruel and no less ugly under sounding names; and recoiled from our false deities.

But seriousness comes most in place when we speak of our defenders. Whoever be in the right in this great and confused war of politics; whatever elements of greed, whatever traits of the bully, dishonour both parties in this inhuman contest; — your side, your part, is at least pure of doubt. Yours is the side of the child, of the breeding woman, of individual pity and public trust. If our society were the mere kingdom of the devil (as indeed it wears some of his colours) it yet embraces many precious elements and many innocent persons whom it is a glory to defend. Courage and devotion, so common in the ranks of the police, so little recognized, so meagrely rewarded, have at length found their commemoration in an historical act. History, which will represent Mr Parnell sitting silent under the appeal of Mr Forster, and Gordon setting forth upon his tragic enterprise, will not forget Mr Cole carrying the dynamite in his defenceless hands, nor Mr Cox coming coolly to his aid.

R.L.S.
F.V.de G.S.[2]

The tales themselves were strung together on the pattern already tried out in *The New Arabian Nights* (1882). The passages relating to Prince Florizel were entirely the work of R.L.S., and served to connect the two volumes together. Mrs Stevenson's stories have a distinctly different flavour from those of her husband. Both 'The Destroying Angel' and 'The Fair Cuban' were her work, and they strike a romantic, almost mystical note, close at times to the early work of Marie Corelli, a note which is entirely lacking in his. The same element of the unsuccessful explosion is to be found in both, but while Robert stresses the comedy Fanny stresses the mystery. Her first tale, the story of a girl growing up among the Mormons in America and then trying to escape, has many of the elements which Arthur Conan Doyle was to use a few years later in his *A Study in Scarlet* (1887). Both writers see the sect as evil, and its leaders as possessing strange powers over their followers' lives. Both are tales of delayed vengeance. Both begin in the alkaline desert of Utah while the conclusion of the tale takes place in London. The fate of a girl destined to become a member of the harem of one of the leading Mormons is described by both Fanny Van de Grift and Arthur Conan Doyle in the same terms: it is seen as a form of prostitution to which death is a happy alternative. 'The Destroying Angel' reads:

> . . . to find favour in the eyes of the President himself. Such a fate for a girl like you were worse than death; better to die as your mother died than to sink daily deeper into the mire of this pit of woman's degradation.[3]

And John Ferrier in *A Study in Scarlet* expresses the same thought:

> He had always determined, deep down in his resolute heart, that nothing would ever induce him to allow his daughter to wed a Mormon. Such a marriage he regarded as no marriage at all, but as a shame and a disgrace.[4]

The chapter heading 'The Avenging Angels' in Conan Doyle's book may also owe something to Mrs Stevenson's title 'The Destroying Angel'. It seems probable that either Conan Doyle had read *More New Arabian Nights* or that both writers drew their plot from a common source, possibly a newspaper or magazine article about the Mormon sect. The similarity of the landscape with its rugged mountains and ash grey glittering alkaline desert inclines me to think that the author of *A Study in Scarlet* knew Mrs Stevenson's work directly, but he did nothing with the dynamite theme that was central to her story.

Had *More New Arabian Nights* contained only stories in her vein the book would have stood in no need of an apologetic preface. For Mrs Stevenson treats dynamite with all due respect as a very awful and mysterious source of power in the hands of the Mormons. Set in a wild and threatening landscape the first dynamite experiment witnessed by the Mormon girl in the house of a scientist known as 'the doctor' links up with the romantic writings of half a century earlier, with tales like Mary Shelley's *Frankenstein* or John William Polidori's *The Vampyre* or *Ernestus Berchtold*. The description of a night journey through the mountains when the girl first sees this terrible power at work (although it is in fact a peccant engine which all but destroys its inventor) has more of the elements of the sublime than of the ridiculous in its telling:

. . . from the great chimney at the west end poured forth a coil of smoke so thick and so voluminous, that it hung for miles along the windless night air, and its shadow lay far abroad in the moonlight upon the glittering alkali. As we continued to draw near, besides, a regular and panting throb began to divide the silence. First it seemed to me like the beating of a heart; and next it put into my mind the thought of some giant, smothered under mountains, and still, with incalculable effort, fetching breath. I had heard of the railway, though I had not seen it, and I turned to ask the driver if this resembled it. But some look in his eye, some pallor, whether of fear or moonlight on his face, caused the words to die upon my lips. We continued, therefore, to advance in silence, till we were close below the lighted house; when suddenly, without one premonitory rustle, there burst forth a report of such bigness that it shook the earth and set the echoes of the mountains thundering from cliff to cliff. A pillar of amber flame leaped from the chimney-top and fell in multitudes of sparks; and at the same time the lights in the windows turned for one instant ruby red and then expired. The driver had checked his horse instinctively, and the echoes were still rumbling farther off among the mountains, when there broke from the now darkened interior a series of yells — whether of man or woman it was impossible to guess — the door flew open, and there ran forth into the moonlight, at the top of the long slope, a figure clad in white, which began to dance and leap and throw itself down, and roll as if in agony before the house. I could no more restrain my cries; the driver laid his lash about the horse's flank, and we fled up the rough track at the peril of our lives . . .[5]

It is in 'The Superfluous Mansion' and 'The Brown Box' sections of this book, which clearly bear the stamp of R.L.S.'s own writing, that the fiasco becomes the whole point of the story. Zero, the mysterious terrorist, whose bombs go off in the wrong way, at the wrong time and in the wrong place, is the anti-hero. We first meet Zero in 'The Squire of Dames' section, and it is enough to put the explosion which occurs in this tale side by side with the one in the Mormon desert, to sense the difference in tone:

As he so stood, he was startled by a dull and jarring detonation from within. This was followed by a monstrous hissing and simmering as from a kettle of the bigness of St Paul's; and at the same time from every chink of door and window spurted an ill-smelling vapour. The cat disappeared with a cry. Within the lodging house feet pounded on the stairs; the door flew back, emitting clouds of smoke; and two men and an elegantly dressed young lady tumbled forth into the street and fled without a word.[6]

The book contains two interviews of considerable interest, for which the details have been gleaned from the contemporary press. Indeed it seems clear that, although the original plots must for the most part have been those invented at Hyères, yet much was added when it came to writing them out, and this new material came from the newspapers of the time. One of the two interviews was with a repentant would-be-assassin and the other with the dynamiter, Zero. Stevenson's quarrel with the press over the frequent use of the term 'dynamitard' is also worth noting. He himself consistently used the term 'dynamiter', and added a note to the effect that 'Any writard who writes dynamitard shall find in me a never-resting fightard'.

The interview with the repentant terrorist stresses the oath that had been taken at the outset, and the impossibility of leaving the organisation after a change of heart — that is to say exactly the situation which Henry James was later to develop in the character of Hyacinth in *The Princess Casamassima*. Stevenson's young man knows too much, he cannot be allowed to leave the group of conspirators. He tries to escape but is tracked down in Paris and brought back into the organisation. He complains: 'That oath is all my history. To give freedom to posterity, I had forsworn my own.' His doubts are moral ones as to the means which the organisation is using: 'Horrible was the society with which we warred, but our means were not less horrible.' The oath separated him from his fiancée and from his family. We are not told what happens to him at the end of the tale, but as he is left with the task of removing the body of his fellow conspirator whom in a moment of conscience he had betrayed, his fate can easily be foretold. His last recorded words are spoken, understandably, 'with a dismal accent'. Here Stevenson is following precisely the scheme laid down in the press: the recruitment of terrorists is attributed to a moment of youthful folly from which there is no possibility of return:

'. . . in surely no ungenerous impatience I enrolled myself among the enemies of this unjust and doomed society; in surely no unnatural desire to keep the fires of my philanthropy alight, I bound myself with an irrevocable oath.'[7]

This dismal young man is almost a stereotype in the dynamite novels: more original is the figure of Zero, the dynamiter himself, who may have been modelled on O'Donovan Rossa's collaborator, Mezzeroff and who is the central figure in 'The Superfluous Mansion'.

Zero loves his job, loves the material he works with, has no qualms whatever about the neighbourhood of the children's hospital to the scene of his experiments. On one occasion, when told that the Red Lion Court bomb had been a failure he indignantly defends his reputation with the statement 'a child was injured'. Zero is a foreigner, he pronounces 'bomb' as 'boom'. When his landlord grows suspicious and penetrates into Zero's room he finds all the paraphernalia that contemporary newspaper accounts would lead us to expect:

> . . . the locks of dismounted pistols; clocks and clockwork in every stage of demolition, some still busily ticking, some reduced to their dainty elements; a great company of carboys, jars and bottles; a carpenter's bench and a laboratory-table . . . On a table, several wigs and beards were lying spread.[8]

The landlord is so deeply engaged in examining these properties that he is caught by Zero himself who, instead of silencing him forever sits down, offers him a drink, and proceeds to give away a great deal of further information. 'The Superfluous Mansion' makes no attempt at realism, except at psychological realism in the megalomania of the dynamiter:

> 'Obscure yet famous. Mine is an anonymous, infernal glory. By infamous means, I work towards my bright purpose . . . I may justly describe myself as being nameless by day. But,' he continued, rising to his feet, 'by night and among my desperate followers, I am the redoubted Zero.'[9]

When he comes to recount his exploits, it is the dangers and difficulties on which he dwells:

> 'In this dark period of time, a star — the star of dynamite — has risen for the oppressed; and among those who practise its use, so

thick beset with dangers and attended by such incredible difficulties and disappointments, few have been more assiduous, and not many — ' He paused, and a shade of embarrassment appeared upon his face — 'not many have been more successful than myself.'[10]

When the landlord, 'speaking as a layman', argues that nothing could be simpler or safer than to deposit an infernal machine and retreat abroad, Zero sets out to enlighten him in somewhat alarming terms:

> 'Do you make nothing, then, of such a peril as we share this moment? Do you think it nothing to occupy a house like this one, mined, menaced, and in a word, literally tottering to its fall?'
> 'Good God!' ejaculated Somerset.
> 'And when you speak of ease', pursued Zero, 'in this age of scientific studies, you fill me with surprise. Are you not aware that chemicals are proverbially fickle as woman, and clockwork as capricious as the very devil? Do you see upon my brow these furrows of anxiety? Do you observe the silver threads that mingle with my hair? Clockwork, clockwork has stamped them on my brow — chemicals have sprinkled them upon my locks! No, Mr Somerset,' he resumed, after a moment's pause, his voice still quivering with sensibility, 'you must not suppose the dynamiter's life to be all gold. On the contrary: you cannot picture to yourself the blood-shot vigils and the staggering disappointments of a life like mine. I have toiled (let us say) for months, up early and down late; my bag is ready, my clock set; a daring agent has hurried with white face to deposit the instrument of ruin; we await the fall of England, the massacre of thousands, the yell of fear and execration; and lo! a snap like that of a child's pistol, an offensive smell, and the entire loss of so much time and plant! If,' he concluded musingly, 'we had been merely able to recover the lost bags, I believe, with but a touch or two, I could have remedied the peccant engine.'[11]

He goes on to suggest that such are the uncertainties of dynamite warfare that the French terrorists are proposing a primitive form of chemical warfare in its place — they are studying a plan whereby the drainage systems of cities can be disrupted and whole populations swept away by typhoid, 'a tempting and scientific project'. Zero, however, refuses to give up dynamite and in an ironic passage weighs up and refuses the alternative attractions of germ warfare:

> I recognise its elegance; but, sir, I have something of the poet in my nature; something, possibly, of the tribune. And, for my small part, I shall remain devoted to that more emphatic, more striking, and (if you please) more popular method of the explosive bomb.[12]

It is declarations such as this, in which the tales abound, which must have caused some hesitation in the authors, and probably also in the publisher, as to whether the book might not give offence at a moment when London was just recovering from the shock of the Fenian bombs at Westminster, the Houses of Parliament, and the Tower.

Not much is said about the purposes behind the bombs. Speaking of his past exploits, Zero says 'I found the liberty and peace of a poor country desperately abused; the future smiles upon that land.' When finally the superfluous mansion is blown high into the air, albeit seven minutes too early, Zero exclaims 'Ah Erin, green Erin, what a day of glory', so the reader is led to think that the foreigner (of German origin?) who pronounces 'bomb' as 'boom' must be working for the Fenians. At the end of the book he leaves for Philadelphia, linking up with the Irish-American connection. Furthermore the man who so desperately carries a time-bomb about London in 'The Explosive Bomb' episode is called M'Guire, which may be a reminiscence of the Mafia-type group of Irish dynamiters, the Molly Maguires, who operated in the Pennsylvania mining district but whose ringleaders had all been hung in the 1870s. Originally a popular movement working in the interests of Irish immigrants, they became a terrorist power group and were put down by Major Allan Pinkerton (known as 'the eye that never sleeps') who started the United States secret service. Their dynamiting activities terrified the whole countryside in 1871–2 and they were finally given away by a supergrass called James McParlan.[13] Some account of their activities, like that of the Mormons, may have been circulating in England and have furnished material to dynamite novelists, as Stevenson's use of M'Guire rather than any other common Irish surname might suggest. Nothing else is said in the *Tales* about the ideology behind the dynamiter, because it was the Stevensons' intention to draw a picture of cranks and fanatics rather than of liberators.

One other tale probably drew its origins from newspapers of the time: the very title of 'The Brown Box' recalls the evidence against Cunningham and Burton for the Charing Cross station explosion. Cabmen, porters and landladies were all engaged in identifying the box in which the dynamite cakes were carried, so that Stevenson, writing up his tale, enjoyed making this yet another of Zero's fiascos:

> A dull and startling thud resounded through the room; their eyes blinked against the coming horror; and still clinging together like drowning people, they fell on the floor. Then followed a prolonged and strident hissing as from the indignant pit; an offensive stench seized them by the throat; the room was filled with dense and choking fumes.
>
> Presently these began a little to disperse: and when at length they drew themselves, all limp and shaken, to a sitting posture, the first object that greeted their vision was the box reposing uninjured in its corner, but still leaking little wreaths of vapour round the lid.
>
> 'Oh, poor Zero!' cried the girl with a strange sobbing laugh. 'Alas, poor Zero! This will break his heart!.'[14]

The Stevensons' book is no masterpiece. The tales hang together very badly in the 'Prologue of the Cigar Divan' and 'Epilogue of the Cigar Divan' framework, but it was an interesting attempt to defuse some of the panic that was building up in London and which led to the indiscriminate sacking of many poor Irish labourers who for years had been living and working in England. The new and best story, 'Zero's Tale of the Explosive Bomb' is set right in the middle of the book, and draws upon the May 1884 explosions, particularly the carpet bag at the foot of the Nelson Column which failed to go off. Stevenson, in his usual debunking fashion, shifts the objective from Nelson's Monument to Shakespeare's, and writes:

> 'Our objective was the effigy of Shakespeare in Leicester Square: a spot, I think, admirably chosen; not only for the sake of the dramatist, still very foolishly claimed as a glory by the English race, in spite of his disgusting political opinions; but from the fact that the seats in the immediate neighbourhood are often thronged by children, errand-boys, unfortunate young ladies of

the poorer class, and infirm old men — all classes making a direct appeal to public pity, and therefore suitable with our design.'[15]

If Stevenson wanted to play down the horror of dynamite, there were other novelists of the time who, instead, were interested in playing it up, sometimes going so far as to defeat their own ends and from a very excess of horror falling into the ridiculous. Such is the case of Edward Jenkins's *A Week of Passion or the Dilemma of Mr George Barton the Younger* (1884). This three-volume novel opens with a chapter modestly called 'A Sensation'. The sensation in question is an explosion in Regent Circus one Thursday afternoon on 26 June 188-, at twenty-seven minutes past four o'clock, an explosion which is so complete that all trace of the victim disappears:

> 'Blood!'
> Blood, sprinkled in a fine rain, and here and there in large drops, on faces, on hands, on bright dresses, and light bonnets, and silken sunshades, and delicate-tinted gloves, on shiny hats, and ivory shirt-fronts, and white waistcoats, and with it here and there small knobs and particles of something which made people instinctively shudder and cry out, when they became conscious of its presence on skin or clothing![16]

And once again on the following page:

> There were no palpable signs except that rain of flesh and blood, which had sent a ghastly thrill of horror through the crowd, and a dent in the roadway about the size of a French wash-basin.
> Modern science had achieved a fresh marvel. A horrible crime had been committed in the presence of a thousand people; and there appeared to be no traces left, either of the victim or the perpetrators.[17]

The immediate assumption of the crowd which gathers round the site of the explosion is that a dynamiter has fallen victim to his own machine and the author comments: 'The idea of a Fenian blowing *himself* up in this sensational manner seemed to be diverting.' The first reaction is that this is a political crime which has failed owing to a peccant engine (and Jenkins's book came out a year before the Stevensons' and may have been known to them). The author, however, was writing a novel in which dynamite was being used for private and not for political ends. The whole of the first chapter, which is by far the best in the long novel, is devoted to details of the explosion and the presentation of the mystery which the story goes on to unravel: who was blown up, and why?

The novel is a whodunnit, and is interesting because it introduces a character, Mr Sontag, the chief of the detective department, who carries deduction to a fine art: that is to say he is the forerunner of Arthur Conan Doyle's Sherlock Holmes, who only appeared in fiction three years later. He says of himself, much in the words Dr Watson uses of Holmes:

> The rapidity of observation is the artist's faculty. He has a quick glance, which takes in all the outlines, all the details of form and colour; and the real artist has, besides that, an intuitive sense of the *character* of the object he looks at. Every good detective is an artist with the poetry suppressed.[18]

Mr Sontag is put forward by his author as a model; his astuteness is constantly praised and, with the help of Mr George Barton the younger whose dilemma, in the shape of a young lady, is the source of the many complications enabling Edward to spin out the story to the end of Volume three, he arrives at a satisfactory conclusion in keeping with his early surmise in Volume one. Speaking to Sir Henry, the Chief Commissioner, he opines:

> Take my word for it, the real criminals — for I am sure it was no suicide — are either political conspirators, and that I don't believe, for, if I am not mistaken the man was an Englishman, and neither a Fenian, Nihilist, nor Socialist — or they are people who are of such position and wealth that, when these were menaced, they would hardly hesitate to commit any crime or go to any expense to save themselves from discovery.[19]

What is interesting to us today is the assumption which the author presumed would be shared by his readers, that socialists were among the people who might reasonably be expected to be caught in Regents Circus with dynamite about their persons, and that it was inconceivable that they should be English. This technique of criminalisation of the socialists was so common in the press at the time that a popular writer took it over without question. The quality of Jenkins's writing, and the amount of thought that he put into this novel, can be judged from the contradictory nature of two passages which follow hard on each other's heels on page 115 and page 118 of Volume one. Both are descriptions of interviews between Le Breton, a British nobleman, and the son of the exploded George Barton. In the first Le Breton is presented as possessing traditional British phlegm: 'It was thoroughly English sympathy and reserve, deep and hot as a sleeping volcano, the top of which is covered with snow.' But three pages later this perfect gentleman goes to pieces to such an extent that he not only babbles (and it would be difficult to find a less dignified form of utterance) but he drops that symbol of his British taciturnity, his pipe: 'The horror and pain which appeared on Le Breton's face were indescribable. He attempted to babble out a few words, but his voice died upon his lips. The pipe dropped out of his hands upon the floor.' In this novel the aristocracy certainly does not stand up well under strain; again in the first volume Lord Selby breaks down at the mere idea that he could be suspected of a dynamite crime: '"Good God!" he murmured, "the boy thinks me a murderer!" Tears shot from his eyes like rain. But for that relief he must have fallen to the floor, as if struck by a thunderbolt.'[20] Notwithstanding his own evidence to the contrary, the author remains firmly convinced of the peculiar *sang-froid* of the English, and a few pages later comments in all good faith, 'This strange and proud reserve is unknown to any other race'.

Clearly the author's main concern was to get on with his story at any price, even that of consistency, so that it would be unreasonable to look for any but superficial impressions. Yet just for this reason his book is interesting, because what he gives us are the accepted clichés that the subscribers to Mudie's library, who formed the bulk of the readers of these three-volume novels in the 1880s, would not think of questioning. His biography of a dynamiter, Schultz, the man who made the Regents Circus bomb, contains all the stereotyped details:

He is, however, a German, a man of good education — graduated at Bonn — took to chemistry, in which he became very strong — and might have made a fortune, for he is immensely clever . . . no sooner had he invented anything than he sold the patents, rioted away till the money was spent, and then set his wits to work to devise some new sensation in chemistry or crime. He was a

Socialist and Anarchist, or professed to be — had to cut for his life once from Berlin, where he was mixed up in a plot to kill the Emperor.[21]

The starting point is a chemist, of German origin. Politically he is that popular hybrid, the socialist *and* anarchist. The popularisation of this composite figure did much (together with a uninominal electoral system) to ensure that the Social Democratic Federation stood no chance in the elections of the following year, 1885. He is directly involved in 'a plot against the life of the German emperor', suggesting that Jenkins, like Henry James in *The Princess Casamassima*, had the Reinsdorf-Küchler-Rupsch conspiracy of 1883 in mind, although as his book came out in 1884 he was unable to follow all the details of the trial, and Schultz, unlike James's Hoffendahl, is given no ideological reasons for his actions. While Hoffendahl has been subjected to imprisonment and torture for his political convictions, Schultz is no more than a common criminal, spending his substance in riotous living and then selling his ideas and his dynamite to private operators in the field of crime, in this case to a firm of defecting solicitors.

Jenkins goes on to dot the i's of his belief in the immorality of socialism as such, attributing a long tirade on the subject to no less a person than Mr Sontag the detective, who is presented as the most intelligent character in the book, and therefore as a man whose opinion is to be taken seriously. Discussing the crime and using his famous method of deduction, Mr Sontag ties up socialists and criminals as one and the same:

'They [the men who ordered the dynamiting] must be very rich persons, capable of commanding the assistance of the ablest of those secret criminal organizations which are always existing in the great Continental cities, some of which conceal vulgar criminal objects under the disguise of political associations, others of bogus international financial or commercial companies, wherein we sometimes find men of exceptional intellect and education engaged. Many of these men are really political agitators as well. They have so befogged themselves with Socialistic ideas, that they have actually succeeded in persuading themselves that there is no difference between *meum* and *tuum*. A man when he is persuaded of that is, so far as all human law is concerned, already a criminal in principle. Some go no further —

but it is not wonderful if many do not stop there, but become criminals in practice.'[22]

For good measure Mr Sontag throws in at this point also the Irish agitators, who have nothing whatever to do with this crime:

'The Irish agitator, for instance, in the House of Commons, says that the land which belongs to the Irish landlords is that of the Irish tenants. The Irish agitator in Ireland really believes this doctrine, and falls back on it to justify shooting the landlord. I am not a politician, but I simply take note of a fact, which, as a policeman, I am bound to note, and which is to me an alarming one, and it is this — that the Socialistic ideas now allowed to be freely propagated in all free countries, and which are being propagated in spite of authority in others, are developing and producing a large number of criminals, not of the ordinary kind — low, vulgar, uneducated villains, but men of intelligence and resources.'[23]

In point of fact the real criminals in the book are a long-standing and eminently respectable firm of solicitors who have been mismanaging an estate and speculating disastrously with the proceeds. They employ the German chemist, Schultz, as a technician to get rid of the estate agent who has begun to investigate their misdeeds. Jenkins is not writing a political novel, but he is nevertheless manipulating public opinion so that the incautious reader, instead of drawing the obvious moral of 'put not thy trust in firms of respectable solicitors' is encouraged to attribute all the evil in the world to dynamiters — socialists, anarchists and Irish agitators.

The note of mystery and horror which is struck in the first chapter is not kept up throughout the whole, much of which is concerned with the feelings of the juvenile lead for a heroine (appropriately called Blanche to emphasise her purity) whose father he erroneously believes to be responsible for the 'ghastly and original exit from London society' of his own father. Elements of the Gothic novel and even of Jacobean tragedy are also exploited, particularly in the dismembered hand which is found on the following day on a window-ledge 250 yards from the scene of the explosion 'bearing evidence of having been violently torn from the wrist of the proprietor'. This hand is the only clue to the identity of the victim of the peccant engine, which by blowing up before its due time failed to kill also a second victim designate; and most conveniently the little finger has a slight congenital deformity, besides belonging to a 'muscular man of past middle age, who, however, was not accustomed to manual labour'. These clues enable Sherlock Holmes's predecessor to trace the identity of the victim and thence the motive and the perpetrator. Had Jenkins been content to follow up these threads in one volume he would have produced a very readable story, but Mr Sontag's researches are interspersed with long and complicated love passages and misunderstandings in which the psychology is as unacceptable as the dialogue. It is nevertheless a typical example of the popular dynamite novel, where the explosive, packed into a watch (of which a fragment of the enamel face conveniently carries a piece of the maker's name — just enough to enable the sharp-eyed detective to trace the customer) is immensely powerful and is being used by ordinary criminals, in spite of Jenkins's attempt to provide them with political affiliations.

It is nevertheless with relief that we turn to another example of the peccant engine, by far the best in the English novel, to be found in Joseph Conrad's *The Secret Agent*; here, too, dynamite is used ironically, but whereas Stevenson's irony was of the most obvious kind, and Jenkins's was extremely heavy-handed, that of Conrad is exquisite in its varying layers of subtlety. Like Stevenson, Conrad refused to take his anarchists seriously. The plot of his novel was based on an actual event which took place in Greenwich in 1894, although Conrad wrote the novel later, and published it in 1907. As George Woodcock points out in his book on *Anarchism*: 'The only victim of anarchist violence in England was a Frenchman named Marcel Bourdin, who in 1894 accidentally blew himself up in Greenwich Park with a homemade bomb intended for use abroad.'[24]

Reading the novels of the 1880s and 1890s we get the impression of a whole network of anarchist activity in England and particularly in London, but Bourdin, as Woodcock points out, was the *only* casualty in fact as distinguished from fiction. In Conrad's novel the peccant engine is not even carried by a real anarchist — he narrates an explosion caused by an *agent provocateur* in the pay of a foreign embassy which desires to move the British to adopt strong antiterrorist measures. The tale is potentially comic, and many of the elements out of which it is constructed are in fact the elements of comedy. The choice of the Greenwich Observatory as the objective of the explosion with its implied attack on science is very like the attack on Shakespeare's Monument as the representative of culture in Stevenson's tale. Both writers are decidedly tongue-in-the-cheek with regard to the presumed reaction of the British public in the face of the selection of these historic locations. Another potentially comic element is Conrad's description of the London anarchists themselves, the group which the secret agent is paid to frequent and on whose activities he reports. The total absence of any real activity and the inconclusiveness of their tirades takes us forward to Jack London's *The Assassination Bureau* (where the anarchists employ a firm of professional assassins) and back to the club at the Sun and Moon in Henry James's *The Princess Casamassima* which is only the façade and recruiting ground for real conspirators. Looking back over English novels of the nineteenth century these meetings can be seen to be a modernisation of those early Chartist and trade union meetings which were so often presented (even by 'sympathetic' novelists) as comic. The difficulties of uneducated speakers trying to express themselves in Queen's English were often parodied, as were defects of mannerism (as Slackbridge in *Hard Times*). And the leaders were further rendered ridiculous by physical deformities. Slackbridge, badly dressed and 'wiping his forehead from left to right' (how else, if we stop to think about it, should a speaker wipe his forehead if the heat of the crowded room renders this operation necessary?) is picked up and multiplied in Gissing's *Demos* where not one of the leaders is presented as physically normal.

Conrad was drawing on this tradition of class caricature when he described the London anarchists in *The Secret Agent* as being not only ineffectual but also physically repulsive. It is the kind of manipulative humour which he had learned from his predecessors and which he uses remorselessly throughout *The Secret Agent*. There is also a kind of macabre humour conforming with the popular horror tradition in the relentless details of the peculiar violence of the Greenwich Park explosion. The horrific description given by the Chief Inspector is very like the rain of blood described in the first chapter of Jenkins's *A Week of Passion*. The Chief Inspector communicates the news to the unhappy Verloc: "'Blown to small bits: limbs, gravel, clothing, bones, splinters — all mixed up together. I tell you they had to fetch a shovel to gather him up with.'"[25]

Yet in Conrad all these potentially comic elements take on a subtle difference — they all effectively enhance the tragedy of a most tragic story. Into this melodramatic framework of a bomb outrage effected not by the anarchists themselves but in such a way that it would inevitably be attributed to anarchists, and which in any case was not intended to do more than token damage, Conrad introduces four very real and convincing characters, motivated by feelings which are wholly credible and often creditable, and who are in one way or another all totally destroyed by the peccant engine. In the preface which he wrote much later, in 1920, Conrad sets out to justify his use of irony:

> Even the purely artistic purpose, that of applying an ironic method to a subject of that kind, was formulated with deliberation and in the earnest belief that ironic treatment alone could enable me to say all I felt I would have to say in scorn as well as in pity.[26]

Unable to provoke the anarchists to action, as the representative of the foreign embassy insists that he must do: 'The proper business of an "agent provocateur" is to provoke', Mr Verloc is driven to the expedient of procuring a bomb himself and giving it to his idiot brother-in-law Stevie to place at the Greenwich Observatory. The bomb, going off before its time, kills Stevie and blows to pieces all the tranquil domesticity of Mr Verloc's home life. In destroying Stevie, albeit inadvertently, Mr Verloc destroys the axis of his family, for his wife, Winnie (who had in fact been in love with an impecunious butcher in the next street) had only married in order to provide a home for her young brother, the gentle idiot whom she treats with more than maternal affection. Her mother too had voluntarily gone into exile to a distant almshouse so that the burden of her family should not be too much for the easy-going Mr Verloc, sacrificing herself so as not to jeopardise Stevie's chances of future protection. Mr Verloc, the lazy, home-loving, uxorious husband who from innate indolence and detestation of the idea of regular work had chosen the unsavoury profession of informer which he carries on behind the façade of a small back-street shop, never having realised that all his comforts depended on the fact that the two women saw him as the provider for Stevie, sees his world crumble about him when he is traced as the organiser of the outrage through the address tag that his anxious wife has attached to Stevie's overcoat; and when his wife eavesdrops on the shocking account of Stevie's end given by the Chief Inspector. For Mr Verloc, tracked down by the police, is stabbed to death by his wife, while she, after a pathetic attempt to elope with the nastiest of the anarchist group (who, learning that the police may be after her, hurriedly drops her and leaves her penniless) jumps overboard at night from a cross-channel steamer.

The most interesting character study is that of Stevie himself; the docile boy with a penchant for endlessly drawing circles with a compass, who loses his head at the sight of injustice and suffering. There is, as so often in Conrad, a double irony in the portrait of Stevie, for while what is stressed is always his gentleness and docility, rendering him an easy tool for his brother-in-law, yet at the same time he is seen as himself a potential dynamiter. We are told, when he is introduced to us in the first chapter, that he had at the age of 14 lost a job as an office boy given to him by a friend of his father's by letting off fireworks on the staircase: 'He touched off in quick succession a set of fierce rockets, angry catherine wheels, loudly exploding squibs — and the matter might have turned out very serious. An awful panic spread through the whole building.'[27] He was unable to explain why he had taken this action, and it was only later that Winnie obtained from him a misty and confused confession, suggesting that he had recourse to fireworks in much the same spirit as anarchists had recourse to dynamite: 'It seems that two other office-boys in the building had worked upon his feelings by tales of injustice and oppression till they had wrought his compassion to the pitch of that frenzy.'[28] This frenzy is repeated when, shortly before destroying Stevie for good, Conrad describes the boy's reactions at the sight of a cabman beating a horse:

At the bottom of his pockets his incapable, weak hands were clenched hard into a pair of angry fists. In the face of anything which affected directly or indirectly his morbid dread of pain, Stevie ended by turning vicious . . . The anguish of immoderate compassion was succeeded by the pain of an innocent but pitiless rage.[29]

Like Jenkins and Stevenson, Conrad is not averse to trying to shock the reader by his description of the gory result of the explosion:

Another waterproof sheet was spread over that table in the manner of a tablecloth, with the corners turned up over a sort of mound — a heap of rags, scorched and bloodstained, half concealing what might have been an accumulation of raw material for a cannibal feast. It required considerable firmness of mind not to recoil before that sight. Chief Inspector Heat, an efficient officer of his department, stood his ground, but for a whole minute he did not advance. A local constable in uniform cast a sidelong glance, and said with stolid simplicity,

'He's all there. Every bit of him. It was a job.'[30]

And the deliberately shocking cannibal image is repeated in a more domesticated form on the next page:

And meantime the Chief Inspector went on peering at the table with a calm face and the slightly anxious attention of an indigent customer bending over what may be called the by-products of a butcher's shop with a view to an inexpensive Sunday dinner.[31]

Yet towards all his protagonists, including the old lady who incarcerates herself in an almshouse in the hope of thereby helping her idiot son, Conrad, however macabre his humour, shows the pity and comprehension of a great tragic writer and reveals how they are led as much by their virtues as by their weaknesses to their inevitable doom.

He reserves a very different treatment for his anarchists: Comrade Ossipon, Michaelis the ticket-of-leave man and Karl Yundt. In order to communicate the disgust and repulsion with which he regards their ideas, Conrad resorts to the old technique of making the men themselves disgusting and repulsive. In the case of Karl Yundt 'the all but moribund veteran of dynamite wars', the insistence is on his toothlessness, implying his inability to bite: 'with a faint black grimace of a toothless mouth', 'a dried throat and toothless gums which seemed to catch the tip of his tongue', 'the venomous splutterings of the old terrorist without teeth'. He has, in fact, never been dangerous: 'the famous terrorist had never in his life raised personally as much as his little finger against the social edifice. He was no man of action; he was not even an orator of torrential eloquence.' This very old man who can hardly move of his own volition ('He got in motion slowly, striking the floor with his stick at every step. It was rather an affair to get him out of the house because, now and then, he would stop, as if to think, and did not offer to move again till impelled forward by Michaelis') is denied any touch of sympathy by his author, his physical disintegration is simply a reflection of his moral disintegration.

Michaelis, the ticket-of-leave apostle is disgusting in a different way: obese and bloated, 'He had come out of a highly hygienic prison round like a tub, with an enormous stomach and distended cheeks of a pale, semi-transparent complexion, as though for fifteen years the servants of an outraged society had made a point of stuffing him with fattening foods in a damp and lightless cellar.' Comrade Ossipon, an ex-medical student without a degree, 'author of a popular quasi-medical study (in the form of a cheap pamphlet seized promptly by the police) entitled "The Corroding Vices of the Middle Classes", although younger is hardly more attractive: 'with a flattened nose and prominent mouth cast in the rough mould of the negro type' — a description based on the classification of Lombroso[32] which incidentally casts some light on Conrad's attitude to race as well as class distinctions. All three men are morally degenerate, all are living off women. Karl Yundt is nursed by a bleareyed old woman ('a woman he had years ago enticed away from a friend, and afterwards tried more than once to shake off into the gutter') with the implication that she earned her, or their, living as a prostitute. Michaelis is living off a wealthy old lady who sends him to Marienbad for health cures, and supports him in a cottage in the country. Comrade Ossipon 'was sure to want for nothing as long as there were silly girls with saving-bank books in the world.'

Having drawn these anarchists as physically and morally repulsive, Conrad denies them that sympathy due to the weaknesses of old age or ill health. He then goes on to deny them any saving grace that might spring from wholehearted dedication to an ideology. They are revolutionaries, he points out, above all because they are too lazy to take on any responsibilities, including the responsibility of work, though vanity may also have played a part in their choice of career:

For obviously one does not revolt against the advantages and opportunities of that state, but against the price which must be paid for the same in the coin of accepted morality, self-restraint, and toil. The majority of revolutionists are the enemies of discipline and fatigue mostly. There are natures, too, to whose sense of justice the price exacted looms up monstrously enormous, odious, oppressive, worrying, humiliating, extortionate, intolerable. Those are the fanatics. The remaining portion of social rebels is accounted for by vanity, the mother of all noble and vile illusions, the companion of poets, reformers, charlatans, prophets, and incendiaries.[33]

One of the concluding ironies, therefore, of Conrad's tale, is that the only real anarchist is the idiot Stevie, who, hypersensitive to the injustice which exists in the world, is filled with helpless rage against it, and who inevitably falls a victim to the dynamite he is obediently carrying with perhaps only a vague idea of its purpose as a social protest, a purpose which links back to his own protest with the fireworks a few years earlier.

The 'dangerous man' in Conrad's novel is the chemist, the man whose fixed idea is to provide the perfect detonator. He it is who furnishes the dynamite which so successfully if inopportunely blows Stevie to bits. This chemist goes around London sure that he is safe from arrest because he has made himself into a walking bomb: 'To deal with a man like me you require sheer, naked, inglorious heroism.'[34] Physically he also is repulsive:

> His flat, large ears departed widely from the sides of his skull, which looked frail enough for Ossipon to crush between thumb and forefinger; the dome of the forehead seemed to rest on the rim of the spectacles; the flat cheeks, of a greasy, unhealthy complexion, were merely smudged by the miserable poverty of a thin dark whisker. The lamentable inferiority of the whole physique was made ludicrous by the supremely self-confident bearing of the individual. His speech was curt, and he had a particularly impressive manner of keeping silent.[35]

Yet Conrad makes a distinction between this man and the comrades of the Red Committee: he has the arrogance of the dynamitard. As is usually the case both in fact and fiction, his background is chemistry. He is nicknamed Professor: 'his title to that designation consisted in his having been once assistant demonstrator in chemistry in some technical institute'. The Professor, like Stevie, is filled with a great sense of injustice, but unlike Stevie who resented injustice and cruelty to others, the Professor's is a private, not a public grievance: 'His struggles, his privations, his hard work to raise himself in the social scale, had filled him with such an exalted conviction of his merits that it was extremely difficult for the world to treat him with justice.'[36] He enjoys giving Ossipon technical details about the Greenwich bomb:

It gave me some trouble, because I had to cut out the bottom first and solder it on again afterwards. When prepared for use, the can enclosed a wide-mouthed, well-corked jar of thick glass packed around with some wet clay and containing sixteen ounces of X2 green powder. The detonator was connected with the screw top of the can. It was ingenious — a combination of time and shock. I explained the system to him.[37]

The Professor is saddened by the failure but attributes it to Verloc and Stevie rather than to his invention: 'He either ran the time too close, or simply let the thing fall', and goes on: '. . .there are more kinds of fools than one can guard against. You can't expect a detonator to be absolutely fool-proof.'[38]

Conrad chooses to end his book, which after all has taken the form of a morality (the anarchists are not so much characters in the round as 'vices') not with the act of madness and despair which is Winnie's suicide, but with the Professor continuing to walk around London, a threat to established society. It is he who speaks the epilogue: 'Madness and despair! Give me that for a lever, and I'll move the world.'

Conrad's novel is substantially a defence of the Establishment. He sides with Chief Inspector Heat, the policeman who infinitely prefers thieves to dynamiters because thieves have, after all, the greatest respect for property. They are an integral part of a society based on the rights of property; they are not challenging the basis of the social structure; they accept that when they are caught they must pay the price of seven years hard. The members of the Red Committee (the name suggests that Conrad is perpetuating the usual confusion between socialists and anarchists) puzzle and disgust the policeman, but he has society on his side: 'All the inhabitants of the immense town, the population of the whole country, and even the teeming millions struggling upon the planet, were with him — down to the very thieves and mendicants.' This is clearly Conrad's own conviction, but the novel ends ambiguously for not only is the Professor left a free man but he has just obtained the promise of payment for 'certain chemicals which I shall order tomorrow', and in the very last paragraph of the book is prophetically projected into the future:

And the incorruptible Professor walked, too, averting his eyes from the odious multitude of mankind. He had no future. He disdained it. He was a force. His thoughts caressed the images of ruin and destruction. He walked frail, insignificant, shabby, miserable — and terrible in the simplicity of his idea calling madness and despair to the regeneration of the world. Nobody looked at him. He passed on unsuspected and deadly, like a pest in the street full of men.[39]

Notes

1. Preface to *Collected Works of Robert Louis Stevenson*, Vol. 6, Edmund Gosse (ed.) (London, 1907).

2. Preface to Stevenson, *More New Arabian Nights*.

3. Ibid., p. 228.

4. Arthur Conan Doyle, *A Study in Scarlet* (London, 1887). Quotation from 1891 edition, p. 147.

5. Stevenson, *More New Arabian Nights*, p. 214.

6. Ibid., p. 197.

7. Ibid., p. 287.

8. Ibid., p. 312.

9. Ibid., p. 315.

10. Ibid., p. 316.

11. Ibid., pp. 316-7.

12. Ibid., p. 317.

13. See Arthur H. Lewis, *Lament for the Molly Maguires* (New York, 1964) for a full account of the activities of this early group of dynamiters.

14. Stevenson, *More New Arabian Nights*, p. 397.

15. Ibid., p. 320.

16. Jenkins, *A Week of Passion*, Vol. 1, p. 7.

17. Ibid., Vol. 1, p. 8.

18. Ibid., Vol. 1, pp. 58-9.

19. Ibid., Vol. 1, p. 55.

20. Ibid., Vol. 1, pp. 217-8.

21. Ibid., Vol. 2, p. 56.

22. Ibid., Vol. 2, pp. 133-4.

23. Ibid.

24. George Woodcock, *Anarchism* (Harmondsworth, 1962), p. 414.

25. Joseph Conrad, *The Secret Agent, a Simple Tale* (London, 1907). This and all subsequent quotations unless otherwise stated are from the Everyman edition (London, 1961), p. 210.

26. From preface to *The Secret Agent*, in the *Uniform Edition of the Works of Joseph Conrad*, 22 vols. (London, 1923-8).

27. Conrad, *Secret Agent*, p. 9.

28. Ibid.

29. Ibid., p. 169.

30. Ibid., p. 86.

31. Ibid., p. 88.

32. Norman Sherry in his exciting exploration of Conrad's sources in *Conrad's Western World* (Cambridge, 1971) draws attention to the influence of Cesare Lombroso's classification of criminal types in *L'Uomo delinquente* (Rome, 1875). Sherry notes that Lombroso's work was not translated into English until 1911, but

adds that his views were widely known before that date. It seems clear to me from *The Secret Agent* that Conrad had not only absorbed Lombroso's general views but had studied his text which was easily accessible in the French translation of 1887. Paola Marcari and Matilde Ricci who wrote under my supervision their doctorate dissertations for Rome University on this subject are of the opinion that not only the anarchists but also the character of Stevie was suggested by the theories of Lombroso.

33. Conrad, *Secret Agent*, p. 53.

34. K. R. M. Short in *The Dynamite War* convincingly suggests that the anarchist François Polti (see Chapter 2 of the present book) may have given Conrad the idea of the man who is a walking bomb.

35. Conrad, *Secret Agent*, p. 62.

36. Ibid., p. 75.

37. Ibid., pp. 75-6.

38. Ibid., p. 76.

39. Ibid., p. 311. Probably Conrad had in mind the figure of Souvarine the anarchist in *Germinal* as he walks out of Zola's novel. It is worth noting that the holocaust in the mine at Monsou was caused not by dynamite but by deliberate weakening of the props and flooding the pit. It is only at the end of the novel (completed in January 1883) that Zola adds this reference to dynamite: 'Alors, sur le terri ébranlé, Souvarine se leva . . . Et il jeta sa dernière cigarette, il s'éloigna sans un regard en arrière, dans la nuit devenue noire. Au loin, son ombre diminua, se fondit avec l'ombre. C'était là-bas qu'il allait, à l'inconnu. Il allait, de son air tranquille, à l'extermination, partout où il y auriat de la dynamite, pour faire sauter les villes et les hommes. Ce sera lui, sans doute, quand la bourgeoisie agonisante entendra, sous elle, à chacun de ses pas, éclater le pavé des rues.' p. 459.

4 'GOD BLESS THIM GUNS!'

Frances Trollope, Anthony's mother, had written earlier in the century one of the first social protest novels, *Michael Armstrong*. This story of a factory child, with its anger against the inhumanity of contemporary working conditions for children, its attempt at sociological inquiry and its awareness of industrial exploitation, was the forerunner of a whole series of nineteenth-century novels of social protest. Anthony Trollope himself, besides being the chronicler of Barsetshire and the writer of entertaining social novels, had attempted, with some success, a serious social criticism of the contemporary English economic system in *The Way We Live Now* (1875). It is therefore all the more disappointing to turn to his little-known Irish novel, *The Landleaguers*, published in 1883, and to find him presenting the Irish question so unremittingly from the viewpoint of the landlords.[1]

The family with which the novel is chiefly concerned is the Jones family of Castle Morony in County Galway, and the story was left unfinished at Trollope's death in 1882 although as he was drawing to the end of Volume three (only eleven chapters to go) it is quite clear who will marry whom, and who will be hanged, even if his son, Henry M. Trollope, had not added a note to this effect. The very last words with which the novel breaks off, spoken by an old peasant, Con Heffernan, are indicative of the tone of the whole: "'What with Faynians, and moonlighters, and Home-Rulers, and now with thim Laaguers, they don't lave a por boy any pace.'"[2] The story is set in 1880 when Mr Jones's meadows are flooded by the tearing down of the sluice gates by a landleaguer who has been influenced by teachings from America, and who does not want to pay his rent. Much stress is laid in the book on the evil doctrines coming from America. On page two of the first volume, that is to say at the very outset of his tale, Trollope informs the reader of the sad change that has come over a 'poor and obedient tenantry':

> Not only have they in part repudiated the power of the priest as to their souls, but, in compliance with teaching which has come to them from America, they claim to be masters also of their bodies.

Never were a people less fitted to exercise such dominion without control.

The youngest son of Mr Jones, a 10-year-old boy called Florian, has turned Catholic, and when he inadvertently witnesses the flooding of his father's land he is compelled to swear an oath to reveal nothing. In this Trollope is following the convention of the terrorist secret society novels, for the oath is extorted by a man in a mask:

> But just at that moment the man in the mask, who had not yet spoken a word, extemporised a cross out of two bits of burned wood from the hearth, and put it right before Florian's nose; one hand held one stick, and the other, the other. 'Swear', said the man in the mask.[3]

The Catholic curate, Father Brosnan, to whom the boy then turns for advice, tells him that his oath to the leaguers is binding: 'Then you must hould your tongue. In such a case as this I cannot absolve you from your word.' The boy for many months follows this counsel but in the end, under pressure from his family, reveals what he has seen, and is then shot and killed on his way to the trial to give evidence. This crime of the flooding of the meadows is the main plot-thread running through the novel, but there are numerous other murders besides Florian's, culminating in the assassination of five out of a family of six 'to stop the tongue of one talkative old woman'.

The hero, Frank Jones, is allowed to obtain his reward, marrying the American daughter of an Irish landleaguing member of the British Parliament, but not until she has most opportunely lost her voice so that he will not be embarrassed by a wife who is a public singer. Trollope's orthodoxy can be traced not only in the rewards he distributes (a bride for Frank and a bullet for Florian) but in the very names he gives these characters: Florian, fussy and foreign for the Roman Catholic 10-year-old who lied to his family and Frank, a name which speaks for itself, for his Protestant anti-landleaguing brother.

Toward the end of the third volume Trollope comes back to the point which he had made at the very beginning — and once more places the responsibility for Irish unrest in the 1880s with the Irish emigrants to America:

> A sweeter-tempered people than had existed there had been found nowhere; nor a people more ignorant, and possessing less

of the comforts of civilization. But no evil was to be expected from them, no harm came from them . . . The tuition had come from America! That, no doubt, was true; but it had come by Irish hearts and Irish voices, by Irish longings and Irish ambition.[4]

Reading the newspapers and the novels of the time the most striking thing about the Irish question, or rather about the way in which it is presented, is that the fundamental conflict is seen as being neither national nor religious but economic, although the fact that the tenants were mostly Catholic and a number of the land-owners were Protestant mixed the religious question inextricably with the social. Black Daly, the master of the Galway hounds in *The Landleaguers*, lays down the law unequivocally: 'It was the business of a Protestant to take rent and of a Roman Catholic to pay rent.' Both Trollope's novel and George Moore's *Drama in Muslin* tell the story of what is really a class struggle in a prevalently agricultural society between landlords and tenant farmers over the ownership of the land, a struggle made increasingly bitter by the failure of potato crops. A crop failure meant that the peasant farmer, unable to pay his rent, was evicted, leaving the young with no alternative but emigration with its attendant exploitation (the influx of cheap Irish labour was used by British manufacturers to weaken the bargaining power of local workers) while the old were left with no alternative to starvation.

The administration of the laws governing eviction had long been in the hands of local magistrates, all drawn from the landed gentry, so that during the nineteenth century more and more evicted tenants took the law into their own hands, and terrorism had increased to such an extent that no member of the land-owning classes felt safe, and the risk was even greater for the hated agents of landed proprietors, especially of absentee landlords living safely in London. So great was the lawlessness that the British Parliament passed a Coercion Act in 1881 setting up a rent committee known as the Land Commission, a court of appeal to judge between landlords and tenants, protecting the latter against exorbitant rentals and consequent eviction on non-payment, a measure bitterly resented by the local landlords as an unwarranted interference with their rights. This was the situation when in 1883 Anthony Trollope's *The Landleaguers* was published.

Trollope knew Ireland well. He had lived and worked for many years in Ireland as an administrator in the postal service (he states in the novel that he has known Ireland from 1842 to 1882) and naturally

the people with whom he came into contact socially were the landowners. That Trollope should sympathise with his friends over the
constant threat to life and property constituted by the Land League
is only to be expected, as is his detestation of the acts of terrorism
perpetrated by the leaguers, ranging from boycotting and the
burning of ricks or the admonitory docking of the tails of cattle
belonging to new tenants who took over land after an eviction, to the
dynamiting or burning of farms and shooting of the agents of landed
proprietors. But that he should fail so completely to look for the
causes, to try to analyse what was driving men to such desperate
measures, is only too typical of the centuries-old English approach
to the problems of Ireland. With his local knowledge Trollope might
have written a book about Ireland that could stand comparison with
The Way We Live Now: had he looked as closely at Irish economics
as he did at the English he might even have made a contribution (the
diffusion of information being a very relevant contribution) to the
solution of the Irish question.

Possibly such was his intention when in the third volume of his
long and not very readable novel he introduced a chapter called 'The
State of Ireland', which he advises readers who are only interested in
sensational incidents to skip. In this chapter he lays the story aside
completely and outlines his own views on Ireland which, as they are
typical of the approach of much of the British press at the time, it
may be well to quote.

He begins by the incontestable statement that things in Ireland are
very bad indeed:

> There can be no doubt that Ireland has been and still is in a most
> precarious condition, that life has been altogether unsafe there,
> and that property has been jeopardised in a degree unknown for
> many years in the British Islands.[5]

He continues, speaking of the decrease in the population which
followed the potato famine of 1846, with an open defence of Malth-
usian reasoning:

> The famine and its results were terrible while they lasted; but they
> left behind them an amended state of things. When man has failed
> to rule the world rightly, God will step in, and will cause famines,
> and plagues, and pestilence — even poverty itself — with His own
> Right Arm.[6]

It is shocking to think that Trollope is here writing of the results of famine not from hearsay but from personal observation, because in 1846 he was actually living and working in Ireland, where the estimated deaths from famine in the decade were 800,000.

Arguing against the reduction of rents in cases of hardship, a measure which the Coercion Act empowered the Land Commission to effect, Trollope falls into a semi-biblical preaching style in order to deliver the same hard-hearted message: 'Shall the idle man be made equal to the industrious, — or can this be done, or should it be done, by any philanthropy?'[7] He has no qualms about putting such principles as the work ethic or property rights even higher than the right of survival, and goes on to argue: '. . . the new law [creating the Land Court] will be felt to have been unjust as having tampered with the rights of property, and having demanded from the owners of property its sale or [*sic*] other terms than those of mutual contract.'[8] Trollope is here making a firm stand for the Liberal principle of non-interference by the state in economic questions: a principle which regarded the protection of the weak as ultimately harmful if it disturbed what was thought to be the balance of nature, and he strengthens his case by arguing that the British Parliament should never have given way to external pressures or taken such decisions at a time when the Land League was determined to exact them:

> Whether these concessions be good or bad, this was, at any rate, no time for granting them. They seem to me to amount to wholesale confiscation. But supposing me to be wrong in that, can I be wrong in thinking that a period of declared rebellion is not a time for concessions?[9]

His own party leader, Gladstone, was to answer this last question for him: when it seemed that under the pressure of the landleaguers in Ireland, and the Fenians in America, Ireland would break away altogether from the United Kingdom, then Gladstone who had earlier been an opponent of Home Rule for Ireland changed his position and in 1886 proposed a Home Rule Bill which, unfortunately for the subsequent history of both countries, was defeated. This shift in Liberal policy must have been difficult for many die-hards such as Trollope to accept, for he had written of the Irish home-rulers that they 'brought their politics, their aspirations, and their money from New York, and boldly made use of the means which the British Constitution afforded them to upset the British

Constitution as established in Ireland'. Trollope's strongest argument was the cruelty of the methods used by the landleaguers, an argument to which almost all the Irish dynamite novels revert, and which he summarises in the following lines of his chapter on Ireland:

> And their anger turned not only against their landlords, but against those who might seem in any way to be fighting on the landlords' side. Did a neighbour occupy a field from which a Landleaguing tenant had been evicted, let the tails of that neighbour's cattle be cut off, or the legs broken of his beasts of burden, or his sheep have their throats cut. Or if the injured one have some scruples of conscience, let the oppressor simply be boycotted, and put out of all intercourse with his brother men. Let no well-intentioned Landleaguing neighbour buy from him a ton of hay, or sell to him a loaf of bread.
>
> But as a last resource, if all others fail, let the sinner be murdered.[10]

The desolation of this last picture where each man's hand was raised against his brother, and where the victims were often the families or the very cattle, is the dominant mood conveyed in one of the best British novels of the 1880s, George Moore's *A Drama in Muslin* (1886).

Like Trollope, Moore is concerned with contemporary Ireland, but unlike Trollope who was preaching a doctrine of repression Moore has no solution to offer. His novel is essentially a tragedy and his message is a message of pity. The only way out he can offer to his heroine is the one so many of the Irish were finding for themselves: at the end of the story she leaves Ireland for good to settle in England. Moore's novel is an extraordinarily sensitive piece of writing; he blends symbolism and realism in much the way that Gissing was doing in the same years. Social problems are explicit, particularly the problem of the marriage market that Gissing was to tackle in *The Odd Women* a few years later. But unlike Trollope Moore does not interrupt the story with a chapter that the reader is invited to skip if he feels so inclined, the interpolated essay beloved of the moralising Victorians. In Moore social and political questions are discussed and debated by the characters themselves, are lived as an integral part of their lives and make a very different impact on the reader — they have become the very essence of the novel.

The story opens on prize day in a girls' convent school, and the reader is introduced to the girls whose stories are the basic plot material of the novel. The relationship between five girls is sketched: Alice Barton, plain and extremely popular who wrote the school play of *King Cophetua*; Lady Cecilia Cullen, deformed, with a strong lesbian attraction toward Alice and a marked disgust with men; Violet Scully, thin and elegant, destined to carry off the matrimonial prize of Dublin society; May Gould, a sexy type; Olive Barton, beautiful and empty headed. They move about in their white dresses among the nuns, *jeunes filles en fleur*, and attend the benediction in the convent-church: 'A real young-girls' church: trim, delicate pillars rising like uplifting arms, arches gracefully turned as adolescent bosoms, an altar fanciful and light coloured as a toilet-table.'[11] These girls, seen in the idyllic setting of the convent grounds, are about to be driven off to the marriage mart in Dublin Castle where the available men with money are either ageing roués or young profligates. Moore moves with assurance from the symbolist picture of the virgin girls in their white dresses to the realism of their conversation which, although not as slangy as their contemporary Agatha in Shaw's *An Unsocial Socialist*, is nevertheless often reduced to bickering. The drama of the wasted lives of these girls is set against the troubled background of Ireland in 1882. Moore shows us many scenes of contrast, of conspicuous waste against a background of poverty and want, and is constantly reminding the reader, not by comment but by contrasting scenes, that the money bled out of the peasantry goes to support such worthless creatures as the local aristocracy — Lord Dungory the elderly Frenchified beau or Mr Barton the inconclusive artist and musician.

The spinsters' ball at Ballinasloe, held in the old schoolroom, impresses Alice (the girl who became a writer, and with whom Moore often identifies himself in the novel) by the sinister and threatening sense of the poor pressing round the windows: 'There were hedges on both sides, through which vague forms were seen scrambling, but May humorously explained that as no very unpopular landlord was going to be present, it was not thought that an attempt would be made to blow up the building.'[12] The festivities are undisturbed by dynamite, but the presentiment voiced by Alice is verified by the arrival of a telegram announcing that the brother of Mr Burke, the Marquis of Kilcarney, has been shot. Alice had sensed something 'sinister' in the pressure of the poor people to catch a glimpse of the ball:

'But look!' said Alice, 'look at all those poor people staring in at the window. Isn't it dreadful that they, in the dark and cold, should be watching us dancing in our beautiful dresses, and in our warm bright room?'

'You don't want to ask them in, do you?'

'Of course not, but it seems very sinister; does it not seem so to you?'[13]

I have examined elsewhere the significance of windows as marking a sense of separation and exclusion,[14] and this novel of George Moore's often uses the same technique. It is repeated, this time in the more deliberate form of author-to-reader, when he describes the carriages on their way to the drawing room at Dublin Castle, where the girls are to be officially presented to the Lord Lieutenant.

Never were poverty and wealth brought into plainer proximity. In the broad glare of the carriage lights the shape of every feature, even the colour of the eyes, every glance, every detail of dress, every stain of misery were revealed to the silken exquisites who, a little frightened, strove to hide themselves within the scented shadows of their broughams: and in like manner, the bloom on every aristocratic cheek, the glitter of every diamond, the richness of every plume were visible to the avid eyes of those who stood without in the wet and the cold . . . you see also the Irish-Americans, with their sinister faces, and broad-brimmed hats, standing scowling beneath the pale flickering gas-lamps . . .[15]

These are the Fenians, the dynamitards, yet the sense of fear they arouse is also a sense of guilt. The economic theme is ever-present, even in the description of the visit of the girls to the dressmaker's to choose the materials for their ball-dresses for the Drawing room, the Irish equivalent for presentation at court: they are being decked out for sale:

The beautiful silks hissed as they came through the hands of the assistants, cat-like the velvet footfalls of the velvet fell; it was a witches' Sabbath, and out of this terrible cauldron each was to draw her share of the world's gifts. Smiling and genial, Mrs Symond stirred the ingredients with a yard measure; the girls came trembling, doubting, hesitating; and the anxious mothers saw what remained of their jeopardised fortunes sliding in a thin golden stream into the flaming furnace that the demon of Cork Hill blew with unintermittent breath.[16]

All the time that the girls are getting ready for their first Dublin season the threat of dynamite is in the air. Women talking in the Shelbourne Hotel comment that murder was more common in Dublin than in the country, and that the Lord Lieutenant dared not stir a yard without an escort of soldiers: 'Consolation was, however, found in Mrs Gould's remark, that if the Castle were blown up with dynamite the conspirators would probably choose the day of the Levée rather than that on which the Drawing-room was held.'[17] Mrs Barton makes much the same comment, after she has brought her girls to what she had imagined was the comparative safety of Dublin:

'I assure you, my dears, we are all on the brink of ruin, we are dancing on the edge of a precipice. In flying from Galway we thought we had fled from the Land League; but I was talking to Lord Dungory this morning, and he says that the city is under-mined, that a network of conspiracy is spread all over the place. He says there are assassins waiting and watching night and day to kill the Lord Lieutenant, and that there are so many plots hatching for the blowing up of the Castle, that even now it is doubtful if it will be considered safe to hold a Drawing-room.'[18]

George Moore, in this most experimental of his novels, conveys the sense of imminent danger not only by means of the clumsy if authoritative technique of direct authorial intervention and by comments made by the characters themselves, but also in dramatic form, as when a clap of thunder is mistaken for a dynamite explosion by all present at the Drawing room. Violet Scully has just been presented:

The Lord Lieutenant kissed her, and so warmly that Her Excellency looked up surprised, but her annoyance was lost in the crashing of the thunder which at that moment broke in terrific claps over their heads. Everyone thought instinctively of dynamite, and it was some time before even the voluptuous strains of Liddell's band could calm their inquietude.[19]

The whole Drawing room sequence is the high point of the novel:

everything in the girls' lives is seen as a preparation for this moment, which with its pageantry hardly conceals the fact which Moore is bent on revealing — for all practical purposes it is a high-class cattle market at which the mothers barter their daughters to the highest bidders. In the most daring passage (heavily laden with horticultural symbolism) he likens the shoulders of the women to roses, revelling in their exotic names, and by means of the relentless cataloguing of flower after flower suggests a sense of the unbearable crush in which the women were standing to await presentation:

> The beautiful silks were hidden by the crowd; only the shoulders remained, and, to appease their terrible ennui, the men gazed down the backs of the women's dresses stupidly. Shoulders were there, of all tints and shapes. Indeed, it was like a vast rosary, alive with white, pink and cream-coloured flowers: of Maréchal Niels, Souvenir de Malmaisons, Mademoiselle Eugène Verdiers, Aimée Vibert Scandens. Sweetly turned, adolescent shoulders, blush white, smooth and even as the petals of a Marquise Moretmarle; the strong, commonly turned shoulders, abundant and free as the fresh rosy pink of the Anna Alinuff; the drooping white shoulders, full of falling contours as a pale Madame Lacharme; the chlorotic shoulders, deadly white, of the almost greenish shade that is found in a Princess Clementine; the pert, the dainty little shoulders, filled with warm pink shadows, pretty and compact as Countess Cecile de Chabrillant; the large heavy shoulders full of vulgar madder tints, coarse, strawberry colour, enormous as a Paul Neron; clustering white shoulders, grouped like the blossoms of an Aimée Vibert Scandens, and, just in front of me, under my eyes, the flowery, the voluptuous, the statuesque shoulders of a tall blonde woman of thirty, whose flesh is full of the exquisite peach-like tones of a Mademoiselle Eugène Verdier, blooming in all its pride of summer loveliness.[20]

Then, even more daringly, but in a natural transition from the rose imagery, he passes on to the stifling scent of the crowd, with all its cattle market implications and criticism of the aristocratic pretensions of this mass of perspiring humanity:

> An hour passed wearily, and in this beautiful drawing-room humanity suffered in all its natural impudence. Momentarily the air grew hotter and more silicious; the brain ached with the dusty

odour of *poudre de ris*, and the many acidities of evaporating perfume; the sugary sweetness of the blondes, the salt flavours of the brunettes, and this allegro movement of odours was interrupted suddenly by the garlicky andante, deep as the pedal notes of an organ, that the perspiring arms of a fat chaperon slowly exhaled.[21]

As social criticism a passage of this kind is more devastating than whole chapters of analysis; it is a forerunner of Aubrey Beardsley and the *Yellow Book* aesthetics where fastidious taste takes a shocked delight in carefully chosen vulgarities. But it is more than this: set against a background of the Irish troubles it is a biting indictment of folly and waste.

The girls, returning home after leaving their English convent school, are totally incapable at first of comprehending the troubled state of their country. The first introduction of politics shows Moore's sense of the irony of their innocence: 'Mr Barton commented on the disturbed state of the country. Olive asked if Mr Parnell was good-looking.' But soon they become aware of the economic repercussions of the Land League activities, by which they are directly affected:

> 'Oh, yes, is it not dreadful?' exclaimed Mrs Barton; 'I don't know what we shall do if the Government don't put down the Land League; we shall all be shot in our beds some night. Did you hear of that murder the other day?'
>
> 'And it is said there will be no rents collected this year,' said Mr Barton, as he tightened one of the strings of his guitar.
>
> 'Oh! do cease that noise!' said Mrs Barton. 'And tell me, Lord Dungory, will the Government refuse us soldiers, and police, to put the people out?'
>
> 'If we go to the Castle, we shall want more money to buy dresses,' said Olive.[22]

Throughout the novel this is the central debate of the landowners: how to exact rents from their tenant farmers, some of whom appealed to the Land Commission for reductions, and some of whom followed the advice of the leaguers by refusing to pay at all. The proprietors, most of whom had no profession or income other than their rents and whose property was often heavily mortgaged, were at their wits end, but social *mores* had to be observed. More than ever it behoved the young, whether girls or men, to marry money, and the novel is concerned with the delusions and disappointments they encounter in attempting to comply with this obvious social duty. While the men discuss assassinations and evictions, the girls, who have been brought up to think only of spending, find it difficult to come to terms with the new realities. Over and over again Moore reports conversations like the following, between May Gould and her mother:

> 'I can't sit here all day listening to you lamenting over the Land League; and, after a certain number of hours, conjecturing whether Mickey Moran will or will not pay his rent becomes monotonous.'
> 'Now don't vex me, May; for I won't stand it,' said Mrs Gould, getting angry. 'When you ask me for a new dress you don't think of what you are saying now. It was only the other day you were speaking to me of refurnishing this room. I should like to know how that's to be done if there was no one to look after Mickey Moran's rent?'[23]

Throughout the novel there is a gradual change in all the girls as they learn to accept the bitter realities of their existence. At the beginning Moore says of them: 'On their young hearts the shadow of calamity fell lightly.' For a while they continue to think only of marriage, not from heartlessness but because that is the way they have been conditioned. The mother of Alice and Olive Barton tells them categorically 'I would sooner have the worst husband in the world than no husband,' and at first they hardly question the truth of Mrs Barton's teaching: '. . . they dreamed unflinchingly of their white dresses, while the island rocked with the roar of five million peasants claiming the right to own the land that they tilled.'[24]

Page by page Moore implacably destroys their social and their sexual illusions, and on both heads he is far more outspoken than his contemporaries (with the possible exception of the early novels of George Bernard Shaw). Mr Barton reads aloud from the *Daily Express* the account of a dastardly murder in Kerry:

> A bailiff's house had been broken into by an armed gang, and the unfortunate man had been dragged out of bed and shot before his own door. In Meath an attempt had been made to blow up a landlord's house with dynamite; in Queen's County shot had

been fired through a dining room window, and two large hay-
yards had been maliciously burned; in Wicklow forty head of
cattle had had their tails cut off; in Roscommon and in Galway
two men, occupying farms from which tenants had been evicted,
had been so seriously beaten that their lives were despaired of.[25]

George Moore, in the plain language of newspaper reporting, gives
us here a short chronicle of the times, but then he goes on, some 30
pages later, to reinterpret the same news items in poetic language,
evoking the emotional mood into which the lives of his characters
were plunged. The repetition of the onomatopoeic key-word
'gloom', the alliteration of 'deadly deeds done in the darkness' is
communication on a poetic level, and the last 20 words of the
passage (which in their earlier journalistic formulation read 'At
Wicklow forty head of cattle had had their tails cut off') seem to me
among the best that have ever been written on the tragedy of
Ireland:

> Gloom, gloom, January gloom, and yet no gloom to deaden the
> cries for vengeance for the assassination of landlords, of agents —
> for the cold-blooded torturings of bailiffs, caretakers, and other
> deadly deeds done in the darkness; no gloom to hide the
> informer, and the peasant cruelty that fell upon defenceless
> cattle; not gloom enough to stifle the lowing of the red-dripping
> mutilations that filled the humid darkness of the fields.[26]

The sadness of the girls' initiation into Irish politics is comparable
to the disillusion of their initiation to sex. At last in the 1880s and
1890s men were beginning to question the long-established
relationship between the sexes, a subject which had hitherto
concerned only women novelists. While Mary Wollstonecraft, Mrs
Gaskell, Charlotte Brontë and George Eliot all contested the
economic and sexual subjugation of women, the problem had hardly
seemed to exist for their male contemporaries. George Moore was a
pioneer in this field, and could allow himself to be much more
explicit in the discussion of female sexuality than his feminine
forerunners. We have to wait for D. H. Lawrence (and not even the
early Lawrence) for any advance beyond Moore in open debate on
the question of desire in women, as directed toward either their own
or the opposite sex. Henry James's Olive Chancellor or Gissing's
Rhoda Nunn are much less openly lesbian than Lady Cecilia Cullen,

nor were illegitimate babies ever produced by débutantes in novels before Moore's time. Even Grant Allen's *The Woman Who Did* did it some 14 years later, and on the highest feminist principles, not driven by unsatisfied desire.

After Fred Scully's seduction of May Gould, to which she was a willing partner, and the subsequent pathos of her lonely retirement and the birth of her unwanted child who dies, as the bastard in *The Mummer's Wife* was to die, of neglect (not deliberate neglect but rather shiftlessness and lack of love), May does not, like all earlier and many later heroines, dedicate the rest of her life to chastity and good works. The last we hear of her, toward the end of the novel, after her affair and illegitimate baby from Fred, is the following conversation with Alice, tragic in its stark realism, which makes Moore's point about the situation of supernumerary women better than any statistics:

> 'Oh, no; but I am dreadfully sinful. If you knew *all* you would not speak to me: and if I died now I should go straight to *Hell*!'
> 'I did not know Fred Scully had come back.'
> 'Nor has he. It was not he.'
> 'Who was it?'
> 'Don't ask me — what does it matter?'
> 'I am very sorry . . . Do you love him very much?'
> 'No, no; it was an old man.'[27]

This seems a far cry from dynamite, and yet it is just one of the individual human tragedies which were being played out against the backcloth of the national tragedy, suggesting the break-up of the values of a society which the British Parliament was being called upon to uphold.

Mr Ryan speaks for the whole land-owning class when he expresses satisfaction upon hearing the news of the Phoenix Park murders in Dublin of Lord Frederick Cavendish and Mr Burke: 'I'm glad they were murthered, for if they hadn't been, we'd have been.' At last the British Parliament, with the assassination of the Lord Lieutenant, would be forced to legislate and put down the rebels. 'The implacable certainty which forced itself into every heart that he spoke but the truth' is the message we might find expressed by any of the proprietors in Trollope's *The Landleaguers*. But Moore, unlike Trollope, gives us a picture also of the other side: what was driving the peasantry to arson, assassination and dynamite? Towards the end of the book, when the heroine, the only character who solves all her problems and who helps the others to struggle with theirs, on her way to leave Ireland for ever is faced with the reality of an eviction, the reader sees this eviction through her eyes. She has solved the problem of her own identity, of what to do with her life, by becoming a writer. She has solved her economic problem in the same way by becoming self-supporting; she has solved her sexual problem by becoming the wife of a middle-aged doctor, and by producing a son, and her marriage relationship has a sound basis in her own financial independence: unable to do anything about solving the Irish problem she leaves it behind her. On her way to the ship she and her husband are witnesses of this scene of man's inhumanity to man under the pitiless rain which, rather than a romantic trimming, is felt to be part of the very nature of the Irish scene:

Suddenly the carriage turned up a narrow road. The coachman stopped to inquire the way, and our travellers were the unwilling witnesses of one of those scenes for which Ireland is so infamously famous — an eviction. The cabin was a fair specimen of its kind. It was built of rough stone without mortar, and through the chinks all the winds of heaven were free to wander. There was a potato-field at the back, and a mud-heap in front, and through the slush the shattered door was approached by stepping-stones. From the exterior it is easy to imagine the interior — a dark, fetid hole, smelling of smoke, potato-skins, and damp. And about this miserable tenement there were grouped a dozen policemen armed with rifles, two men in pot-hats and long ulsters, and a dozen or fifteen peasants come to watch the proceedings. An old woman of seventy had been placed for shelter beneath a hawthorn-bush; six young children clung about their shrieking mother; the man, with nothing but a pair of trousers and a ragged shirt to protect him from the terrible rain, stood a picture of speechless despair on the dung-heap, amid a mass of infamous bedding, and a few wooden stools that had been dragged from the house by the landlord's agents.

'Is it not terrible that human creatures should endure such misery?' exclaimed Alice.

'Yes, it is very shocking, it is horrible, let us do something for them; suppose we pay the rent for them, it cannot be much, and restore them to their miserable home. We cannot leave Ireland with such a shocking picture engraved on our minds for ever.'

'Yes, yes, Edward, do pay the rent for them — it is too terrible.'

The transaction was soon concluded, the man was handed a receipt, and told he might put his things back into his house.

. . . The agents laughed coarsely. One said: 'There are plinty more of them over the hill on whom he can exercoise his charity if he should feel so disposed!'

'It would save us a dale of throuble and ixpense if he would; but to whom do we go next? Mick Flanagan! Where does he live?'

'I show you, yer honour,' exclaimed half a dozen peasants, 'this way, not a couple of hundred yards from here, close to the public, where we may have a drap if yer honour feels so inclined.'

'And to think,' said Dr Reed reflectively, 'that they are the same peasants that we once saw so firmly banded that it seemed as if nothing would ever again separate them, that nothing would ever again render them cowardly and untrue to each other.'[28]

The problem is projected interminably into the future. The ultimate uselessness of the single act of charity towards the evicted crofters, except as a salve to the conscience of the givers, and the reminder that there are plenty more over the hill whose cottages will be made roofless to prevent their return is a social indictment, but George Moore was no preacher, he did not offer the reader any solution to the problems of Ireland as so many novelists, forgetting their role, were inclined to do. Rather he presented a picture, as truthful as his own kind of realism with its sudden transitions into symbolism (the techniques are complementary rather than contradictory) could make it. This last view of Ireland is the picture the emigrants took with them to the United States; some of them turning over bitter memories became Fenians, and others plunged their hands into their pockets, no longer empty, and provided the money to pay for the dynamite with which to blow up the British Parliament.

Moore's *Drama in Muslin* was eminently a book written by an Irishman as opposed to Trollope's *Landleaguers*, a book by an Englishman who had lived and worked in Ireland for many years. In 1886 a curious book was published, by an Englishman who knew how Ireland should be dealt with, Colonel Fred. Burnaby, under the title *Our Radicals*. The book was left unfinished by Colonel Burnaby, who was killed on 17 January 1885 in the advance on Khartoum. The manuscript had travelled with him in camel bags across the desert and reached the hands of his personal secretary, J.

Percival Hughes, much torn and stained. Hughes completed the novel, which is full of Fenians and dynamiters, and the plot of which is laid in the near future. In every sentence the reader is aware that this is the work of a military man. His treatment of women, who are not allowed to take up much space, is excessively stereotyped when we remember that he was writing at the same time that Moore was creating Alice Barton and May Gould. His heroine, appropriately named Blanche to imply her virginity, is so delicate that she is unable to receive a proposal of marriage standing on her own two feet:

> 'Tell me — oh, tell me, I may still love on!'
> She was very pale, as she heard him declare his passion, and would have fallen to the ground had he not caught her in his arms. She turned her eyes to his face, suffused as they were with happy tears, and allowing her head to fall gently upon his shoulder, she whispered one word of consent.[29]

As is to be expected, great attention is paid in the novel to military manoeuvres. The story is laid in the near future, before the beginning of the twentieth century. Ireland has already obtained local government and Britain is governed by the Radicals, under Mr Jonas Cumbermore (= Joseph Chamberlain), an arrangement of which the Colonel strongly disapproves. Opposed to the Radicals is Lord Cromer (some analogy with Cromwell?) whose doctrines would today be termed Fascist, and whose bid for power is made by calling a rally of all the military who are loyal to him and to his ideas. Twenty thousand men gather at his country house. The Prime Minister sends the head of the police to arrest him for treachery, but the forces ranged around Lord Cromer are such that the head of police attempts instead to anaesthetise him and carry him to London before he marches on the town. This attempt is foiled, and at the end of the novel Lord Cromer and his 20,000 picked troops carry the day, with the full approval of the author and consequently of the population.

Ireland is linked to England by a tunnel under the sea (another consequence of the invention of dynamite). The Fenians are extremely active, plotting to destroy the Radical government, but also to thwart the strong man, Lord Cromer. Metrale, the head of the police, has an extremely busy time, and enjoys his author's sympathy when acting against the Irish, though not when supporting the legitimate British government against Lord Cromer:

Then there were the daring Fenian plots. Several explosions had taken place in the military barracks, and other public buildings had to be watched day and night.

Over and above these things, there were the persons of the Ministers to guard, Lord O'Hagan Harton, the Lord Chancellor, having been fired at on one or two occasions . . .

Several attempts had been made on the Prime Minister's life. On one occasion a torpedo had been discovered in his cellar.[30]

Furthermore a new technique had been evolved by the Fenians: they had taken to kidnapping both to extort money and to obtain political leverage. Colonel Burnaby's imagination is here running some hundred years ahead of his time for this was not a method commonly used by nineteenth-century terrorists. Nevertheless the mere possibility must have caused his readers to shudder. 'In one case the body of a little girl was found at her mother's door. It is a deplorable state of things. There is only one way to stamp out secret societies, and that is by force . . .'[31]

Metrale goes into great detail when reporting to the Lord Chancellor on the techniques of one of the dynamite plots. His use of a female spy, an expert in the art of seduction, points forward to a whole series of detective stories, but seems in sad contrast with the ideal of feminine purity represented by Blanche. Perhaps the fact that the spy was an Irishwoman called Moloney meant that in the eyes of the colonel a different set of standards would apply. Kipling had not yet pointed out that the colonel's lady and Judy O'Grady are sisters under their skins. The plot is described as follows:

'The Fenians are becoming more daring every day,' continued Metrale. 'Hitherto, as you know, they have made attempts to destroy buildings by putting dynamite in the cellars, or against the walls. They have learnt that we know most of these devices. They therefore changed their tactics, and hit upon the following plan. They determined to destroy Mr Cumbermore's house, not from below, but from above. It appears that there are some explosives which ignite so rapidly that their effect is just as great in a downward as in an upward direction. This fact established, one of the Fenians obtained access to the roof of Mr Cumbermore's house, and placed 50 lb weight of fulminating mercury on the slates, in a straight line above the room where a Cabinet Council was to be held. He connected his infernal machine with the telegraph wire that runs over Belgrave Square, and tapped that same wire about two miles further off, where it communicates with another building. His emissaries were on the watch to signal to him when the Ministers arrived in Belgrave Square. His intentions were, after allowing you half an hour to settle down to business, to connect the wire of his battery, and explode the fulminating mercury. If this had been effected the whole building would have been rased to the ground.'

'How did you detect the plot?' asked the Lord Chancellor.

'By the merest accident,' answered Metrale. 'I had desired a female decoy, named Moloney, to ingratiate herself with O'Brien, a suspected Fenian. She did so successfully . . .

The evening before last O'Brien took her to his rooms in the Strand. She saw some coils of wire lying about, and asked their use. At first O'Brien would not tell her. She managed by those arts which a woman has the power to employ, supported by his belief that she was devoted to the Fenian cause, to get the secret of the plot from him. I learnt the whole of it four hours before the explosion was to have taken place, and I surrounded the house in the Strand, and succeeded in arresting three of the rebels, including Mrs Moloney, whom I was obliged to take into custody for her own safety.'[32]

The last lines are a reminder of the dangers constantly run by spies and informers; the leader of a Fenian group specifically reminds them of their oaths, and that 'the most fearful death the ingenuity of man can devise shall be the punishment of all who betray their associates'. The Colonel has also another axe to grind in his novel: there had recently been a newspaper campaign on police expenditure in relation to police efficiency; Burnaby comes to the defence of the officers of law and order, letting Metrale plead his own cause: '"If I had had money at my disposal I could have picked up all the links of the chain of conspiracy years ago; but no, I am stinted on every hand, and am therefore unable to employ a secret service."'[33]

The police are certainly shown as working hard for their living, for the book is full of ingenious plots and conspiracies. The Colonel is particularly captivated by a new technique, that of attacking the objective from above, rather than from below. He did not go so far as some of his contemporaries and propose airborne troops or bombs (possibly he found the idea of replacing naval and land forces with an air force uncongenial) but the Foreign Office, like the Prime

Minister's house, is attacked from the roof. His plan is to fill the plumbing system with petroleum instead of water:

> The large cistern on the roof of the Foreign Office had been out of order for some time, but had recently been put into repair. The pipe for filling it with water was attached, but the cistern itself was empty. Barry received this information from a Fenian in his service, who had been employed as a plumber in the work. By means of a plan of the sewers and underground communications of London, in the conspirator's possession, he had ascertained the exact position of the pipe that supplied the Foreign Office with water. His men had taken a house, beneath which the pipe passed. They had orders at a certain time to tap it, and then, by means of a small but powerful steam-engine, to force petroleum into the cistern. It was further arranged that at a given signal the plumber, who had arranged to secrete himself on the roof, was to turn a tap which, for the extinction of fire at the Foreign Office, was connected with the reservoir on the roof. The building would at once become fairly saturated with petroleum, and, what with the fires and the gas burning below, it would be indeed strange if a single person within the walls were to escape the conflagration. Never had a more diabolical plan been formed . . .[34]

The material used in this case is no longer dynamite, but the effect is much the same: 'A crash was heard, and there rose a vast crimson lake of fire to the heavens above, lighting up the faces of the crowds in the streets with a lurid glare.' England becomes a warning to the rest of Europe. Continental statesmen are described as viewing the situation there with incredulous astonishment. The horrors in Ireland are described as surpassing the Reign of Terror in Paris. Yet Burnaby stresses, as did many other writers, the substantial indifference of the English people to what was happening, and one passage reminds us of the population dancing on the lid of a trapdoor in James's *The Princess Casamassima*, published in the same year as *Our Radicals* but written later. The two passages are quite independent of each other; it is the basic idea which is the same. The Colonel writes: 'Yet the people of England did nothing. They ate, they drank, they smoked, they slept, and were indifferent to all the murder and confiscation of property going on around them.'[35] And again some twenty pages later: 'It was the height of the season. The fashionable world had commenced to give its dinners, parties and balls, as if no great disaster was impending.'[36]

What really concerned Burnaby was, as for all Conservatives, the threat to property. He tells us that:

> London was in a very unsettled state. The minds of the unfor-
> tunate men who had been thrown out of work by the principles of
> the Government had been excited by revolutionary speeches to
> robbery and plunder.
>
> The Irish had taken advantage of these doctrines for some
> years past, and had possessed themselves of land that belonged
> legally to English people . . .[37]

And again, to stress the lawlessness which he felt was bound to follow on the heels of a Radical government, he goes on: 'Judging from the reports in the papers, London was in the hands of a mob, who, incited to rebellion by Socialistic leaders, were plundering every place that was worth the sacking.'[38] It is hardly surprising that 'the reports in the papers' in Burnaby's novel should contain this kind of information, in the first place because this was the tone of the press of his own time, and in the second because Lord Cromer had taken steps to establish a monopoly of the mass media. When Mr Cumbermore, the Radical leader, to secure a large circulation of the *Rattlesnake* reduced the paper from twopence to a penny, slightly decreasing the size, Lord Cromer increased the amount of matter in the *Sovereign and People* and sold it for a halfpenny. Colonel Burnaby shows his awareness that some battles can be better fought by investment in the media than in armaments.

While vastly amusing himself by placing his military training at the service of his conspirators, the Colonel could rely on setting all to rights in the end, restoring law and order under the dictatorship of Lord Cromer, a general who had distinguished himself in India. In the event this task was left to Burnaby's secretary, who followed up his chief's notes and closed the novel with the Radical government setting sail for a trip round the world, after being totally disillusioned by their failure to achieve popularity by giving the populace every-thing they wanted. As a piece of special pleading, the following conversation between the Chancellor and the Prime Minister of the Radical government is worth quoting:

> 'What terrible days we live in! Who would have thought that
> under a free and enlightened Radical Government England

would be on the eve of a revolution?'

'Yes,' replied the Prime Minister, 'and what perplexes me is that the movement is not against the Crown — I wish it were — but against ourselves; against us, who have enfranchised the lower classes because we thought it would keep us in office — who have given up the colonies because we thought it would be economical to do so — who sold Gibraltar to the Spaniards, and were able in consequence to abolish the income tax; against us, who strive daily to do away with that costly appendage Royalty — who have abolished the Household Troops, nominally on the ground of expense — who gave the people caucuses to save them the trouble of even thinking for themselves: and it is against us that the popular feeling is directed.'[39]

Under Lord Cromer as Governor-in-Chief Colonel Burnaby foresees a very different order of things:

Martial law had been proclaimed. All delinquents had been brought before courts presided over by Lord Cromer's officers. One man had been hanged for arson, and several thieves severely flogged for violently robbing people in the streets. In each case the punishment had followed the sentence within the space of six hours.[40]

This is a cautionary tale in more senses than the Colonel intended.

The most pro-Irish of the dynamite novels that I have read was written at about the same time as *Our Radicals* but published a year earlier in 1885. This is Tom Greer's *A Modern Daedalus*, one of the first books in the 'superman' genre. Tom Greer, an Irish doctor who, like Trollope, stood unsuccessfully for election to the British Parliament, and who later moved to England to a practice in Cambridge, (a career not unlike that of the fictional Dr Reed, Alice's husband in George Moore's *A Drama in Muslin*) was a very humane man. Lest the motives which led him to write of dynamite should be misunderstood or misinterpreted he added a preface to dissociate himself from the attempts of the Fenian dynamiters:

Let no reader suppose that this book is the work of an enemy of England. On the contrary, though a native of Ireland, I am a lover of England, and a believer in the necessity of a firm and lasting union between the two countries. Nobody more deeply deplores the disunion at present so apparent between them. For the objects, and still more for the methods of the so-called 'dynamite party', I have the deepest abhorrence. It is necessary to point out to any candid reader how widely different is the employment of dynamite in open war from its use as the instrument of secret murder and assassination, and of the destruction of public monuments which are a heritage and possession, not of the English people alone, but of all mankind.[41]

The plot of the book is simple, and turns on the invention of a primitive flying machine in the form of a pair of wings strapped on the shoulders of the hero, John O'Halloran. John tells his own story, which is dated in the near future, beginning on 30 April 1887. The cover shows a splendid batman figure, and it has been conjectured by both Patrick Parrinder and Giorgio Melchiori that this Irish tale may have been read by the young James Joyce and have influenced his choice of pseudonym under which the first stories of *Dubliners*, published in *The Irish Homestead* in 1904, appeared. Certainly the kind of pacifism expressed in the novel and the hero's determination to use his invention for the benefit of all mankind and not for the aggrandisement of a single nation, is in keeping with Joyce's own internationalism.

John's invention which enables him to fly like a bird along the rocky coast and over the hills of Ireland, and which fills him with dreams of becoming a benefactor to mankind, is at once seen by his family as a potential and powerful weapon. The O'Hallorans are Donegal peasants involved first in a rebellion against evicting landowners and their agents, later against British government forces and finally in open war against the British army. John's elder brother, Dan, is a leader of the rebels. Returning home from his first successful flight John has a serious quarrel with his family, particularly with his father. While John has been away at the university his family has been falling under the influence of revolutionary doctrines:

> I returned to find them gloomy, idle, suspicious, filled with a literature of whose very existence I was previously unaware, but of which they were as keen students as I myself was of mathematical and physical Science. The whole history of Russian Nihilism, of German Socialism, of the Italian Carbonari, of the French Commune, was at their fingers' ends.[42]

It is interesting to find Dr Greer, with his personal knowledge of the background of the Irish nationalist movement, documenting the theoretical preparation of the peasant leaders in these terms. He also describes, right at the beginning of his story, the repressive measures to which Ireland was subjected and which led to the rebellion, a rebellion which he foretold as taking place some 30 years before the historical event. He records that the Tory Prime Minister:

> . . . reversed at once the action of the land-courts, suppressed the 'disloyal' newspapers, and forbade public meetings, filling the country with police and soldiery, and preserving a tranquillity to which he triumphantly pointed as a proof that nothing was needed but the strong hand. Rents rose above their old figure, evictions were of daily occurrence, capital was attracted in abundance, and the Tory millennium of wealthy landlords and a starving peasantry began to be realised. But deep mutterings of discontent filled the country, rising to a sustained scream of indignation in Parliament, where the Irish Leader, at the head of a compact brigade of seventy members, revelled in a perfect carnival of obstruction, and for the time united both English parties in stern opposition to any and every Irish demand.[43]

Like George Moore, Greer lays stress on the economic factors of the conflict between the Irish and the British government, seeing the Irish question as essentially a class struggle, and this is also true of the analyses offered by Trollope and Burnaby, who took the other side. Relatively little is said about Catholics and Protestants: much is said about the payment or non-payment of rents.

John O'Halloran, Greer's flying man, continues his tale and tells how he came back from the university to find that his home had become the scene of secret meetings and the storehouse for an immense armoury of modern weapons 'including dynamite bombs of New York manufacture'. John has no wish to join his father and brothers in their rebellion — his head is full of the possibilities that his wonderful invention will open up for the future of mankind. Not that he ignores the realities of the Irish situation; at the beginning of the book he declares that he has been filled with 'most unscientific sorrow and indignation' at the sight of roofless cottages where he remembers to have seen happy families, and in a passage which recalls George Moore he describes his feelings:

. . . when the cabin stood roofless as the result of a recent eviction; when, as on one occasion, I actually caught sight of the smoke rising from the still smouldering thatch that had been stripped off by the 'crowbar brigade', and saw the houseless wretches who had lived under it standing like statues of despair upon the roadside among their broken and worthless furniture . . .[44]

Despite his sympathy with the evicted peasants John is shown as undergoing a revulsion of feeling on the occasion of his first successful flight. Alone, flying like a bird, he has great visions of the future:

What additions to the sum of human pleasure; what an extension of mutual knowledge and brotherhood among nations; what new and higher forms of civilisation; what a revolution in the social and political conditions of the race seemed now about to be inaugurated![45]

As he glides home from this experimental flight he witnesses the killing of an agent returning from an eviction. He sees two armed men in a trap with the dark speck a hundred yards in front which he can identify as a mounted policeman, with another following at the same distance behind. Then he sees the ambush, two men in the hills waiting with their rifles levelled, and sees the flash of a shot and the fall of the agent. It is significant that, although he refuses to join the rebels, he has no doubts as to which side he is on: 'I did not feel called upon to give any information, with the certainty of having to explain the very peculiar circumstances under which I had witnessed the crime, to an incredulous judge and a probably hostile jury.'[46]

In fact he learns later that one of the murderers was his own brother. It is on the evening of the same day that he has a serious quarrel with his father and determines to leave home. The father is delighted with his invention but at once sees the possibilities of its application in warfare:

'This will ensure the triumph of Old Ireland. You must keep it a secret; you must set yourself to train your brothers and other young men, till we have a flying brigade that can go anywhere and do anything! Nothing will be able to stand against it, and you will have the glory of delivering your country and striking the chains from her hands! Oh! Jack, I am a proud man to see this day!'[47]

John, however, speaks with the voice of his author and holds very firmly to his original idea:

'Oh, father,' I answered, 'how can I make the first use of my discovery in causing war and bloodshed? It is not for war, it is for peace! It is not for one people only, it is for all the world! I would rather bury it in the sea than that one life should be sacrificed, much less a bloody war provoked.'[48]

And he goes on with reasoning that is very close to that of James Joyce, expressing an idea of universal brotherhood, the natural reaction of an idealistic youth surrounded by angry patriots:

'Never will I join in such a mad and hopeless and wicked enterprise!' I rejoined hotly. 'I don't believe that men are parcelled out into tribes and nations, one all good and the other all bad. It is by drawing out the good in all, and not by setting one against another, that anything can be done.'[49]

At this point John, like the heroes of so many boys' adventure stories, runs away from home, leaving his flying machine behind him. With the help of university friends he constructs another and sets off to fly to London to offer his invention for commercial development. Here he meets with a great disappointment. In the first place the crowds who see him fly over the town and settle on the dome of St Paul's are certain that he has gone there as a dynamiter. The *Globe* and the *Echo* carry a full description of the flying man, with the captions 'Sixteen people trampled to death in the streets!!!' and 'Great Dynamite Plot to blow up St Paul's'. This is not the reception that he had bargained for. The newspapers, as Greer notes, had overstated the case:

No lives had actually been lost, though several accidents were reported. But the inventive genius of the writers had no difficulty in discovering the motive that had prompted me. Undoubtedly it was part of a dynamite conspiracy, and the police were at that moment on the roof of St Paul's, searching for the infernal machine I had been seen to carry there.[50]

John suffers great disillusion at Parliament's reception of his invention. They are afraid that such a revolutionary form of transport will
cause financial havoc and a ruinous monetary crisis, with panic
among the railway shareholders. They determine not to permit the
use of the invention, or to place it under such restrictions that it
cannot come into general circulation. John reflects that he might do
well to go elsewhere: 'What is to hinder me from crossing yonder
"silver streak" that shines on the far horizon? ay, or even the
Atlantic itself, to the home of freedom beyond?'[51] While negotia-
tions seem to be at a stalemate, news comes through that open war
has broken out in the north of Ireland. Things are going badly for the
British, who decide to offer John a thousand pounds for his
invention to be used for military purposes. This is exactly the
situation that he had left Ireland to escape, but as he plans to offer
his invention to other purchasers the British capture him and lock
him in prison to prevent it falling into the hands of political enemies.
John is rescued by one of his brothers who had learnt to manoeuvre
the flying machine that he had left at home, and at this point he
determines to give his invention without payment to the cause of the
Irish people. He supervises the production of Irish flying machines
in large numbers and he undertakes the training of special squad-
rons. The first attack described leaves from St Stephens Green to
bomb Dublin Castle from the air:

> . . . at the appointed hour the little squadron mustered, and I
> looked with some anxiety to their equipments, which were of a
> novel character. They carried neither rifles nor sidearms. Each
> man was provided with a broad belt and sling, in which were
> suspended three dynamite bombs weighing five pounds each.
> And each had a plumb-line, consisting of a leaden weight
> attached to a cord six feet long, to enable him to judge accurately
> when a given spot was exactly beneath him, so that the bombs
> could be dropped with unerring aim.[52]

The extremely primitive equipment, particularly the plumb-line
to make certain that the bombs will arrive exactly on target, is part of
the traditional nineteenth-century boys' story, which encouraged
initiative and inventiveness. What is unusual is the amount of space
given by the author to deploration of the result of the attack and to
pacifist reasoning:

'The whole business is inexpressibly shocking and revolting to me. I could never bring myself to do it, if it were not that I am sure the best way to bring the whole thing to an end quickly is to strike the very hardest and heaviest blows we can while it lasts . . . I hate the soldier's trade from the bottom of my heart.'[53]

Dick, his brother, replies by describing some of the horrors of war in detail:

'There were some gruesome sights. One fellow was dug out with almost his whole face blown away — hardly the semblance of a feature left — and yet he was alive, and the doctors say will be likely to recover . . . The sight of the surgeons working away in the courtyard, with their knives, and saws, and probes glittering under the electric light, and their horribly cool and business-like air, was worse than the bloodiest field of battle could be.'[54]

As a doctor himself Greer was naturally led to envisage the work of the surgeons. John O'Halloran refuses to join in the public thanksgiving proclaimed by the Catholic bishop for the destruction of the hostile garrison and the raising of the blockade. Instead he makes his way, alone and unrecognised, to the castle:

Here I was known to the officer in charge, and was admitted to gaze on the ghastly heaps of ruins, the broken walls, the shattered windows, the blood-stained tables where the surgeons had been at work, and last and worst of all, the chamber into which the mangled bodies of the slain had been gathered and piled in heaps, awaiting burial. What a grim commentary it was upon the tramp of church-going feet outside, and the joyous clang with which the air was palpitating![55]

Nevertheless, once involved in the war, John sees it through, hating every minute of it and cursing the irony of fate which has driven him to be the inventor of a 'new and unprecedentedly destructive method of warfare'. He organises his flying squad in an attack on three British warships lying in the roads outside Dublin Bay, and blows them up most effectively by dropping dynamite bombs down the funnels to explode in the heart of the furnaces. He then organises an expedition which is to prove decisive for the outcome of the war against a British army which has landed in the north. Again the equipment is extremely primitive:

> Every man was supplied with a belt containing twelve dynamite
> cartridges of one pound each. The whole force was then told off
> into squads of six, of which half were supplied with three four-
> pound shells per man, the rest with watering cans of petroleum,
> containing a gallon each. In addition every man was armed with a
> revolver.[56]

The watering cans prove particularly effective, for after dousing
the enemy troops and their equipment, the bombs set fire to
them, and no more British are to be seen in Ireland. We are
reminded of Colonel Burnaby's plan to syphon petrol into the
fire-extinguishing system of the Foreign Office. The result of
the attack in *A Modern Daedalus* is described in terms of Dante's
Inferno:

> It lasted only a minute, but what a minute! I have not the imagi-
> nation of Dante, and I cannot picture to my readers a scene such
> as even the author of the 'Inferno' could not have painted,
> although it has never ceased to haunt my memory since. I still
> seem to feel the hot and suffocating rush of smoke and vapour
> that swept upwards to the very heavens, forcing us to fly wildly to
> windward to escape its scorching breath.[57]

Greer uses his novel not only to describe but also to theorise about
war. He declares that 'I hate the necessity of war. I have no pride in
victory', which is a very different stance from that taken in most
books for boys where the emphasis is placed on glory and conquest.
Greer prefers to dwell on the destruction caused by war, and
although not a pacifist-at-any-price he encourages his readers to
meditate on the whole question and not to fall into easy patriotism.
He puts in a plea, however, for dynamite, arguing that war is not a
game, the rules of chivalry cannot apply:

> But when men do make war, they ought to be in earnest. Their
> weapons should be the deadliest they can use; their blows the
> heaviest they can deal. To say that they may make war, indeed,
> but that they must not make it too effectively; that to kill a man
> with a solid bullet is legitimate, but to wound him with an
> explosive one is atrocious; that to blow your enemy to fragments

with gunpowder is civilised warfare, but to employ dynamite for the same purpose is worthy only of savages; is a species of cant born of the idea that war is a magnificent game for kings and nobles, and must be carried on under rules that disguise its essentially revolting nature, and prevent it from being too dangerous or disagreeable to them.[58]

Although not a revolutionary Greer is an idealist and reverts to irony at the end of his story in defence of the idea of international co-operation among the workers of the world:

In short, the Radical and Republican prints, which advocated such Utopian and Socialistic (and therefore wicked) dreams as universal peace and co-operation among working men of all countries, irrespective of the Imperial schemes of sovereigns and statesmen, were found to be unexpectedly and disgustingly popular among the masses.[59]

Sympathising with this concept, Greer's hero nevertheless does not throw himself into the conflict to achieve this union. What matters for him is the idea of individual liberty, and John's flying machine was born as much from the sense of the poetry of flying as from scientific curiosity. At the very opening of the book the reader is told:

. . . one of my earliest recollections is of the wonder and interest with which I used to watch for hours the gliding flight of the sea birds which made their homes by millions on the inaccessible cliffs and lonely stacks of that bold front which the headlands of Donegal present to the Atlantic waves. Their easy, graceful motion — ascending and descending invisible spiral stairs without a tremor of the wing — had an irresistible fascination for me.[60]

The story ends with the war with England over, thanks to the flying machines, and Ireland free to govern herself. The inventor then sets off to realise what had been his dream at the beginning. After a long lyrical passage where he describes himself as flying 'with all the free and careless facility of a bird' he sets off on his worldwide travels, and this is the ambition which he is proposing to his readers; not the joys of conquest but the joys of knowledge:

I share in all the life that goes on under the sun. I trace the footsteps of British civilisation in India, of Russian civilisation in Tartary. I see everything, I sympathise with everything, I love everything.

It is a dream, I know.[61]

It is curious to note how this honest and unpretentious book was received by a contemporary reviewer in the *Spectator*, a review published on 21 March 1885. The reviewer ignores the political issues raised to concentrate instead on the invention of the flying machine, and somewhat shortsightedly thanks his stars that any such invention is impossible:

> The truth seems to be that the designs of Providence require such beings as men to be tied by the leg to the earth, and to be unable to approach any spot except by a few well-defined routes — otherwise we should be simply helpless against even a very feeble conspiracy of evil. Conceive only what a very few Nihilists could do with such powers of flying as Mr. Greer here assigns to his modern Daedalus . . . we may congratulate ourselves that, so far as we have the means of judging, human beings will never acquire the powers with which Mr. Greer has amused himself by investing them.

His thought turns at once to the danger of such an invention falling into the hands of the Nihilists, which is an interesting shift of focus. The real threat to England at the time came not from Nihilists but from Fenians, and Tom Greer had been prospecting the use that Irish nationalists could make of it. But the *Spectator* reviewer substitutes Nihilists, presumably in an attempt, conscious or not, to keep the whole Irish question at bay.

Donald Mac Kay's *The Dynamite Ship* (1888) was written some years earlier, in January, February and March of 1884. It is another story set in the near future, and describes the bombardment of London which the author imagines taking place on 4 July 1889. The frontispiece draws attention to the main point of the story: the blowing up of the Houses of Parliament, not from within but from without, in an attack from dynamite guns stationed on the dynamite ship moored on the Thames. Like Greer's *A Modern Daedalus* this novel, the work of an Irish American, is highly politicised, and uses dynamite in much the same way; that is to say in open warfare (albeit by a very small group) and not in conspiracies: it is a far cry from the Guy Fawkes syndrome. The plot, which again like Greer's has only a minimum love-interest (a sure sign that it was intended mainly as boys' reading) is the story of three men, Heyward an American, Alexander an Englishman and Lubin an Irishman who build a steam ship fitted with dynamite guns. They have the financial support of the Irish League, and they set out from the United States to hold up London and to obtain the freedom of Ireland. They also take on board two young English princes, who are most conveniently bathing off the south coast at the time; another indication that the story was directed towards boys.

The first part of the book, during which the ship is being built, is full of political debate, setting forth the wrongs of Ireland and at the same time condemning the Fenian dynamite movement. Naturally enough the Englishman is the most severe against the conspirators, while Lubin, the Irishman, although condemning them, at the same time puts forward the argument of the provocation to which they are subjected as being at least some justification. There is a long discussion between the Englishman and the Irishman on this subject, which recalls the discussions in the press regarding the part played by the secretary of the Fenian movement in the United States, O'Donovan Rossa, at the time when Mac Kay was writing. Lubin makes a clear distinction between the mass of Irish patriots and Rossa's followers:

'He believes that dynamite bombs, secret murders, and miscellaneous butcheries will intimidate England. So long as he does nothing but believe and make a noise, let him go on. He distracts public attention from the real work that is being pushed forward.'

'Does he represent any one but himself?'

'There are a few notoriety-loving persons that advocate dynamite warfare, secret explosions, miscellaneous killing, and all that sort of thing; and, of course, this being a free country, they are entitled to their opinions; but the great mass of Irish patriots do not hold any such views.'

'But still,' said Alexander [the Englishman], in a tone of impatience, 'the killing of innocent men and women is countenanced to some extent by the Irish in this country, and, I confess, it is not pleasant to think of your relatives — I have some relatives in the suburbs of London — being blown to the moon by a gang of midnight conspirators. These blatherskite orators say in defence, that any war will make widows and orphans, and that a dynamite war is exempt from no horrors attending an armed rebellion. It is simply atrocious.'

'None of these incendiary orators would put into practice the barbarous doctrine that they preach.'

'But they encourage weak or vicious minded persons to carry their teachings into effect. The result is the same either way. I attended a meeting of a small dynamite club, a few evenings ago, in company with a few friends, and the threats and speeches, there, made my blood run cold!'

'What did you hear?'

'A number of arguments claiming to show that secret killing was justifiable, that England herself had countenanced midnight assassination, and that, in the recent civil war in this country [America], bombs and other explosives had been used, secretly, to destroy human life. One speaker said that he could manufacture an explosive that would kill a man at the rate of two hundred thousand miles a minute. He has the insolence to ask Ireland to send him five hundred young men to learn to manufacture and use his explosive, with a view to blowing up English cities. Is that a rational way of carrying on warfare?'

Lubin's face became grave almost to sternness. 'My dear Alexander,' he said, slowly, 'your points are well taken, and I must accept them as my own reasoning. But you forget, for a moment, what great provocation the Irish people have had for more than six hundred years. They have been wronged, oppressed, insulted, robbed, and murdered. Were you an Irishman, and had you suffered as I have suffered, did you look forward to no hope this side the grave, no justice this side of Heaven, you, too, would rise up and cry, "Kill!"'[62]

Both the Englishman and the American are moved to join the attack by a sense of justice. Heyward states that as an American his sympathy must go out to any people in distress. Lubin is even more strongly motivated in that his grandfather died from British persecution and his father is at present in a Dublin prison.

Another political question which is also given considerable space is the function of the Irish League. In England there were many accusations that the League of Irish Americans was financing the dynamiters. The author explicitly states that, so far as the general public knew, or could from any surface indication imagine, the Irish

League confined its attention to the work of relieving distress in Ireland. He is most anxious to avoid the criminalisation of the League, though he does not deny that some of its funds may have found their way to assist the Fenian conspirators. However, even if this is so 'it was not known, or even suspected, that any of the members of the League held views other than that by judicious and persevering contributions of money, and the unending agitation of all questions touching upon Irish wrongs, the freedom of Ireland might ultimately be secured'. Such a passage as the above, introduced into a book which is presented substantially in the form of a boys' adventure story, means that the author had the Irish question very much at heart and was taking precautions to avoid discouraging any right-thinking American who was contributing to the League.

The dynamite guns, with their eight-mile range, are the invention of a Russian, Mellerkoff [Mezzeroff?], who proudly illustrates his work:

'This cylinder, by means of compressed air, will, with perfect and unvarying certainty, throw a dynamite explosive — bomb, cartridge or shell — eight miles so accurately that it will hit the object aimed at. The projectile will then explode with dreadful force. In fact, it will kill a man at the rate of two hundred thousand miles a minute!'
It was the dynamite gun.[63]

This invention, which at the time belonged to the sphere of science fiction, makes the attack on the British Parliament possible. The idea of the conspirators is to steam up the Thames to just below London Bridge, and when they are within striking distance of their objectives, the Houses of Parliament, the Bank of England and the Tower, to send a messenger to Parliament with an ultimatum demanding the freedom of Ireland.

Everything goes according to plan. The Speaker of the House reads out the message and specifies:

'. . . this expedition has no connection with the skulking secret-killing dynamiters that have infested the British kingdom for several years. The members of this expedition denounce the secret system of warfare, and propose to meet us openly and above board, face to face. They will meet us like Englishmen, in a fair field, with no favor.'[64]

But Parliament, notwithstanding their shudder when the word dynamite is uttered, send back a message proposing to keep Ireland but to pay a sum of money in return for a ceasefire. Disdainfully rejecting this humiliating offer the crew open fire, and the effect of the dynamite shells on the Houses of Parliament corresponds with the book's dramatic frontispiece:

> The soaring shell hovering for an instant in air above the buildings of Parliament had fallen with awful force upon the roof.
> In the explosion that followed like ten thousand bolts of lightning, the roof melted away and went flying skyward. The walls wavered for a moment, and then stood still.
> Before the shower of fragments fell, countless numbers of people, who had disregarded the warnings to keep aloof from the neighbourhood of the official buildings, scurried away to places of safety as rapidly as their trembling limbs would carry them.[65]

A counter-attack is attempted but fails, significantly killing however the Irish member of the organisation, who lives long enough to hear the news that the attack has obtained its objectives:

> Lubin grasped the precious roll of parchment, hugged it to his bleeding breast, and raised his glazing eyes to Heaven.
> 'Ireland is free!' he cried. 'Ireland is free! I die — I die — in peace.'
> Falling back upon the sofa, he smiled faintly, and sighing deeply as though weary with the heat and burden of the day, closed his eyes.
> Lubin was dead.[66]

The political purpose behind the book is underlined by an epilogue in which the rejoicing over the liberation of Ireland is wholly unequivocal. Unlike Greer, Mac Kay spares no thought for the victims of the attack but thinks only of the successful outcome:

> The great city of Dublin was aglow with gladness. The Irish people were free . . .

Prisons were thrown open, work-houses were emptied of their inmates, and people everywhere were freed from British influence and British power. It was one great day of rejoicing and thanksgiving. It was the new birth.

. . . Then the great IRISH REPUBLIC was formed.[67]

The lyrical tone of this passage looks forward to the words of another Irishman, William Butler Yeats, who was also a strong supporter of Irish independence and who was to use this concept of 'the new birth', the beginning of a new cycle, in a number of his more memorable poems. And this new birth is to be heralded by what Burnaby had called 'the star of dynamite', used not in conspiracies but in open warfare: 'Used openly, and in the sight of all men, it is as fair as the sling of David' says Heyward, and 'The gun's all right' says Mellerkoff 'The gun is not to blame.' But it is the old Irish servant, Larry, the only one who is recorded as speaking in brogue, who goes the furthest:

'Wud yez till me, an ould frind, what thim guns might be for?' Heyward hesitated only a moment. Then he said: 'To give Ireland her liberty, Larry.'

The faithful old serving-man's face was intensely illumined with joy. 'To free ould Ireland — my Ireland?' he asked eagerly . . . 'God bless you, Misther Heyward; God bless us all.' Then, a moment afterward, 'God bless thim guns!'[68]

Notes

1. In his first two little-known Irish novels published many years earlier, *The Macdermots of Ballycloran* (London, 1847) and *The Kellys and the O'Kellys or Landlords and Tenants* (London, 1848), Anthony Trollope dealt with the problems of Irish tenantry from a much more sympathetic point of view.
2. Trollope, *The Landleaguers*, Vol. 3, p. 291.
3. Ibid., Vol. 1, p. 40.
4. Ibid., Vol. 3, p. 229.
5. Ibid., Vol. 3, pp. 142-3.
6. Ibid., Vol. 3, p. 147.
7. Ibid., Vol. 3, p. 157.
8. Ibid., Vol. 3, p. 161.
9. Ibid., Vol. 3, p. 164.
10. Ibid., Vol. 3, pp. 167-8.
11. George Moore, *A Drama in Muslin* (London, 1886), pp. 15-16, later published in a revised edition as *Muslin* in 1915 with significant cuts, showing that Moore had

undergone a political change of heart in the intervening years. The passages quoted here are taken from the first edition.

12. Moore, *Drama in Muslin*, p. 86.
13. Ibid., p. 87.
14. See my essay 'The Windows of the Victorians' in *English Miscellany*, vol. 25 (Rome, 1975-6), pp. 335-54.
15. Moore, *Drama in Muslin*, p. 171.
16. Ibid., p. 164.
17. Ibid., p. 154.
18. Ibid., pp. 157-8.
19. Ibid., p. 176.
20. Ibid., p. 172.
21. Ibid., p. 173.
22. Ibid., p. 29.
23. Ibid., p. 83.
24. Ibid., p. 95.
25. Ibid., p. 104.
26. Ibid., p. 144.
27. Ibid., p. 318.
28. Ibid., pp. 322-4. This sympathetic description of an eviction is almost completely excised in the 1915 edition.
29. Burnaby, *Our Radicals*, Vol. 2, pp. 226-7.
30. Ibid., Vol. 1, p. 49.
31. Ibid., Vol. 1, p. 55.
32. Ibid., Vol. 1, pp. 78-9.
33. Ibid., Vol. 1, p. 82.
34. Ibid., Vol. 1, pp. 187-8.
35. Ibid., Vol. 2, p. 68.
36. Ibid., Vol. 2, p. 87.
37. Ibid., Vol. 2, p. 178.
38. Ibid., Vol. 2, p. 196.
39. Ibid., Vol. 1, pp. 206-7.
40. Ibid., Vol. 2, p. 228.
41. Greer, *A Modern Daedalus*, preface.
42. Ibid., pp. 6-7.
43. Ibid., pp. 8-9.
44. Ibid., p. 14.
45. Ibid., p. 17.
46. Ibid., p. 23.
47. Ibid., pp. 35-6.
48. Ibid., p. 36.
49. Ibid., p. 37.
50. Ibid., pp. 81-2.
51. Ibid., p. 131.
52. Ibid., p. 199.
53. Ibid., p. 214.
54. Ibid., pp. 214-5.
55. Ibid., p. 222.
56. Ibid., p. 235.
57. Ibid., pp. 237-8.
58. Ibid., p. 247.
59. Ibid., p. 251.
60. Ibid., pp. 1-2.
61. Ibid., p. 259.

62. Donald Mac Kay, *The Dynamite Ship* (London; New York, 1888), pp. 53-5.
63. Ibid., p. 94.
64. Ibid., p. 178.
65. Ibid., p. 186.
66. Ibid., p. 203.
67. Ibid., pp. 206-8.
68. Ibid., p. 103.

DYNAMITE FALLS ON CASTLE WALLS

A lone poet, John E. Barlas, in 1887 wrote both the poem 'A Vision of Vengeance' and a sonnet sequence *Holy of Holies: Confessions of an Anarchist*. Under the influence of William Blake's 'London' he describes a city awaiting destruction:

> . . . And spirits about that town
>   Went up and down,
> Each swathed, as 'twere, in a pale cloud of pain,
>   Some scored with seam and gash;
>   Some bore the lash:
> Some lips were sad, some curled with proud disdain,
> But all shed tears of blood thicker than rain.
>
>   And spectral women there,
>   With braided hair,
> Went up and down, and sold their feverish lips,
>   Which many with strange thirst
>   Tasted, and cursed:
> And maniacs, wild-eyed as the moon's eclipse,
> Wandered adrift like conflagrated ships.[1]

Barlas shares Blake's vision, but not his power of expression. His up-to-dateness consists in the fact that the 'fieriest cloud' which is to put an end to all evils, including the evil of prostitution, seems to be an anarchist dynamite attack. The stress on the exploitation of women, which he found in Blake, was possibly reinforced by W. T. Stead's series on 'The Maiden Tribute of Modern Babylon'[2] which caused such an outcry in 1885, linking as it did the names of leading politicians with the trade in girls under the age of consent (at the time 13). The 'fieriest cloud', by putting an end to politicians and prostitutes alike, cleanses the city:

> Slowly it sailed, and came
> A sheet of flame,
> High o'er that city's topmost column-peak, —
>   The town lay still as Death:

I held my breath:
The blood-red deluge fell. Without a shriek
The town was cleansed of all that made it reek.

Then changed those furial gleams
To mild moon-beams.
And in that city, late those demons' lair,
Angels went too and fro . . .[3]

The same idea of the moral nature of anarchist destruction[4] is to be found in the sonnets, all addressed to 'Violet', their main message (a secondary one is the loneliness of the anarchist) condensed into the last lines:

Then with a roar as of the crashing sky
We sweep the liar and coward from the world.[5]

The theme is essentially one of regeneration, and the anarchist is presented as an idealist: a destroying angel.

The science fiction dynamite novels also lean toward this idealistic interpretation of the initial motivation of the dynamitards, and often give considerable space to the ideological background of their anarchist protagonists. Unlike the Nihilist novels, however, the authors never give their whole-hearted support to the movement, and when they come to describe the secret meetings held by the members of the organisation the novelists convey their disapproval in a number of ways: apart from the ritual trappings of terror, the hoods or masks, there are mysterious passwords and binding oaths, and the conspirators are always watching each other and being watched in their turn. Almost every such meeting carries a sentence of death to some defecting member, a sentence against which there is no appeal and which is carried out as swiftly and secretly as possible. The conflict between the high humanitarian aims expressed and the way in which the organisation actually sets to work is implicitly and often explicitly conveyed to the reader.

The ideological basis of anarchy was under discussion in the last 20 years of the nineteenth century in many theoretical treatises and pamphlets, to which the writers of novels could turn for clarification. Apart from the basic ideology elaborated by Kropotkin, pamphlets and essays on the subject were published by persons as different as Robert Buchanan, George Bernard Shaw and the Archdeacon of

Westminster. The confusion evident in the novels often stems from a tendency to confound the issues involved, a tendency which is to be found in these very pamphlets. Shaw, who even as a young man could both think and write clearly, in *The Impossibilities of Anarchism* (published by the Fabian Society in 1893, but first drafted in 1888) points out, as I have tried to do in the first two chapters of this book, that:

> . . . no distinction is made in the newspapers which support the existing social order between Social Democrats and Anarchists, both being alike hostile to that order. In the columns of such papers all revolutionists are Socialists; all Socialists are Anarchists; and all Anarchists are incendiaries, assassins and thieves.[6]

Shaw himself was a Marxist, for a time a member of the Fabian Society founded by Beatrice and Sidney Webb and later joined the ranks of the Communist Party, as did H. G. Wells. His quarrel with anarchy is that, having a more realistic idea of human nature than Kropotkin, he does not believe that once the pressures of an unjust society have been removed man will automatically become honest; that is to say he sees the need for institutions, democratic institutions, which will organise the relations between man and man:

> Krapotkine, too optimistically as I think, disposes of the average man by attributing his unsocialism to the pressure of the corrupt system under which he groans. Remove that pressure, and he will think rightly, says Krapotkine . . .[7]

Shaw is by no means so sure of this, and sees the problem as being particularly acute immediately after the abolition of the capitalist system, before there has been time to educate men and women along new lines and in obedience to new principles: 'The practical question remains, could men trained under our present system be trusted to pay for their food scrupulously if they could take it for nothing with impunity?'[8] Shaw's answer to this is that they could not, and he foresees the necessity of enforcement of law and order, a concept refused by anarchists and Nihilists alike, because the origins of these movements were to be found in countries where the police and army were regularly used in support of injustice and repression. Shaw believes, as a socialist, in centralised state power and institutions, with the difference that it is to be a completely democratic state, and, having no experience of secret police, he places his trust in the British bobby and Tommy Atkins for seeing justice done:

> Fortunately, there is, as we have seen, a fine impartiality about the policeman and the soldier, who are the cutting edge of State power . . . If his orders were to help the police to pitch his Lordship into Holloway Gaol until he had paid an Income Tax of 20 shillings on every pound of his unearned income, the soldier would do that with equal devotion to duty, and perhaps with a certain private zest . . . Now these orders come ultimately from the State — meaning, in this country, the House of Commons. A House of Commons consisting of 660 gentlemen and 10 workmen will order the soldier to take money from the people for the landlords. A House of Commons consisting of 660 workmen and 10 gentlemen will probably, unless the 660 are fools, order the soldier to take money from the landlords for the people.[9]

Not all the novelists dealing with anarchists had read George Bernard Shaw. Some may have read Robert Buchanan, who in 1891 published *The Coming Terror: A Dialogue between Alienatus, a Provincial* [with whom Buchanan identifies], *and Urbanus, a Cockney*. Apart from the country versus city theme which surfaces in the title and choice of protagonists, Buchanan is writing an anti-socialist pamphlet essentially attacking Shaw's idea of state socialism. But he confuses the issue by calling his state socialists anarchists and defining as socialist what is essentially an anarchist programme of freedom from control, and he makes confusion worse confounded by putting forward a liberal programme of *laissez faire* as being the one which meets with his full approval. It is useful, I believe, to quote from the beginning and from the end of his pamphlet, to give an idea of the terms in which the theoretical discussion at the time was being carried on, and the confusion engendered:

> **Urbanus** Possibly, with your prophetic faculties, you can tell me what shape that Terror will assume?
> **Alienatus** The shape it has assumed always, that of Anarchy, that of the Demogorgon, who is all-creating yet all-destroying. In simpler words, Humanity will arise and rend itself. The present Order will vanish, like a house built on sand, but with it will vanish every vestige of a social cosmos. The triumphant majority

of human beings will trample down all the rights of minorities, all the privileges of individuals, all the moral differentiation of the human race. No man will breathe freely in his own dwelling. No personal life will grow, upward or downward, its own way. There will be universal legislation, expressed in a creed which shall base the salvation of the State on the destruction of the individual. . .

Urbanus I hardly follow you. Let me ask you, to begin with, to explain the paradox which represents Legislation and Anarchy as convertible terms?

Alienatus . . . The tyranny of a majority, however beneficient in intention, becomes of its own nature anarchic. Anarchy, politically speaking, is a condition of things representing the triumph of communities over the wills and wishes of individual men. There is the anarchy of Despotism, the anarchy of Parliaments, the anarchy of the Bureau.[10]

And at the end:

Alienatus . . . I have defined true Socialism, not as the arbitrary will of those who would altogether destroy institutions and crush freedom of individual action, not as the rule of the Mob and its mouthpiece the Demagogue, but as the combination of free individuals to limit general legislation wherever it paralyzes personal endeavour and destroys personal rewards. I am therefore a true Socialist; that is, a man eager for the common good, but one who believes that good can only be attained by such complete freedom in life, morality and religion as is compatible with the general growth and welfare.[11]

The Archdeacon of Westminster, writing ten years later on the occasion of the assassination of the American President McKinley by an anarchist, has his own solution to offer, and, although naturally enough he turns his argument to the ends of the church, it is significant that he proposes to look for the cause of anarchism and finds them in the commercial system (= capitalism). His proposed solution, the christianising of commerce, amounts in fact to the destruction of monopolies and Combines which 'enhance the price of the necessities of life', and he goes so far as to denounce speculators as being worse than the anarchists, their sin is of 'a far deeper dye':

. . . But if you execute to-morrow every known Anarchist in the world you have not really touched the evil. The same causes will produce the same effects. The wise in all countries will labour to counteract the causes. The causes of Anarchism are twofold . . . Anarchism is the fruitage of Atheism . . .

The second cause of Anarchism is the instability of the equilibrium of the whole commercial system of civilized nations . . . In no country in the world has it been more manifest that national prosperity [in the United States] has enriched, not the many, but the few . . . Where it [individual wealth] is the result of 'rings', 'corners', 'combinations', all tending abnormally to enhance the price of the necessities of life for the masses, it strikes at the root of civilized life, sins against the brotherhood of the race, and becomes a plague centre of furious vitality prolific of the disease of Anarchism . . . base and brutal as is this crime of the assassin Czolgosz, I consider that the speculators who, for their personal aggrandisement, were prepared to bring to the verge of starvation thousands of their fellow-men, are criminals of a far deeper dye.[12]

These debates are far from irrelevant to the more serious dynamite novels. Writers like George Griffith in *The Angel of the Revolution* and E. Douglas Fawcett in *Hartmann the Anarchist* had to take into consideration not only the world they were destroying but also what they were planning to put in its place. There had been a spate of minor utopias in 1885-6 which, as they did not pass society through the holocaust of regeneration by dynamite, do not directly concern us, except in so far as the social criticism they offered contributed to the general debate. These utopias do not call for the sudden and violent destruction of society as we know it, as they are geographically located Elsewhere, or are set so far in the future that, though the world is the same, everything has changed. Edward Bellamy's *Looking Backward*, the best of this group and published a year or two later, in 1888, is set 113 years in the future, bringing us up to the year 2,000. None of these writers show anything like the range of imagination which in 1895 enabled H. G. Wells to write *The Time Machine*: they were simply concerned with criticising the social and political institutions of the present day, often in a very uninspired way.

A Radical Nightmare, or, England Forty Years Hence, published anonymously in 1885 but signed by 'an ex-MP', describes how Lord

Carlton fell asleep on the eve of the November 1885 general elections and woke up 40 years later in 1925. His disappearance from the political and domestic scene, as he learns later, was 'put down to the Irish dynamiters' whose party he had always strongly opposed in the House and elsewhere. The scene in the future is set in France, which has been laid waste by civil war. Why exactly the Irish dynamiters should have taken part is not clear, but the author seems to imply that they came in, with their efficient dynamite techniques, as mercenaries:

> Millions of people were massacred wholesale, large towns were in a moment destroyed by dynamite laid by Irish Americans, who had made this sort of destruction their means of livelihood. Nobody was spared; children, women, and aged persons of both sexes were mercilessly destroyed; and France became a dreadful waste.[13]

The author gives a panoramic view of the disastrous state of Europe (the King of England very wisely emigrates to India, where he is shortly afterwards proclaimed king). The only country which thrives seem to be Ireland, busy exporting dynamite:

> Mr Carnal [= Parnell] proclaimed Ireland independent, and installed a parliament of his own at Dublin, with himself as Prime Minister . . . Mr Bosher [Rossa?] was invited to leave America and take the post of Minister for War; this he at once accepted, and soon afterwards started a large dynamite manufactory at Bray, for the better protection of Ireland against her enemies. I may add that the Communists in France largely added to the prosperity of Ireland by the employment of skilled dynamitists and infernal machine manufacturers, in their little differences with the French Conservative Party of 1895.[14]

The author is very much preoccupied with this theme of dynamite, even though he has other things to say. His main attack against the Radicals is directed against their stress on education: '. . . England is now the least desirable abode on the face of the earth. Over-education now fills the lunatic asylums.'[15] The work of the School Board is also responsible for the development of the new woman, whose flat figure the author describes with relish, fearing that she will soon make the English race extinct: 'She, or it, whatever you like to call it, is an anti-matrimony party, drinks illicit gin, and swears in Greek and Latin.'[16] This unattractive female is given a voice like 'an apologetic frog', and is a fair warning of what schooling will lead to. The whole book can barely be considered a novel, although it is given a fictional framework, but is rather a pamphlet for the times written from a strongly conservative point of view. In his radical nightmare it is significant that the author sees Ireland as independent from England — indeed all communication, except that of the fishing boats, has been cut off: 'The steamers had stopped running many years ago, and the submarine cable had been destroyed by dynamite.'

A Fortnight in Heaven (1886) by Harold Brydges is, like Buchanan's pamphlet, and like the *Radical Nightmare*, an attack on state socialism. In a variant of the dream technique, the narrator leaves his body behind on earth while he studies the 'Pecooliar institootions' of the planet Jupiter and is greatly inconvenienced when he returns to earth to find that meantime he has been certified as dead and his body buried. Heaven consists in a larger-than-life Chicago and New York, but the novel is more a *divertissement* than a serious consideration of alternatives, the only major proposal being government by plebiscite.

Falsivir's Travels (1886) by Thomas Lee describes the discovery of a warm country at the North Pole, reached by crossing a ridge of mountains in a balloon. It is a topsy-turvy utopia, a point emphasised by the craze of the inhabitants for standing on their heads which he describes as 'the national vice'. Some of the features of his new world are similar to those Wells was later to describe in the Eloi and Morlocks of *The Time Machine*, particularly the division of the inhabitants into two races, men and giants, the giants being servants or slaves. Social criticism of existing society in England is implicit in much of the reasoning, and the story is told from the viewpoint of the workers whose obedience is ensured, as the author illustrates, by religious teaching:

> The priests tell the giants that if they humbly obey their masters, the men, and do their bidding in this life, then they, in the next state of existence, will be men, and beautiful as the men are, for, say they, 'We were giants in our first state of existence, but we obeyed our masters, and now we are men;' and the poor foolish giants, having no sort of book learning, believe this, and do not only blindly submit, but almost worship the men as a superior race of mortals, when, in point of fact, the giants are, in my

opinion — except book learning — quite as intelligent as their masters, only their knowledge is of a different sort. The men are clever at any light or fancy work; they are good at poetry, prose, or painting; but at making a road, building a bridge or houses, or anything wherein labour is required, they are useless. The giants build all their houses.[17]

This novel probably owes something to Butler's *Erewhon*, but while Butler had used the allegory of the musical banks to exemplify the role of the church in nineteenth-century society, Lee is even more outspoken, showing how Christian thought is distorted by the teachings of the church in the interests of the privileged classes: 'If their great philosopher were now amongst them, he would fail to recognize the doctrine he had taught.' Not until Robert Tressell's *The Ragged Trousered Philanthropists* was published in 1915 can we find such a downright and explicit attack on the part played by both church and chapel in upholding the existing social structures, but this novel of Lee's, of which the writing is very simple, differs in tone from most nineteenth-century novels and seems to be written from a genuinely working-class point of view.

Max Adeler's *The Drolleries of a Happy Island* (1886) is a very slight sketch indeed, intended prevalently as a satire on the woman's emancipation movement along the same lines as *The Radical Nightmare*. It contains a number of topical references: the Fenians are called Finny-yuns; there is a student song about a mule blown up by dynamite. Chapter V, called 'The Female Parliamentary Session', which is set in the House of Uncommons, shows the women's parliament doing little except changing its clothes at frequent intervals and legislating on tax relief for 'any gentleman, on showing that his wife's dressmaking and millinery expenses absorbed two-thirds of his income'.

The Phantom City, a Volcanic Romance (1886) by William Westall is really a boys' adventure story, where the narrator recounts in the first person a balloon flight into phantom-land, which with its high priest and temple of the sun bears little relation to contemporary events, with the exception of a chapter called 'The Maiden Tribute' describing the yearly sacrifice of a maid of high degree and marriageable age to the volcano in return for its quiescence. The tale is a socio-anthropological fantasy of the kind which in years to come were so often to alternate or even to interweave with socio-political fantasies.

Edward Bellamy's *Looking Backward* (1888) jumps a long way forward and forestalls many modern science fiction tales by preserving the narrator alive and intact in a sealed underground room for something over a century. The explanation is typical of its time: the miracle is the work of a mesmerist, and the room was simply soundproofed to combat insomnia. He wakes up in a world where, as his host explains to him:

> 'The industry and commerce of the country, ceasing to be conducted by a set of irresponsible corporations and syndicates of private persons at their caprice and for their profit, were intrusted to a single syndicate representing the people, to be conducted in the common interest for the common profit.'[18]

Bellamy is using the framework of the novel for a serious analysis of the working of a socialist state. He too, like Max Adeler and the 'ex-MP', is interested in the role of woman in the future, and finds a new fiancée for his narrator (for the purposes of the story she is a descendant of the old one) who is a far more rational creature.

The author turns the tables on his readers at the end of the book, by waking up the narrator back in the nineteenth century. He is very distressed when his attempts to communicate the kind of socialism he has seen in his dream lead to his being thrown out of a dinner party accused of being an 'Enemy of Society'. At this point he wakes up again and finds that it was his excursion backwards that was a dream and he is allowed to live out the rest of his natural life in the socialist utopia of the year 2,000. This reversal mechanism is more than a mere trick to hold the attention of the reader; it is rather Bellamy's view of his own predicament, the man who has seen a vision but who cannot persuade his contemporaries to listen to him.

It may have been the approach of the end of the century that turned men's thoughts so persistently to the future. A number of dynamite novels were set in the twentieth century, overlapping with the older genre of the utopia and the newer one of science fiction. *A Modern Daedalus* and *The Dynamite Ship* had both been dated a few years forward, but were concerned with the contingent situation in Ireland. George Griffith, instead, in his *The Angel of the Revolution* (1893) is concerned with world politics, and in this long and well-written novel he makes use of a fleet of airships and of dynamite on an unprecedented scale. In intention the work is pro-Nihilist, ending in the creation of a world federation under central Nihilist control, although there are a number of inconsistencies, suggesting that the author had by no means fully absorbed the doctrine that he was preaching and was often unable to escape from the structures and values of middle-class nineteenth-century society. Much of the story takes the form of science fiction concerned with the invention and building of a fleet of Nihilist airships: the inventor is the hero of the narrative which is told in the third person, a technique implying that the author must take more responsibility for the ideas expressed than when he can shield himself behind a fictional narrator.

A world war is allowed to build up between the *League* (English, Germans and Austrians) and the *Alliance* (French, Russians and Italians), and it is when they have almost destroyed each other that the Nihilists intervene. America is taken over by the millions of Nihilists living there, and the Nihilists in other countries join them so that the nations of the Western world are brought to their knees by force and formed into a Federation which crushes also the Moslems when, at the end of the novel, they attempt an attack. In a number of ways this novel is an interesting forerunner of H. G. Wells's political science fiction novels: *The War of the Worlds* and *The World Set Free*, and even his *A Modern Utopia* has some of the same features.

Apart from the speed and destructive power of the new machines, far exceeding anything existing in fact or fiction before this date, and apart from the apocalyptic vision of the devastation of modern warfare, Griffith's novel is a blend of the traditional dynamite conspiracy novel, the historical romance (in its study of the background of the conspirators) and the utopia, this last confined to the epilogue entitled 'And on Earth Peace!'.

The trappings of the conspirators' meetings are very much the same mixture as before. At the very beginning of the novel we hear of the Brotherhood (organised in inner and outer circles) condemning a member to death for collusion with the Czar's secret police:

'No; Ainsworth met his death in quite another way. He accepted from the Russian secret police bureau in London a bribe of £250 down and the promise of another £250 if he succeeded in manufacturing enough evidence against a member of our Outer Circle to get him extradited to Russia on a trumped-up charge of murder.

The Inner Circle learnt of this from one of our spies in the

Russian London police, and — well, Ainsworth was found dead with the mark of the Terror upon his forehead before he had time to put his treachery into action.'[19]

The swiftness and sureness of punishment effectively guards the Brotherhood against traitors:

> 'But how do you guard against treachery? It is well known that all the Governments of Europe are spending money like water to unearth this mystery of the Terror. Surely all your men cannot be incorruptible.'
> 'Practically they are so. The very mystery which enshrouds all our actions makes them so. We have had a few traitors, of course; but as none of them has ever survived his treachery by twenty-four hours, a bribe has lost its attraction for the rest.'[20]

The binding oath is an essential feature of initiation, but the romantic hocus-pocus going back to the Rosicrucians and Freemasons has been replaced by a legal document and a bureau-cratic formulation, which is to prove, as Ainsworth found to his cost, none the less deadly. The hero is simply requested to sign on the dotted line:

> I, Richard Arnold, sign this paper in the full knowledge that in doing so I devote myself absolutely for the rest of my life to the service of the Brotherhood of Freedom, known to the world as the Terrorists. As long as I live its ends shall be my ends, and no human considerations shall weigh with me where those ends are concerned. I will take life without mercy, and yield my own without hesitation at its bidding. I will break all other laws to obey those which it obeys, and if I disobey these I shall expect death as the just penalty of my perjury.[21]

Once Arnold has signed the paper he loses all personal freedom, and Griffith conforms completely to the traditional pattern when he makes Arnold realise his plight and declare: '"You have made a conspirator and murderer of me. How is it possible that, knowing this, I can again become what I was before your infernal influence was cast about me?"'[22] He feels himself to be in the grip of the Brotherhood for ever.

The organisation which he joins is exceedingly wide-reaching:

'In the first place, that which is known to the outside world as the Terror is an international secret society underlying and directing the operations of the various bodies known as Nihilists, Anarchists, Socialists — in fact, all those organisations which have for their object the reform or destruction, by peaceful or violent means, of Society as it is at present constituted.

Its influence reaches beyond these into the various trade unions and political clubs, the moving spirits of which are all members of our Outer Circle. On the other side of Society we have agents and adherents in all the Courts of Europe, all the diplomatic bodies, and all the parliamentary assemblies throughout the world.'[23]

But the moving spirit is a Nihilist, Natas, and the broad flag flying from the stern of the *Ithuriel*, the flagship of the air fleet, is red.

Griffith effectively communicates the idea of the background of the Nihilists, the repressions they have suffered and the tortures they have undergone at the hands of the Czar's secret police, by having his narrator describe the 'fine paintings' which are exhibited in the council chamber of the Brotherhood, a little picture gallery 'all faithful reproductions of scenes that have really taken place within the limits of the so-called civilised and Christian world'. This transfer of his message from the spoken onto the visual plane seems in some way to vouch for its truth when the passage goes on: 'There are some here in this room now who have suffered the torments depicted on those canvases, and who could tell of worse horrors than even they portray. We should like to know what you think of our paintings?'[24] Arnold, at least, is convinced, as he looks around the long table where sit 14 masked and shrouded figures, and reflects:

My own reading tells me that they are only too true to the dreadful reality. I think that the civilised and Christian Society which permits such crimes to be committed against humanity, when it has the power to stop them by force of arms, is neither truly civilised nor truly Christian.[25]

When asked whether he would be willing to take action to put an end to the crimes he affirms without hesitation: 'Yes, if it costs the lives of millions to do it.'

Griffith is not really interested in the Russian situation: the cases of injustice and repression which he reports are included in a somewhat perfunctory fashion to account for the subsequent activities of the conspirators. In the first chapter he evokes a scene of torture with the knout which earlier novelists had used so effectively, but in Griffith the whole passage has a second-hand air, and is simply the mechanism by which the inventor of the flying ships is drawn into the group of conspirators, one of whom bares his back to reveal his scars:

> 'That is the sign-manual of Russian tyranny — the mark of the knout!'
> Arnold shrank back with a cry of horror at the sight. From waist to neck Colston's back was a mass of hideous scars and wheals, crossing each other and rising up into purple lumps, with livid blue and grey spaces between them. As he stood, there was not an inch of naturally-coloured skin to be seen. It was like the back of a man who had been flayed alive, and then flogged with a cat-o'-nine-tails.[26]

This is the more shocking in that the victim is an Englishman, so that the reader is filled initially with sympathy with the conspirators: it is clearly time to do something about the regime of the Czar when violent hands can be laid on a fellow-countryman whose only crime was to intervene to prevent an old Jewess from being flogged to death. Russia is far away from the main scenes of action in the novel, but the terrorists acquire a certain respectability from the fact that some of the leaders are fugitives and refugees. The famous pillar of farewells at Tobolsk, which is the classic feature of Nihilist novels, and which was a symbol of the end of all hope for the political exile, is also briefly mentioned:

> Although the railway extended as far as Tomsk, Mazanoff made them disembark here, and marched them by the Great Siberian road to the Pillar of Farewells on the Asiatic frontier. There, as so many thousands of heart-broken despairing men and women had done before them, they looked their last on Russian soil.[27]

At the very end of the novel Griffith pauses, before outlining the structure of the Federation which is to ensure world peace, to devise a fitting punishment for the Czar and his followers, along Gilbert-and-Sullivan lines:

You shall drag your chains over Siberian snows, and when you faint by the wayside the lash shall revive you, as in the hands of your brutal Cossacks it has goaded on your fainting victims. You shall sweat in the mine and shiver in the cell, and your wives and your children shall look upon your misery and be helpless to help you, even as have been the fond ones who have followed your victims to exile and death.[28]

This background relies in part on contemporary newspaper articles reporting repression in Russia, and probably partly on other recent novels such as May's *Love: The Reward* and Hatton's *By Order of the Czar*; the theme of the dramatic painting of the exiles' trek to Siberia may well have been borrowed from the latter novel, where it is central to the plot. The introduction of these Russian dissidents into *The Angel of the Revolution* seriously confuses the basic issues involved, because the mass of the revolutionaries in Griffith's novel are not Russian exiles at all but westerners exploited by the capitalist system, as he states very clearly in an attack on American capitalism. From the point of view of the storyteller this was much less picturesque, so he keeps the more old-fashioned conspiracy setting, while equipping his plotters with modern airships and substituting a new objective in the Ring of Capitalists. The Czar, as the passage quoted above shows, is only recollected and paid off in his own coin in a few lines at the end. Instead the real enemy is identified in the West:

Representative government in America had by this time become a complete sham. The whole political machinery and internal resources of the United States were now virtually at the command of a great Ring of capitalists who, through the medium of the huge monopolies which they controlled, and the enormous sums of money at their command, held the country in the hollow of their hand. These men were as totally devoid of all human feeling or public sentiment as it was possible for human beings to be. They had grown rich in virtue of their contempt of every principle of justice and mercy, and they had no other object in life than to still further increase their gigantic hoards of wealth, and to multiply the enormous powers which they already wielded.[29]

Another modern touch is to be found in a primitive bugging technique which at the time still belonged to the realms of science fiction but which Griffith was farsighted enough to foresee as an appropriate weapon with which to wage war on the new enemy:

> Every one of the cabs is fitted with a telephonic arrangement communicating with the roof. The driver has only to button the wire of the transmitter up inside his coat so that the transmitter itself lies near to his ear, and he can hear even a whisper inside the cab.[30]

The conspiracy itself is organised on a hierarchical basis, all the wires running back into the hands of the great chief, Natas, the mystery man who was to become so popular in subsequent spy stories; the master's power over men is superhuman, and his word is law. Natas belongs to the old romantic tradition rather than the new scientific one, and his gift of hypnotism may have been borrowed from Marie Corelli's Casimir Heliobas in *A Romance of Two Worlds*, another larger-than-life, semi-demonic superman hero who controls his subjects by a similar projection of psychic forces. Natas gives the following demonstration of his power:

> 'Stand there till I tell you to move.'
> As he spoke these last words Natas made a swift, sweeping downward movement with one of his hands, and fixed his eyes upon those of the Professor. In an instant Volnow's muscles stiffened into immovable rigidity, and he stood rooted to the deck powerless to move so much as a finger.[31]

Volnow is the greatest living physical scientist so it is interesting to note that Griffith pits the two men against each other only to show Volnow helpless in the other's hands as Griffith comes down in favour of romantic pseudo-science with Natas as Prospero. Hypnotism, like vivisection, was fascinating the novelists of the period. Readers had recently met not only Marie Corelli's doctor but also the much shadier figure of Verena Tarrant's father in Henry James's *The Bostonians*. The theme was a sign of the times.

The angel-demon dichotomy in Natas, the leader of the revolution, visible in the upper and lower halves of his face, and repeated for good measure in the upper and lower halves of his body, seems to me to symbolise a corresponding dichotomy in the novel itself:

> The face of this man exhibited a contrast so striking and at the

same time terrible, that the most careless glance cast upon it would have revealed the fact that it was the face of a man of extraordinary character, and that the story of some strange fate was indelibly stamped upon it.

The upper part of it, as far down as the mouth, was cast in a mould of the highest and most intellectual manly beauty. The forehead was high and broad and smooth, the eyebrows dark and firm but finely arched, the nose somewhat prominently aquiline, but well-shaped, and with delicate, sensitive nostrils. The eyes were deep-set, large and soft, and dark as the sky of a moonless night, yet shining in the firelight with a strange magnetic glint that seemed to fasten Tremayne's gaze and hold it at will.

But the lower portion of his face was as repulsive as the upper part was attractive. The mouth was the mouth of a wild beast, and the lips and cheeks and chin were seared and seamed as though with fire, and what looked like the remains of a moustache and beard stood in black ragged patches about the heavy unsightly jaws.

When the thick, shapeless lips parted, they did so in a hideous grin, which made visible long, sharp white teeth, more like those of a wolf than those of a human being.

His body, too, exhibited no less strange a contrast than his face did. To the hips it was that of a man of well-knit, muscular frame, not massive, but strong and well-proportioned. The arms were long and muscular, and the hands white and small, but firm, well-shaped, and nervous.

But from his hips downwards, this strange being was a dwarf and a cripple. His hips were narrow and shrunken, one of his legs was some inches shorter than the other, and both were twisted and distorted, and hung helplessly down from the chair as he sat.

Such was Natas, the Master of the Terror, and the man whose wrongs, whatever they might have been, had caused him to devote his life to a work of colossal vengeance, and his incomparable powers to the overthrow of a whole civilisation.[32]

Griffith, that is to say, was of two minds as to how he felt about the conspiracy. On the one hand he sympathised with its ultimate aims; he allows the Brotherhood to completely overturn existing governments. The terrorists were a development of nineteenth-century workers' movements: they were known to the world only under the guise of industrial unionism, but behind them was 'a perfect system of discipline and command which the outer world had never even suspected'. They were not only armed, but trained in the use of firearms to a high degree of skill. Griffith seems to have taken this view of the unions straight from the Conservative press of the time, which saw the union movement as a serious threat to the established political and economic system, and certainly suspected the existence of an international plot and a military organisation in the background. Griffith also takes over the denigratory term 'terrorists' from the press. 'Freedom fighters' had yet to be born, but writers who sympathised with such movements were already using the term 'liberators'. On the other hand, Griffith's revolutionaries 'were nearly all of Anglo-Saxon blood and English speech', which was surely a mark in their favour. The very first clause of the New European Constitution established by the revolution proclaimed 'the supremacy of the Anglo-Saxon Federation in all matters of international policy'. The second clause constituted an 'International Board of Arbitration and Control', and Griffith seems to be quite unaware of any inconsistency in the co-existence of these two clauses, which would inevitably give rise to a conflict over competence.

The twisted and distorted lip of Natas, and his teeth like those of a wolf contrasting with the 'highest and most intellectual manly beauty' of the upper part of his face bring out in visual form, as I said, the conflict in Griffith's own mind concerning the revolution and its actors: although much of the warping of Natas's body and mind is attributable to the tortures he has undergone in Russia, the wolf-like teeth are an innate characteristic. The same kind of ambiguity is revealed by a number of glaring inconsistencies in the narrative itself, particularly in those aspects which concern women and private property. Women, indeed, in this novel as in so many others of the time, can well be classed under the 'private property' heading.

All the women in the novel are incredibly beautiful. A comparison of Lady Muriel Penarth and Natasha is to the detriment of neither: of Lady Muriel's appearance we are told:

It lacked the brilliance and subtle charm which in Natasha so wondrously blended the dusky beauty of the daughters of the South with the fairer loveliness of the daughters of the North; but it atoned for this by that softer grace and sweetness which is the highest charm of purely English beauty.[33]

The reason for this flawless beauty is obvious; Natasha's reception of Arnold's proposal of marriage leaves us with no doubts: woman is conceived as the reward of man, who deserves no less than perfection.

> '. . . when you have made war impossible to the rivalry of nations and races, and have proclaimed peace on earth, then I will give myself to you, body and soul, to do with as you please, to kill or to keep alive, for then truly you will have done that which all the generations of men before you have failed to do, and it will be yours to ask and to have.'[34]

This is a variant of the chivalric quest motif of medieval romance, and its adoption suggests a certain innate conservatism in the author. At the end of the story, shortly after the exemplary punishment of the Czar, we have the exemplary reward of the two heroes:

> And so it came to pass that three days later, in the little private chapel of Alanmere Castle, the two men who held the destinies of the world in their hands, took to wife the two fairest women who ever gave their loveliness to be the crown of strength and the reward of loyal love.[35]

The reason given for Natas's hatred of society, which drives him to dedicate his life to 'a work of colossal vengeance' is that his wife, condemned to exile in Siberia, had been abducted (presumably by one of the provincial governors, as so often happens in stories about Russia) and had ceased to be his own property. Natas himself gives this account of her fate:

> 'Let it suffice to say that my wife was beautiful with a beauty that is rare among the daughters of men; that a woman's honour is held as cheaply in the wildernesses of Siberia as is the life of a man who is a convict.
> The official story of her death was false — false as are all the ten thousand other lies that have come out of that abode of oppression and misery, and she whom I mourned would have been well-favoured of heaven if she had died in the snowdrifts, as they said she did, rather than in the shame and misery to which her brutal destroyer brought her . . . but two years later he visited

Paris, and was found one morning in bed with a dagger in his black heart, and across his face the mark that told that he had died by order of the Nihilist Executive.'[36]

That a real woman might have actually preferred this alternative fate to perishing among the snows is never taken into consideration — the wives created by male novelists as prizes for men were as good as they were beautiful, and being good meant a rigid respect of the laws of property: they knew to whom they belonged.

The whole question of private property is dealt with in a way that is not so much ambiguous as contradictory. Lord Alanmere (Tremayne) who is destined to become the World Governor is shown as taking appropriate steps, on the eve of world war, to safeguard his own very valuable inheritance: 'Within the next six hours Tremayne transferred the whole of his vast property in a single instrument to his promised wife, thus making her the richest woman in England . . .'[37] The Brotherhood instead are working on a very different basis. They declare: 'There is no such thing as private property in the Brotherhood', and we are shown how this works out in practice in an account of the wedding of Radna and Mazanoff:

> One usually conspicuous feature in similar ceremonies was entirely wanting. There were no wedding presents. For this there was a very sufficient reason. All the property of the members of the Inner Circle, saving only articles of personal necessity, were held in common. Articles of mere convenience or luxury were looked upon with indifference, if not with absolute contempt, and so no one had anything to give.[38]

The author himself finds it difficult to believe in such a disinterested way of life, because he immediately, as an afterthought, goes on to add that, with the flying ship in their possession, they could help themselves to anything they liked: 'After all, this was not a very serious matter for a company of men and women who held in their hands the power of levying indemnities to any amount upon the wealth-centres of the world under pain of immediate destruction.'[39] The concept of private property was so deeply rooted in Griffith's world ethos that he could not even write a story in which his characters seriously renounce it; a situation later paralleled in H. G. Wells's *A Modern Utopia*, which allows for bankruptcies and the need for private weapons to safeguard such personal possessions as jewels, etc. Yet neither author is writing ironically: in their attempt to imagine a world functioning on a wholly different economic basis they just could not get away from their own backgrounds.

Another problem for Griffith was internationalism. In theory he accepts it, but in practice he is very strongly pro-British. A thanksgiving service is held in St Paul's near the end of the story: '. . . a brief and simple service of thanksgiving for the victory which had wiped the stain of foreign invasion from the soil of Britain in the blood of the invader, and given the control of the destinies of the Western world finally into the hands of the dominant race on earth.'[40] Why this very mixed group of international terrorists, led by a Hungarian Jew, should have worked towards this end Griffith does not explain. He simply does not seem to see any inconsistency. Yet the book is well written and far from careless. It would rather seem that he shared with his readers a number of basic assumptions regarding the role of women, the rights of private property, the dominant position of Britain and the inalienable nature of monarchy. Nothing had been said in the book about kings and queens and then suddenly in the epilogue there they are, constitutional monarchs ratifying the decisions of Parliament: 'In all countries the Civil and Criminal Codes of Law were to be amalgamated and simplified by a committee of judges appointed directly by the Parliament with the assent of the Sovereign . . .'[41]

Griffith, whose plot purports to turn the world upside down, leaves a great many things in what he considered, after all, to be their right places. The Czar ends down the silver mines, but less tyrannical monarchs sit safe and sound on their thrones, while the superiority of Britain is affirmed.

E. Douglas Fawcett's *Hartmann the Anarchist*, written in the same year as *The Angel of the Revolution* (1893) looks forward well into the twentieth century. The main events take place in 1920, although the story opens in 1918 and reference is made to an outrage in which Hartmann took part in 1910. The narrator is described as a moderate socialist who gets mixed up with Hartmann and his group in their plan to destroy society by organising simultaneous risings in all the capitals of Europe. The narrator's function is that of observer, never of participant. The author (well aware that the majority of readers make no distinction between narrator-characters and effective authors) in this way dissociates himself from the dynamiters and their ideas. The narrator is at pains to explain, right at the beginning of the novel:

> I myself, though a socialist, was averse to barricades. 'Not revolution, but evolution' was the watchword of my section . . . What was socialism? The nationalization of land and capital, of the means of production and distribution, in the interests of a vast industrial army. And how were the details of this vast change to be grappled with amid the throes of revolution?[42]

He turns out to be a very milk-and-water socialist indeed; in the last chapter of the novel when the revolution was over and interest turned to 'the great problems of labour', the narrator drops the whole social question, significantly and unfairly attributing part of the responsibility for this change of heart to his marriage: 'My own connection with these latter [the great problems of labour] was not destined to endure. After my marriage with Lena, my interests took a different turn. Travel and literary studies left no room for the surlier duties of the demagogue.'[43] With his author's full approval he settles down to cultivate his garden.

These two passages sufficiently exonerate the author from any personal involvement in the theories put forward, so that he feels free to expound, or to allow his narrator to expound, the doctrine of destruction and regeneration held by the anarchists. The plot deals with the total warfare waged by the anarchists upon civilisation: they plan, under Hartmann, to destroy society by simultaneous risings in every capital in Europe. They have a flying machine or aëronef which by means of machine-gun fire, dynamite bombs and burning petrol (the idea launched in *Daedalus*) is to give the lead for the destruction of London, while gangs of anarchist incendiaries are at work on the ground. Unlike many of his predecessors, Fawcett clearly distinguishes his anarchists from socialists, and significantly the first aerial bombardment is an attack on a mass demonstration of socialists taking place below. Much of the story is concerned with the science fiction aspect of the invention and functioning of the aëronef, but a great deal of attention is also paid to the views held by the anarchists. Women are kept on the borders of the story, they take no part in the revolution, although Mrs Hartmann *mère* describes how her son came to adopt his peculiar political views, and it is her death in the bombardment, from which she has refused to flee, which drives Hartmann, after the failure of the revolution, to blow up the airship and its crew together in a final triumph of dynamite. The narrator's girl friend, Lena, who is held partly responsible for his renunciation of political militancy at the end of the story, is simply the sympathetic listener so dear to the nineteenth-century male novelist:

> I was very fond of Lena, who was not only a charmingly pretty girl, but, thank goodness! sympathized most cordially with the bulk of my political opinions. She never of course mixed with the peculiar circles I frequented, but dearly loved to follow my reports of the movements which they represented.[44]

The anarchists, in Fawcett's novel, are of two distinct kinds, and their minds are reflected in their bodies as faithfully as in Conrad's *Secret Agent*. There are the idealists, Hartmann himself, and Burnett, the journalist and agitator: neither of these men is described as physically repulsive. The author gives a sense of verisimilitude to the story by showing us, literally, the portrait of the anarchist as a young man:

> . . . a loose photograph marked on the back, 'R. Hartmann, taken when twenty-three years of age', just about the time of the celebrated bridge incident.
> It was the face of a young man evidently of high capacity and unflinching resolution. A slight moustache brushed the upper lip, and set off a clearcut but somewhat cruel mouth. A more completely independent expression I never saw. The lineaments obscured by time defied accurate survey, but the general effect produced was that they indicated an arbitrary and domineering soul, utterly impatient of control and loftily contemptuous of its kind.[45]

And then he compares this with the adult Hartmann, Commander of the *Attila*:

> Seated before a writing-desk, studded with knobs of electric bells and heaped with maps and instruments, sat a bushy-bearded man with straight piercing glance and a forehead physiognomists would have envied. There was the same independent look, the same cruel hardness that had stamped the mien of the youth, but the old impetuous air had given way to a cold inflexible sedate-

ness, far more appropriate to the dread master of the Attila. As I advanced into the room, he rose, a grand specimen of manhood, standing full six feet three inches in his shoes.[46]

Not very different is the description of Burnett, again a fine figure of a man: 'a stalwart individual with a thick black beard and singularly resolute face'. Burnett too as a young man had been 'courteous and argumentative' but on board the *Attila* he reveals the other side of his character, which is 'dogmatic and brutal'. These, the thinkers, are allowed a certain degree of nobility, but the men they employ are desperadoes 'hated by and hating society', 'one and all devoured by lust of blood and revenge'. The third leader, Schwartz, belongs to the latter type, and shows Fawcett conforming to the already well-established pattern of the German dynamiter:

> . . . an elderly man apparently of the higher artisan class. His face was most unprepossessing. There was a bull-dog's obstinacy and attachment about it, but the eyes were unspeakably wicked and the mouth hard and cruel. I diagnosed it at once as that of a man whose past was best unread, whose hand had in dark by-ways been persistently raised against his fellow-men.[47]

The crew of the *Attila* are an unattractive bunch, 'all proscribed men, loathing not only the landlord and capitalist but the workers, who would most of them have rejoiced over their capture', and it is curious to note how completely the Irish have disappeared from the scene. Of twenty-five crew members eight are Germans, six Englishmen, four French, two Russians, one an Italian and the others Swiss, and at the rendezvous in Switzerland they expect to be joined by many Russians, Poles, Austrians, and Italians besides unspecified 'delegates of other nationalities'. There is no trace of the Irish or Irish-Americans.

The aim of these men was to attack not only the abuses and defects but the very foundations of society: 'Their long-cherished thought had been to shatter the trophies of centuries.' Hartmann himself describes his crew as 'fiends of destruction', and has no illusions as to the means he is employing, but attributes the moral responsibility to industrial exploitation which has turned men into maggots:

> 'They are like the creatures generated in decaying bodies. They are the maggots of civilisation, the harvest of the dragons' teeth

sown in past centuries, the Frankenstein's monsters of civilization which are born to hate their father. You have read Milton, of course. Do you recall the passage about Sin and the birth of Death who gnaws his wretched parent's vitals? It is the Sin of this industrial age which has bred the crew of this death-dealing *Attila*.[48]

The Miltonic reference is introduced very deliberately since the author intends to show Hartmann as an 'ethical madman', a term coined later by Jack London in his *Assassination Bureau*.

If this was the crew, the mob who took part in the attack on the ground were an even more repulsive lot, and the author thoroughly approves of the violent handling they receive from their captors, the soldiers, who are to re-establish law and order after one-fifth of London has been destroyed:

> Just then a squad of soldiers passed by escorting some incendiaries, whose faces filthy with grime and brutal to a degree filled us with loathing and anger . . . What kicks their captors were giving them! The faces seemed unfamiliar to me, all alike of a low grade of ruffianism such as every great city breeds, but which never declares its strength till the day of weakness arrives.[49]

It was Schwartz who led astray the youthful Hartmann, converting his healthy optimism and desire for reform into the negative desire for destruction. The philosophical Nietzschean element of late nineteenth-century anarchy is suggested in an account of his education under Schwartz's tuition:

> 'Hartmann, you know, was educated for the profession of an engineer, and was always looked on as a prodigy of intellectual vigour . . . when twenty-three years of age he made the acquaintance of a German exile, one Schwartz, a miscreant of notorious opinions and character. This man gradually inspired him with a hatred of the whole fabric of society, and the end of it was that he became an anarchist. That Hartmann was deeply in earnest seems perfectly clear. He sacrificed to his aim, position, comfort, reputation, his studies — in short, everything. He regarded civilization as rotten from top to foundation, and the present human race as "only fit for fuel". Schwartz was a pessimist, and his pupil became one of an even deeper dye.'[50]

The responsibility for this state of things is traced back by the narrator, who is agitating for moderate reform through traditional parliamentary channels, to

> the extremists — on the one hand the Conservatives, who, to my thinking, were perpetuating the conditions whence anarchy drew its breath, namely, a wretched proletariat exploited by capital; on the other by the extreme socialists, who despaired of effective advance by way of ordinary parliamentary reforms.[51]

The situation, when Hartmann's conspiracy gets under way, is shown as being very much the situation in London in the 1880s and early 1890s. A long list of dynamite attempts, including one at the house of the Home Secretary and another at Mansion House, are described, thereby filling the contemporary reader with a sense of the topicality of the book and making the incursion of the *Attila* seem to be actually at hand.

In a conversation held between the narrator and Hartmann, before the revolution begins, Hartmann affirms that it is indeed his object to wreck civilisation. The narrator very naturally asks what he intends to put in its place: 'But how is the new order to take shape? How educe system from chaos?' and Hartmann states: '"We want no more 'systems' or 'constitutions' — we shall have anarchy. Man will effect all by voluntary association, and abjure the foulness of the modern wage-slavery and city-mechanisms."'[52] To this the narrator raises substantially the same objection that Shaw had put forward in his pamphlet: '"But can you expect the more brutal classes to thrive under this system? Will they not rather degenerate into savagery?"'[53] A timorous reader would hardly feel reassured by Hartmann's answer that 'some supervision must necessarily be exercised, but, as a rule, it will never be more than nominal'.

The book is stronger when it comes to action than when dealing with theory. The opening of the attack is planned to take place inevitably, above the Houses of Parliament, where a blank discharge of cannon from the aëronef will warn all, 'after which my flag will be run out'. One puzzle remains for a logically minded reader who is expecting to see the black flag of anarchy in conformity with all Hartmann's theories and instead, for those looking up at the airship from the London streets 'a blood-red flag was to be seen fluttering at the stern'. There are no socialists on board: they are below among the objectives of the raiders; it would seem that the confusion engendered by the newspapers between the symbols of such conflicting dissident movements as socialists and anarchists had still to be dissipated. If their symbol is a little uncertain, the theme song of the anarchists is the song of a true dynamitard:

> The dynamite falls on castle walls
> And splendid buildings old in story.
> The column shakes, the tyrant quakes,
> And the wild wreckage leaps in glory.
> Throw, comrade, throw: set the wild echoes flying;
> Throw, comrade; answer, wretches, dying, dying, dying.[54]

Notes

1. John E. Barlas, 'A Vision of Vengeance' in *Phantasmagoria* (Chelmsford, 1887).

2. W. T. Stead, 'The Maiden Tribute of Modern Babylon', a series of articles on child prostitution in London published in the *Pall Mall Gazette* on 6, 7, 8, 10 July 1885. These articles caused such an uproar and the paper was so much in request that newsvendors attacked the offices for copies, blocking the street and breaking the windows. The police were called in and suggested admission by one door and exit from another, so order was restored.

3. Barlas, 'A Vision of Vengeance'.

4. The purification theme had been introduced by Zola in *Germinal* two years earlier. The anarchist Souvarine declares (p. 159): 'Oui: l'anarchie, plus rien, la terre lavée par le sang, purifiée par l'incendie! . . . On verra ensuite.' And again (p. 247) 'Oh! du sang, murmura-t-il, qu'est-ce que ça fait? la terre en a besoin.' But while Zola, like Conrad, presents his anarchist as a madman, Barlas seems to be quite serious in his support of this view.

5. John E. Barlas, 'Sonnet 43' in *Holy of Holies. Confession of an Anarchist* (Chelmsford, 1887).

6. George Bernard Shaw, *The Impossibilities of Anarchism* (London, 1893), p. 4.

7. Ibid., p. 14.

8. Ibid., p. 15.

9. Ibid., p. 26.

10. Robert Buchanan, *The Coming Terror: A Dialogue between Alienatus, a Provincial and Urbanus, a Cockney* (London, 1891), p. 8.

11. Ibid., p. 37.

12. *PMG*, 14 Sept. 1901. 'Anarchism. Its Cause and Cure.' Report of an Address made on 13 Sept. 1901 by the Archdeacon of Westminster.

13. Anon. (By an ex-M.P.), *A Radical Nightmare, or, England Forty Years Hence* (London, 1885), pp. 15-16.

14. Ibid., p. 29.

15. Ibid., p. 32.

16. Ibid., p. 39.

17. Thomas Lee, *Falsivir's Travels* (London, 1886), pp. 72-3.

18. Edward Bellamy, *Looking Backward — if Socialism Comes. 2000-1887* (Boston, 1888). Quotation from 1967 edition, Cambridge, Mass., p. 127.

19. George Griffith, *The Angel of the Revolution: A Tale of the Coming Terror* (London, 1893), pp. 18-19.

20. Ibid., p. 26.
21. Ibid., p. 36.
22. Ibid., p. 143.
23. Ibid., p. 32.
24. Ibid., pp. 30-1.
25. Ibid., p. 31.
26. Ibid., p. 14.
27. Ibid., p. 385.
28. Ibid., p. 361.
29. Ibid., p. 278.
30. Ibid., p. 25.
31. Ibid., p. 224.
32. Ibid., pp. 141-2.
33. Ibid., pp. 150-1.
34. Ibid., p. 113.
35. Ibid., p. 384.
36. Ibid., p. 382.
37. Ibid., p. 154.
38. Ibid., p. 199.
39. Ibid.
40. Ibid., p. 362.
41. Ibid., p. 387.

42. E. Douglas Fawcett, *Hartmann the Anarchist; or, the Doom of the Great City* (London, 1893), p. 25.

43. Ibid., p. 213.
44. Ibid., p. 24.
45. Ibid., p. 39.
46. Ibid., p. 79
47. Ibid., p. 29.
48. Ibid., p. 82.
49. Ibid., p. 194.
50. Ibid., pp. 26-7.
51. Ibid.
52. Ibid., p. 84.
53. Ibid.

54. Ibid., p. 63, parodying Tennyson's *The Princess*: 'The splendour falls on castle walls . . ./ Blow, bugle, blow, set the wild echoes flying,/ Blow, bugle; answer, echoes, dying, dying, dying.'

6 THE PILLAR AT TOBOLSK

'To strangle whatever nature is in me; neither to love nor to be loved; neither to pity nor to be pitied; neither to marry nor to be given in marriage, till the end is come.'

These are the terms of the oath sworn by Vera Sabouroff in the prologue to Oscar Wilde's *Vera; or, the Nihilists* (1882) which is thought to have been written in 1876 and which refers to the historical period of 1800.[1] The author was only 22 years old when he wrote this romantic play, which looks back to a period long before the time in which we are interested. Its relevance lies in the extreme simplicity with which all the stock elements exploited in the romantic English Nihilist novels at the end of the century are here set out as the background to a Romeo and Juliet love story between Vera and the Czarevitch. The scene for Act I sets the tone:

Scene. -99 *Rue Tchernavaya, Moscow. A large garret lit by oil lamps hung from ceiling. Some masked men standing silent and apart from one another. A man in a scarlet mask is writing at a table. Door at back. Man in yellow with drawn sword at it. Knocks heard. Figures in cloaks and masks enter.*

While the prologue had related the story of Vera, how she joined the Nihilist movement to revenge her brother Dmitri condemned to the Siberian mines for life, the play proper begins with a conspirators' meeting, with mutual suspicion in the air: 'Can Michael suspect me? There is something strange in his manner to-night.' The infiltration has in fact been more serious than usual, for Alexis turns out to be the adventure-loving Czarevitch who slips out from his palace at night to join the Nihilists, where he falls in love with Vera.

While the romantic scenes are pure melodrama, there are touches of the future brilliance of Wilde in the court scenes, especially in the figure of a decidedly jumpy Czar, afraid to open his own letters, and the caustic Prince Paul, master of paradox.

Marquis de Poivrard. Sire, I have the honour to present to you a

loyal address from your subjects in the Province of Archangel, expressing their horror at the last attempt on your Majesty's life.
Prince Paul. The last attempt but two, you ought to have said, Marquis. Don't you see it is dated three weeks back.[2]

The neurasthenic Czar is shot by the Nihilists, and his son, succeeding to the throne, decides to convert Russia into a democracy. He banishes Prince Paul who at once joins the Nihilists. They determine to assassinate the new Czar, and in the drawing of lots the task falls to Vera. The sign that the assassination is accomplished is to be a bloody dagger thrown from the window of the Czar's apartments to the conspirators below. Vera, instead of stabbing the Czar, stabs herself. The play ends:

> *(Vera snatches dagger and flings it out of window)*
> *Conspirators. (below)* Long live the people!
> *Czar.* What have you done?
> *Vera.* I have saved Russia *(Dies.)*[3]

That the young Oscar should have chosen for this early experiment in drama the Nihilists' fight for freedom is hardly surprising in view of the analogy with his Irish background and the fact that Lady Wilde, his mother, was an ardent defender of the cause of the Irish nationalists. When, in the prologue, Vera asks her brother 'What did you want to do?' he answers 'To give liberty to thirty millions of people enslaved to one man', while Vera's final sacrifice is made not only to save the life of the man she loves, but to give Russia a democratic ruler.

The play presents the regime of the Czar and his ministers as utterly corrupt, 'What is the use of the people except to get money out of?' — a regime of repression and martial law upheld by political exile and banishment to the Siberian mines for any offender. When Vera, who has just been told that it is the duty of the peasants to 'Till your fields, store your harvests, pay your taxes, and obey your masters', asks the colonel 'Who are our masters?' she is told: 'Young woman, these men are going to the mines for life for asking the same foolish question.' Wilde's play is indicative of the mood of general sympathy with the Nihilists in their fight against Romanoff repression in Russia; this sympathy was very widely felt in England in the 1880s, though it was never extended to condone acts of terrorism. In this way it contrasted sharply with the reaction in

Britain to the Fenian movement in the same period, particularly in its disponibility to look behind the terrorist acts for the causes at the root of the distress.

The romantic aspect of Nihilism was exploited in two novels, both by women, published in 1884, *Princess Napraxine* by Ouida (Marie Louise de la Ramée) and *Miss Brown* by Vernon Lee (Violet Paget).

Princess Nadège (Nadine) Napraxine is an aristocratic heroine who suffers from boredom (very like the Christina Light of Henry James's *Roderick Hudson* and *The Princess Casamassima*, whom she somewhat resembles) and who refuses to accept the role of wife and mother moving in the very best society into which fate has cast her. Nor is platonic adultery sufficient to alleviate her ennui — she must dabble in the most exciting movement of the times — Nihilism.

The novel is totally non-political, and indeed her first connection with the Nihilists is merely, in a bored sort of way, to remove a dynamite bomb which she thought had been placed too close to where her children were playing:

> 'Did Nadine ever tell you what she did last year?' said Prince Napraxine. 'She saw by chance a queer-looking can which had been placed by some of those miscreants in a niche of the garden wall of our house in Petersburg; the thing looked suspicious to her, and it had a coil of tubing attached to it. She took the whole affair up and dropped it into the fountain. She forgot to mention it till the next morning. Then when we fished it out, and the chemists reported on it, it appeared that the can was really full of nitro-glycerine as she had fancied. I think that was quite as courageous as going to the guillotine.'
>
> 'Oh, no, my dear Platon!' said his wife, with some annoyance. 'Nothing you have no time to think about is really courageous. The can was suspicious and the children were playing near it, so I thought the fountain was the safest place; it *might* have been only milk, you know.'
>
> . . . [Geraldine] 'Who put the can there?'
>
> [Prince] 'Oh, how should I know. The police never traced it. I do not suppose it was any special design against us as individuals; only as items of a detested whole. And two of the Grand Dukes were coming to breakfast with us that day.'[4]

This passage is followed by a discussion about dynamiters, in the tone typical of Ouida's fashionable novels, in which a group of

aristocrats are very witty at the expense of the Nihilists; a passage
close in tone to Robert Louis Stevenson's account of Zero's exploits:

'What a fuss about an ugly little tin can!' said his wife. 'The really
courageous person must have been the person who brought it
there; misguided, perhaps, but certainly courageous. To drive
through a city in a droschky embracing certain annihilation, in the
form of a little tin pot held on your knee, is a combination of
absolute awfulness and grotesque bathos, which must try all one's
nerves without any compensating sense of grandeur in it. A jolt of
the wheel over a stone and away you fly into the air, a blurred
nothing in a stream of blood and dust! No; I respect the Nihilists
when I think of all they risk for a purely abstract idea without any
sort of personal hope or triumph.'
   . . . [Lady Brancepeth] 'You underrate, too, the immense
fascination of the power to destroy; *on se grise* with that sense of
holding the annihilation of a whole community in their hands.
What made the Roman Emperors mad, — the unlimited power of
destruction, — now intoxicates the mechanic or the clerk who has
the task of planting a can of nitro-glycerine. When statesmen, and
even philosophers, theorize about human nature and all its disor-
ders, they never give weight enough to the tremendous attraction
which pure destruction alone exercises over so many minds.'
   'But they have love, too; love of the poor and of a lofty ideal,'
said the Princess. 'Myself, I forgive their little tin cans, though
they are extremely unpleasant, when I think of their impersonal
devotion. All I wish is, that their warfare was not conducted by tin
cans; the thing has a ludicrous, comical, vulgar side; death
dropped in a little box labelled "glass, with care"! There is no
dignity in it, no grace. Pallida Mors should not crouch under a
cab-cushion!'
   'How can you make a jest —' began Prince Napraxine. She
interrupted him:
   'I am not in the least jesting, I am entirely in earnest. I do not
like being made war on by chemists; I do not like annihilation left
in a paper parcel, it makes one feel absurd, fate seems trifling with
one. A Jacquerie hewing at one with their scythes one would
know what to do with, but who can extract any Sophoclean
tragedy from a Thanatus [*sic*] that looks exactly like a box of
sardines or a pot of *foie gras*? It is not the war that I object to, it is
the form it takes; and our great, grim, ghostly Russia should

evolve out of her soul of ice something much more in consonance with her. Beside the burning of Moscow, the little tin cans and the burrowing like moles underground are commonplace and a little vulgar. Russia is so awful in herself. One thinks of the frozen world of the Inferno, and Dante and Virgil walking in the spectral silence; and then, after all, in hard fact there is nothing but the police, and the drunken moujik, and the man who carries his nitro-glycerine as a baker's boy carries his rolls of bread! It is bathos!'

'One never knows what you mean, Nadine,' murmured her husband. 'If you talk so at Petersburg they will think you are a Nihilist at heart.'

'I imagine half the *noblesse* are,' said the Princess.[5]

This novel is good of its kind: anti-feminist, a study of a *femme fatale*; totally non-realistic, yet very readable. Henry James was to write about the same international European society in a novel like *The Golden Bowl*, and to appreciate James to the full we have to compare his Charlotte Stant with Nadège Napraxine of whom Ouida wrote:

> She had no more rigidity of principle than any other person who has been reared in the midst of a witty, elegant, and corrupt society; but her perfect taste supplied the place of moral convictions, the grossness of vice offended her like a bad odour, or a staring colour; and everything loose or coarse seemed to her an affront to intelligence and to refinement.[6]

Of course, James's Charlotte, like his Kate Croy, was a social climber, which adds a dimension of economic and psychological realism lacking in Ouida's Princess. The interest lies in comparing the very different use by two authors of what were substantially the same materials, to produce novels for substantially the same reading public.

Another contemporary theme that is touched upon more than once by Ouida is that of vivisection. There was an outcry in the press in the 1880s against this practice, a movement centred in Oxford, an outcry that was to lead later to H. G. Wells's very successful early novel *The Island of Dr Moreau* (1896). Two different characters in *Princess Napraxine* liken her cold-blooded treatment of the men who are in love with her to the experiments of the vivisector (and the parallel vivisector-dynamitard is not far to seek, the villain of *Who Was then the Gentleman* (1885) combining both professions). Lady Brancepeth, Nadine's friend, says to her: "'. . . but your kind of coquetry I cannot forgive. It is the exercise of a merciless power which is as chill as a vivisector's attitude before his victim.'"[7] while Melville, the priest, voices the same idea: "'I fear, Princess, that you are like Virschow or Paul Bert, who are so absorbed in cutting, burning, and electrifying the nerves of dogs that the dog, a sentient creature, a companion, and a friend, is wholly unknown to them. Humanity, poor Humanity, is your dog.'"[8]

Ouida gives this spoilt, wealthy and beautiful woman one highly dramatic adventure. When Boganof, a dissident writer, was condemned to political exile in Siberia (and this was the fate of many nineteenth-century Russian writers, including Chernychevski and Mikhailoff), she altruistically pleads his case with the Czar at considerable personal risk because she has to defend the right of freedom of expression (about which Ouida as a writer feels strongly). Obtaining his pardon more by personal charm than by the force of argument, the Princess travels in haste across Russia by sledge in the depth of winter before it is too late to save him. Melville the priest praises her for having done 'a very noble thing':

Nadine Napraxine shrugged her shoulders slightly, with a gesture of indifference.

'It amused me. I had a fancy to see Siberia in winter. The pity was that Fedor Alexowitch Boganof was an ugly and uninteresting fellow — with plenty of brains, indeed, which brought his ruin, but quite ugly, rather misshapen, and blessed with five children. If the hero of my journey had only been a fine officer of cuirassiers, or a romantic-looking revolutionist, the story would have been delightful, but poor Boganof no one could turn into a *jeune premier*; not even the gossips of Petersburg. He was only a clever writer, with a mother and a wife who idolized him. The truth is, I had read his novel and liked it; that is why, when his people came to me, I did what I could. Anybody who knew the Tzar as well as I could have done as much. As for going to Siberia — well, I went myself because I have a profound distrust of Russian officials. Even an Imperial pardon has a knack of arriving too late when it is desirable that it should do so. It was certainly a disagreeable season of the year, but behind strong horses one does not mind that. Very soon Siberia will have lost its terrors and its romance; there will be a railway across the Urals, and all chance of the little excitements attendant on such a journey as mine will be over. When the Governor saw me actually in Tobolsk, he could not believe his eyes. If his beard had not been dyed, it would have turned white with the extremity of his amazement. I think he could have understood my taking the trouble if it had been for a Tchin; but for a mere scribbler of books, a mere teller of stories! I told him that Homer, and Ariosto, and Goethe, and ever so many others had been only tellers of stories too, but that produced no impression on him. He was compelled to let Boganof go, because the Tzar ordered him, but he could not see any valid reason why Boganof should not be left to rot away, brain downwards, under the ice . . . I urged on the Tzar the truth that, when the intellect of a nation is suppressed and persecuted, the nation 'dies from the top', like Swift. I think I convinced him for the moment, but then there were so many other people always at his ear to persuade him that universal convulsion was only to be avoided by corking all the inkbottles and putting all the writers and readers down the mines.'[9]

This romantic and improbable rescue is a popularisation of a story that was often told: the long sledge drive across Russia in the attempt to rescue, or at least to obtain an interview with, a political prisoner. It is a major episode in both Grant Allen's *For Maimie's Sake* and in Eden's *In the Bear's Grip*, while the two outstanding novels about Russia in this period, May's *Love, the Reward* and Hatton's *By Order of the Czar* both describe the long trek of the exiles northward through the snow, a journey on which many of those who set out were destined to fall by the way. Ouida, to show that her heroine can achieve a heroic dimension and is capable of altruism on a large, though never on a small, scale, finds this romantic ride a fitting and topical theme, sure that her readers will share her sympathy with the noble ambition of the Princess to free a writer who had spoken out against the Czar's government.

Vernon Lee in her *Miss Brown*, published in the same year as Ouida's *Princess Napraxine*, is an interesting contrast. It is enough to set the two titles side by side to realise that these two writers, both women, and both, incidentally, preferring to publish under pseudonyms, had very different aims. While Ouida's novel is highly romantic, and centres round a woman who manipulated men for her own amusement, Vernon Lee's is a feminist novel about a girl who was manipulated by Hamlin, an artist, a modern version of the Pygmalion story:

> . . . he had determined exactly where he would send Anne Brown to school, where he would go during her stay there, what settlements he would make to ensure her complete freedom of choice when she should choose him, in what part of London he would buy a house for her, which of his female relations should have charge of her, by whom she should be introduced into artistic society; — he began to imagine all the details of his long courtship.[10]

Everything starts off according to plan. Hamlin, we are told, 'was rather pleased that the creature whom he was going to teach how to think and feel did not manifest any particular mode of thinking and feeling of her own'. However Miss Brown makes a bid for liberty and begins to toy with the idea of Girton or Newnham while going in for political economy, history and the moral sciences. She does consent to marry Hamlin in the end, chiefly in order to rescue him from the clutches of Sacha, his Russian cousin and a Nihilist, but the last sentence of the book is a clear indication of the extent of the sacrifice she is making: 'Miss Brown suddenly shivered, as he put his arm round her shoulder. The flash of a street lamp as they passed quickly, had shown her Hamlin's face close to her own, and radiant with the triumph of satisfied vanity.'[11]

Vernon Lee, who was very young when she wrote this long and deeply committed novel, set out to make Sacha (Madame Elaguine), the seductress who admires the music of Wagner's *Tristram* 'with its strange, insidious faintings and sobbings, its hot, enervating gusts of passion', a thoroughly evil woman, someone from whom Hamlin must be rescued at any price, even the price of her heroine's much-prized celibacy. Vernon Lee therefore, labels this female villain a Nihilist, and Sacha herself gives the following ludicrous account of her involvement with the movement:

> I longed to be of some use, and able to sacrifice myself for something. And a man was sent across my path, twice as old as myself, whom I looked upon as a father, and who treated me as a child; and this man used to talk to me, when my husband left me all alone to run after low women, and tell me all about the

miserable condition of Russia, and how all the good was being
stamped out, and only selfishness, and injustice, and corruption
triumphed. He was a Nihilist himself, and one of their chief men
— a wonderful man, who seemed so cold, and just, and honest.
So, little by little, he converted me to his ideas, and I got to know
other Nihilists, men and women, and heard a great deal about all
sorts of terrible doings. I felt so happy and heroic — I was a fool,
you see. Then I suddenly discovered that my hero was quite
different from what I thought — that he had gained all this power
over me only in hopes of making shameful use of it, and had
compromised me with his party merely to make me his mistress.
When I understood it, I drove him away, and threatened to tell all
to my husband; and then he swore to get the better of me, and to
use all the power of his society to bring me, as he called it, to
reason. For two years, while my husband was alive, I struggled
with him, and he kept on threatening and hoping to frighten me.
But when my husband died, I sold all the Russian property, and
was preparing to leave the country, and then that man who hated
me, just because in his way he had loved me, denounced me to his
society as a traitor to the Nihilist cause, and as a person to be
hunted down. And so, ever since, I have been persecuted with all
the might of the Nihilists wielded by this man; and although I have
been hundreds of times on the point of denouncing him and his
associates to the Government, I have never done so, because I am
still a Nihilist at heart, and hate the Russian Government as much
as I hate him . . .[12]

The idea that an international organisation would waste its time and
energies on such petty persecution could only have entered the head
of such an intellectual and right-minded young lady as Vernon Lee.
At this stage she was sadly lacking in any sense of proportion, as was
shown by her dedication of this novel which satirised many of his
artist friends, to Henry James, without first asking his permission,
leaving that fastidious gentleman considerably embarrassed and
upset. Set beside Vernon Lee's *Sacha* even Oscar Wilde's *Vera*
seems almost credible as a Nihilist. Both these writers were very
young, they were making superficial use of such superficial interpretations of Nihilism as were in the air at the time.

Only one year after *Miss Brown* Philip May published, in 1885,
Love, the Reward, the most sympathetic treatment of Nihilism in the

history of the English novel. While Vernon Lee's Sacha speaks of 'all sorts of terrible doings', May attempts to explain who the Nihilists really were, and their struggle to spread their ideas in a climate where education was restricted by law to certain classes.

This is a most unusual novel, with a structure very different from that of English novels of the period, so that the transitions seem to us inconsequential: it is structurally more like a film by Godard, with a theme overriding the plot, and with many interpolations. In May's case these interpolations include whole passages from other novels, particularly Chernychevski's feminist novel *What Is to Be Done* and Gorki's story 'The Revisor'. As an experimental novel it deserves much more attention than it has received: the central theme, which is an unashamed apology of Nihilism, has perhaps not encouraged its dissemination, for it shows better than any of May's contemporaries the extent of the repression to which the people of Russia were subjected under the Romanoffs, and devotes many pages to descriptions of government corruption at all levels. The whole action of the plot is dominated by the constant intervention of the secret police, and by the threat of the silver mines in Siberia to which characters are constantly disappearing to be heard of no more. Justice is shown to be a mockery and lengthy imprisonment without trial the order of the day.

Other novels of the period were telling the same story of police and military brutality but, contrasted with their highly coloured romanticism, the quiet greys of May's account give an impression of absolute realism and fidelity. Nothing is overstated — it is rather the constant understatement which wears down the reader's preconstituted conceptions.

I have been unable to learn anything about Philip May himself. This is his only recorded novel, and was started in collaboration with T. Aubrey Bryne of Boston, who however dropped out after the first volume, with no noticeable effect on the style or content of the rest, but who kept the copyright in the United States by way of compensation. May's own preface declares that this is a committed novel: 'I have a tale to tell which I beg the critics and the public to allow me to place before them', and states 'The best apology I can offer for the appearance of this novel is that I can promise the reader a vivid description of the Russians and of Russia.' How he came to be so familiar with the country he does not tell us, but reading the novel one is filled with a strong impression that he knew his material at first hand. His familiarity with Russian literature is beyond question, and there are passages in his writing which suggest that he is actually thinking in Russian, as in the following simile: 'In some minds, sorrows melt as does the ice in the spring; but there are other natures which cause sorrow, like the late-autumn snow, to harden, after it falls.'[13]

The climate he has in mind here is the climate of Russia, not England, but how many British writers could make such a thought-transition? The preface tells us nothing about how he came by his Russian experience, mentioning only his indebtedness to many Russian works, to *The Times* newspaper and to many books descriptive of Russia and the Russians written in English, French and German. I have even toyed with the idea that this novel is the work of a Russian exile, a number of whom had settled in London. This hypothetical exile, seeing what avid novel readers the British were, and how much space newspapers and magazines gave to novel reviews, decided that the most useful political work he could pursue in exile was to inform as wide a public as possible of the true state of affairs in his country. This would explain why he started out with a collaborator who was a native speaker and, from his name, an Irish-American, one who might be expected to sympathise with May's aims. There is some internal evidence which tips the scales slightly against this theory. Ivan, with whom the author often identifies, we are told:

> . . . was not a true Nihilist; he had not put away art and senti-ment, as a man may divorce an unfaithful wife; and he was even writing a romance. Of this, certainly, a Nihilist was the hero; but this amongst the Nihilists was no sufficient excuse for one who would waste his time in such an occupation.[14]

And a few pages later Maxim, Ivan's friend, interrupts him with economic theories at a time when the writer's only wish is to get on with his story:

> 'What we require, you know', he [Maxim] would say, 'is a new order of things, and a government which will provide every citizen with bread, work, and instruction, for the development of his being . . .' 'Yes, yes,' Alexandroff [Ivan] would answer, scarcely raising his pen from the paper upon which he was describing a love-scene between his hero and heroine.
> Then Maxim Tsiepherkin would add, 'Remember what

Tchernychevski says in his translation of John Stuart Mill: "Land is the gift of nature to the whole human race; it is necessary for life; it is limited in quantity!"[15]

Would not the thoughts of an English author fly straight to John Stuart Mill, without passing through the medium of Chernychevski's translation? Or is this exceptionally good groundwork by an English author who wishes to make his Russian characters credible, and who wants to point out the European contribution to Russian revolutionary thought? And further questions present themselves: Did May find that his love story between Vera, the daughter of a high official and Ivan, the Nihilist student, was running away with him and feel guilty that he was betraying his main purpose in writing this book? Or was he simply defending the right of the artist to get on with his work in peace?

However we answer these questions this Philip May, unlike the Philip May who edited and wrote in the *Ludgate Monthly* in 1891,[16] did succeed in creating convincing characters, particularly women. The relationship between Vera and her maid Hessy, when Vera becomes converted to the Nihilist cause, encouraged by Hessy's doctrines but also by the fact that she has fallen in love with Ivan, is sketched delightfully:

> There was her father, a most stubborn adversary for a daughter to subdue; and Hessy, the maid, who had ideas upon the subject of social and political equality, and who was bent upon a redistribution of all the good things of this world, wished to be the equal of all men, and above all, of all women. Vera was to be the only exception to this rule; for the mistress was to become a convert to the cause of humanity, and be an humble follower of Hessy, the maid.[17]

Hessy, a real hard-liner, is shown as being much more useful to the Nihilists than Vera Michailovna who: '. . . would be more useful to their lodge as a goose laying golden eggs, than as a propagandist who would wish to preach the doctrines of social equality in a silk dress.'[18] They therefore encourage Vera, an aristocrat by birth, to marry the old roué, Prince Potemkin, in compliance with her father's wishes, so that she can provide the movement with funds. This sacrifice Vera is very loath to make. She has read Chernychevski's *What Is to Be Done?*[19] and has learnt the lesson that for a woman independence must be, first and foremost, economic independence: 'She wished to learn some trade; to be independent of father, lover, and husband in the future.' Her thoughts turn to the stage, and she considers the possibility of making her living as an actress, but Hessy, on sound principles, discourages her: '"The stage . . . can do no good, unless it be used to convey a moral or a social lesson; and as the actress is neither free to choose the play, nor the lesson which she would teach the audience, in the present state of society, she is likely to do harm."'[20] Vera is not attracted by another enterprise for women that is described in some detail in May's book: dressmaking and tailoring workshops run on co-operative principles, educational in so far as the work is accompanied by reading aloud. The idea came in the first place from *What Is to Be Done?* where the heroine establishes not only her own independence but that of many other women by founding a similar enterprise. The heroine of Walter Besant's *All Sorts and Conditions of Men* (1882) sets up an educational workshop along the same lines.

All three writers, Chernychevski, Besant and May, have the same thing in mind: women, to achieve independence, must work on co-operative lines, breaking away from male schemes of commercial exploitation, and their work should be coupled with educational, recreational and cultural activities.

It is interesting to find, in May's Nihilist novel, this linking of feminism to a social and cultural revolution. Historically in Russia a number of educated girls joined the Nihilist movement, the daughters of the aristocracy or, like Vera, of senior officials in the bureaucracy. Women of the middle and upper classes in the late nineteenth century were much less satisfied with their lot than were the men of the same classes. While the latter were anxious to defend a system which established and protected their privileges, thinking women were looking for a different system and some were ready to join hands with other revolutionaries, even with those who, like the Nihilists, challenged the entire social and economic basis of society.

It is refreshing in May's book, after the stereotyped revolutionaries of most romances with Russian settings, to meet real people struggling with real ideas, sure of some things, uncertain about others. May draws attention to the strong Anglophile and Francophile trend of the intelligentsia and the tentative approach of the more liberal among these to the views the Nihilists were so enthusiastically preaching. A conversation between Ivan, the Nihilist hero, and General Lertoffski whom he knew socially, is a

good sketch of the cautious civil servant's reaction to Nihilist
doctrines: not total refusal, but the admission that, some time in the
future, a very long way off and after the population has been
educated, they might make sense. At the same time official
measures were being taken, as May tells us, to ensure that education
should not spread. At the University of St Petersburg there were less
than 300 students and the total number of students in Russia was
restricted to about 1,700.

> 'From education,' Ivan said, taking advantage of the gallant
> general's confusion, 'from education of the masses, I expect
> everything.'
> . . . 'Well, well, Ivan Ivanovitch,' answered Lertoffski, his
> Liberal platitudes returning to his mind; 'it will be a happy day for
> Russia, Emperor and People, when the latter have prepared
> themselves for the enjoyment of a temperate and legitimate
> freedom.'
> He spoke so slowly that he seemed to be studying each word as
> he uttered it. He finally allowed the word 'freedom' to come out
> of his mouth; it was very bad to admit freedom into his library, but
> it was worse still to have it sticking in his throat.[21]

The main stress throughout the book is on education rather than
revolution, and dynamite and assassination are shown as playing
only a marginal role in the political change for which the Nihilists are
working. After the death of Czar Nicholas, at the end of the Crimean
War, we are told:

> Into the hands of youth longing with an ardent desire for change,
> were placed the text-books of Socialism which were to
> revolutionise the world. Amongst their instructors were three
> able men, Herzen, Bakunin, and Tchernychevski, who have been
> aptly termed the *fathers* of the political economy designed for the
> people, so inaptly termed *Nihilism*.[22]

There is a great deal of violence in the novel, but it is violence
against the Nihilists, the violence of repression, that is narrated. Yet
the book shows the members of this movement, however serious
their involvement, as being by no means devoid of humour, as on the
occasion of a police raid on the Nihilists' rooms:

The Nihilists at once began to sing *Bozhe Zaria Khrani* [the National anthem]; the privy councillor was forced to take off his hat out of loyalty, and the police did the same. They all stood still and sang, for the police were glad of an opportunity to show a privy councillor how truly loyal they were.

The national anthem was repeated, once, twice, thrice; then, Lertoffski's suspicions were aroused by such an excess of loyalty on the part of the Nihilists . . . They searched for Hessy everywhere, and though they failed to discover her whereabouts, they found, in a grate, the charred remains of a number of papers which had evidently been burned whilst they had been raising their voices in more or less tuneful song . . .

Alexandroff's companions were all resigned; and some were even prepared for the worst. They talked of statistics with reference to suicides in prison; they discussed the best ways of ending life that were open to a prisoner; and wondered how many days, months, or years it would be before they should be tried.[23]

What the Czar and his government are shown as being most afraid of is not, as most English novels dealing with the subject suggest, assassination or dynamite attacks, but rather the work of education and the instilling of new ideas among the peasants in which the Nihilists were engaged, and to which most of the members of the movement were dedicated with total abnegation and at great personal risk:

The leaders of the Nihilists knew that the ignorant peasant could not at once be made to understand the works of Bakunin, Herzen, and Tchernychevski. They contented themselves with teaching the people little fables, something like their own folk-tales which were handed down from father to son. Folk-tales were usually circulated without the stamp of the censor; and these tales were nothing more, without the explanations which the propagandists gave in person.[24]

This was, after all, the teaching method used so successfully by the early Christians, and repressive measures could do but little to block this grass roots approach. The stress in the novel is rather on propaganda than conspiracy, although it does contain certain descriptions of secret meetings, but without the mummery of hooded and masked figures. On one occasion a realistic sentinel is described, keeping watch at the door, but with no mysterious password. He is simply there to warn of the approach of any stranger or to recognise the members of the group, a wholly credible figure:

> At the door of a large room above, in which there were three billiard tables, stood a man busily engaged in chalking his cue. He was outside the door, which was closed; but he kept steadily at work, chalking, and chalking away, as if that were his chief business in life. He had some resemblance to a supernumerary in a Drury Lane play; he seemed to say, 'Here I am; and here I intend to stop as long as possible.' Still, he did not speak to anyone; he only smiled, and applied the chalk more vigorously.[25]

Just as we can believe in the sentinel, May leads us to believe in the aspirations of the Nihilists. In the first volume he says of them:

> There were then, and still are, but few who approve of murder and assassination; but when men become desperate, through being treated like savage beasts by those who have no legal or moral right to rule over them, they may sometimes be forced like beasts to turn in self-defence.[26]

In the second volume he enlarges on the social-service aspect of the movement, and particularly on the role played by women, which is one of the distinguishing features of his book:

> The Nihilists do not aim at the destruction of all things; some of their actions, indeed, would not be unbecoming in a devout believer in any accepted religion. Charity is their chief virtue, and even women are encouraged to devote their energies to the advantage of humanity, especially of suffering humanity; and the female Nihilist can go with safety into the midst of the poor, for she is known as the friend of all those stricken by misfortune or distress.[27]

In the third volume May puts forward an essentially pacifist message, which, like many things in his book, connects him to Greer, the author of *A Modern Daedalus*. May writes:

> The Nihilists have a hatred of war; it is one of the evils which they would destroy, wishing, as they do, reason, and not brute force,

to reign. Still, life, even to them, was precious; and they fought for self-preservation, for liberty and freedom.[28]

The same question is debated at a key point right at the end of the novel, when Vera and Ivan, forced to leave their own country, are emigrating to America to set up a colony run on communal lines. Ivan prophecies the coming of the Russian revolution, while Vera hopes for a peaceful solution:

> 'Before our eyes,' said Ivan, 'a terrible spectacle must be enacted. An uprising of the People of Russia will stamp an indelible mark upon the history of the world; there will be a new baptism of blood, a regeneration of the country, and a sweeping away of despotism.'
>
> 'Liberty,' said Vera, 'is the mother of Peace, not the daughter of War. If Russia were free from Autocrat and landlords, she would do well. The peasantry would hold the land in common, each taking as much as he could cultivate, as was done before the time of Boris Gôdunoff, who introduced serfdom; there would be free schools, universities, libraries, and hospitals, and the People would rule in the interest of the People.'[29]

Both at this point turn their eyes to the Statue of Liberty (which, when May's novel was published, was still in the process of erection at the entrance to the New York harbour):

> 'What is that rising out of the water?' she asked a moment later.
> 'That', he answered, 'is the Statue of Liberty!'
> He walked aft to the steerage; and when the Russian men and women there knew what it was, they cheered. Thus they greeted the goodly land of Freedom.[30]

Charles H. Eden's novel *George Donnington, or In the Bear's Grip* was first published in 1885 and is the story of an Englishman who is arrested in Russia as a Nihilist on the information of a certain count Bodiskoff. The evidence against him is fabricated because he holds a bill of Bodiskoff's and furthermore is interested in the same girl, a Pole called Yanina.

Finding himself, however unjustly, in the same boat as the Nihilists he gets to know them and Eden gives on the whole a very sympathetic presentation of their work and aims, especially in a chapter entitled 'With the Nihilists'. Donnington is believed in England to be a prisoner of the Nihilists whereas in fact he has fallen into the hands of the dreaded III Section, the Czar's secret police. He is condemned to Siberia and the last part of the book is the story of how his English friend succeeds in bringing pressure to bear on the embassy in London to secure his pardon, and then makes the long trek across Russia to Siberia in order to find and rescue him. Eden stresses the fact that this rescue can be effected because he is an Englishman, but that innocent Russians have no such possibility of escape. The author even goes so far as to condone a political assassination, though wrapping this up in a sentimental appeal to the reader's better feelings. In a chapter called 'Criminal or Heroine' he recounts how Bertha Nikitsky, after her father had been beaten to death in prison, shot General Berstel, and he ends with the following apostrophe to the reader:

> Bertha Nikitsky's deed was unwomanly and unchristian; but can we, reader, who are happy in having loving fathers, or who can can dwell with subdued pleasure on the memory of a lost dear one, can we, I say, wholly blame this wild act of retributive justice?[31]

This passage gives the measure of how standardised are the author's attitudes: he puts 'unwomanly' before 'unchristian', and assumes that a father must of necessity be either loving or dead. It is all the more interesting, therefore, to find that when he comes to write about a Nihilist meeting, which is reported in full in Volume 1, Chapter 12, he is willing, despite his conventionality, to go surprisingly far in presenting the aims of the Nihilists. True, he is distressed at the unwomanishness of the women, but even this is set down as a black mark against the Czar:

> The women, mostly under twenty-five years of age, some mere girls, were at the first glance undistinguishable from the men, for their hair was cut short; the majority wore spectacles of blue or neutral tint, which concealed the eyes; long dark cloaks shrouded their forms; their gait was awkward and ungainly, as though they were imitating the movements of the sterner sex; no little decoration — no flower in the hat, no scrap of coloured kerchief or ribbon — betrayed the feminine instinct; their garb was dull,

sombre, and unattractive, their faces fixed and resolute, wholly devoid of womanly grace or softness. Yet many of these young girls were of noble family, had been cradled in every luxury, were still rich in worldly possessions. Surely, something must be very faulty in the government of a country when all the thinking power of the rising generation is driven to such expedients to secure the one desired end — liberty of thought and action.[32]

The meeting is held in the workshop of a Nihilist printer, Anton Petrovitch, and the cover offered is ingenious: a chess championship. The leaders sit at a table with a chessboard before them so that should they be interrupted their audience are simply there to witness the game. No less than 13 pages of the novel are devoted to the speech of Ivan, their leader, whose main argument is in favour of moderation:

'All who are here present are pledged to assist in bringing about a revolution. Ignorant people accredit us with seeking to destroy all existing institutions. They say that our aim is solely destructive; that we would pull down the monarchy, root up religion, sweep away at one swoop administrations, armies, priests, judges, and the monopolists of privileges. Those who say this traduce us.'[33]

The emphasis is on the fact that power must pass into the hands of the workers, and the doctrine he is preaching is that of class warfare:

Only the working-man, as a class, is to be depended upon. The others — monarchs, nobles, priests, landowners, and the bourgeoisie — hold their very existence staked on a continuance of the present system; their surroundings, their education, their prejudices, their possessions, render them conservative and averse to change; whilst the dread of losing these advantages makes them fearful — fills them with a sordid timidity . . .'[34]

Considerable space is devoted, as in all English novels about Russia, to stories of martyrs to the cause, with accounts of the injustices and hardships suffered, and many of these martyrs are described as being women of the upper classes who have joined the movement:

'Wassily Lichareff and Valérie von Rosenberg were both arrested on suspicion, and detained for more than two years in a horrible dungeon whilst the authorities were trumping up a case against them. Valérie, the daughter of a Lieutenant-General in the Russian army, a fragile girl, but one whose spirit was indomitable, had relinquished her friends, her home, her position, for the sake of our holy cause. She had clad herself in the miserably-insufficient raiment of a factory operative, and had worked for sixteen hours a day at a machine, herding with hundreds of the lower orders, sharing their hardships, their privations, their filthy accommodation — even going bare-footed to the river and drawing water when her turn for the performance of such menial offices arose. This she did; such surroundings she endured cheerfully, to preach the gospel of Freedom amongst a class that could not otherwise be reached. Let us rejoice that we have many such noble women in our ranks!' a murmur of applause ran through the listeners.[35]

The writer is here falling back on the vocabulary and tone of sermons, with which he was clearly more familiar than with revolutionary teaching, and he seems to observe that the garments of the factory operatives are 'miserably insufficient' only when they are donned by a lieutenant-general's daughter. While it is true that many such women were giving either active or financial support to the movement, English novels on the subject give perhaps excessive space to this aspect, seeing it as a form of romantic escapism for their stay-at-home readers, with possibly too a word of warning in the descriptions of the hardships these female revolutionaries are called upon to endure. Nothing is spared, not even that fate worse than death, though Eden is too gentlemanly to be more explicit than 'the official had assaulted her with more than the usual brutality of his class'.

Another cruel aspect of Russian repression, the way in which the relatives of prisoners were themselves subjected to prison or exile, particularly offended the English sense of fair play, and is to be found in all the novels about nineteenth-century Russia. Eden is no exception. After describing the barbarous execution of Lichareff, he goes on to show the cost to his mother and little sister:

'He was publicly hanged, but — refinement of barbarity! — the knot of the rope was so adjusted that he continued to struggle for more than thirty minutes before death by slow strangulation put an end to his sufferings.

But with his death were his persecutors contented? Not so; I have more to add. Simply to exact payment of the last debt of Nature does not satisfy the vengeance of a Government such as ours. The criminal's mother and little sister, who had travelled far to bid him farewell, were both arrested immediately upon their arrival in the town, forbidden to see him, and thrown into prison. The wretched mother was set at liberty after the execution, and returned to her home with a double sorrow bowing down her aged head; for not only had she lost her noble son — the bread-winner of the family, but she had also to bewail the unhappy fate of her daughter, a child of thirteen, who was driven on foot, and in chains, to the banks of the Don, seven hundred dreary versts from her kindred, there to repent at leisure the crime of being sister to a man whom the authorities had unjustly doomed to death. Valérie von Rosenberg is at this moment on the road to Siberia, unless death, more merciful than the Third Section, has put an end to her sufferings.'[36]

The fate of Augusta von Wisen and her sisters, the three daughters of a nobleman of high rank and large fortune, the eldest of whom had distributed prohibited books propagating socialist ideas, is also narrated: 'These delicate girls with heavy chains on their arms — fetters uniting them to criminals of the lowest order and worst type — were hurried off on foot to their living death.'[37] A number of narratives of this kind are used by the author to introduce the basic argument of the Nihilists: that it is repression which has given rise to terrorism, or to what is here called 'retributive justice':

> By tyranny a peaceful socialism has become developed into a state that can be best described as a terrorism. Our harmless aspirations for freedom were checked with an iron hand, and from repression has sprung a system of retributive justice which has carried fear into the very strongholds of our enemies. Why should we, of all European nations, be the only one in which liberty of thought is sternly prohibited?[38]

The chapter ends with an appeal to readers of 'more favoured nations' to try to understand the causes of Nihilist terrorism in Russia, and not to withdraw their sympathy and support because of the methods the Nihilists find themselves constrained to resort to:

'The authorities must be taught to recognize that they cannot arrest, imprison, starve, persecute, and torture us with impunity to themselves. It is the chiefs of the Reactionary party that we must seek to terrify; and, if the means we adopt are deprecated by the citizens of more favoured nations, we must ask them to place themselves in our position, and then see if they would manifest more patient endurance of great wrong than we have done.'[39]

That such a writer as Eden, through the mouthpiece of his protagonist George Donnington, is willing to give the Nihilists and their doctrines a hearing, is indicative of the general sympathy that was felt in England for the lot of the Russian people under the regime of the Czar, a sympathy which the novelists themselves were partly responsible for creating.

In the same year as *Love, the Reward* and *In the Bear's Grip* two important historical books were published in Britain: a pro-Nihilist account by Edmund Noble under the title *The Russian Revolt* which carried terrible reports of repression, of conditions in Russian prisons and of Siberian exile, and a book by Augustus J. C. Hare, *Studies in Russia*, which defended the Czar's regime. Even the cautious *Annual Register* comments that this latter author, when in Russia, saw only what the officials wanted him to see. His defence of the Czar and his officials against accusations of cruelty, however well intentioned, raises more doubts than it allays. He writes:

Most of the punishments still in use in Russia are of Tartar origin, the most terrible being that of the knout, introduced under Ivan the Terrible . . . Gogol declares, however, that many Russians become quite indifferent to floggings, and only think them 'a little stronger than good brandy and pepper.' Exile to Siberia, which sounds so terrible to us, is also less appalling to Russians, from their having none of the home-sickness which affects English in exile. But much naturally depends upon whether the exile is to north or south Siberia; as, in the latter, there are many very pleasant places of residence, and its towns are said to be much more lively than many Russian cities.[40]

Nor is his account of the journey to Siberia, with chains of *only* 4 lbs weight on hands and feet, as heartening as he intended it to be:

They journey from eight to twelve miles a day, and have regular sleeping places. They only carry chains of four pounds weight upon their hands and feet on their march; but patriots, murderers, thieves and conspirators, are all chained together. Formerly about sixty thousand exiles to Siberia passed through Kazan; now the number is perhaps ten thousand. About fifteen per cent still probably die on the road, but formerly only a third reached their destination . . . The exiles are allowed to talk to one another on their journey and even to sing their sad wailing choruses . . .[41]

Although the novels by May and Eden both attack the cruelty and injustice of the Czar's regime, Joseph Hatton's *By Order of the Czar* (1890) achieved a peculiar distinction: the title page of the first edition bears a little yellow label with the words: 'Prohibited by the Government of the Czar from Circulation in Russia'. There may be several reasons why this novel, rather than its predecessors, was singled out as being particularly objectionable to the regime. In the first place its author was much better known (for years he was editor of the *Sunday Times*), so his book was destined to receive wider critical notice, and to reach a more ample reading public. Secondly, though certainly not a better novel than May's, and decidedly less realistic, it was written to a best seller formula. Furthermore the increasing unpopularity of the Romanoffs throughout Europe may have led the Czar's diplomatic representatives in the capital cities to show concern over his international image. Lastly, internal opposition to the regime was increasing and it was also feared that such a novel would foment discontent if widely disseminated in Russia. The prohibition is in itself indicative of the power of novels to influence public opinion, communicating more subtly and at a less conscious level than the sermon, essay, lecture, debate or interview, and (at least in the nineteenth century) with a far wider audience.

Joseph Hatton's three-volume novel is the tragic story of Anna Klosstock, the queen of the Ghetto. The author himself adds a note giving a long list of books which he consulted, including Stepniak's *Russia under the Czars* (1885). He was influenced particularly by a pamphlet published by *The Times* in the summer of 1889, giving an account of the persecution of the Jews in Russia in 1881. At about the same time he read in the *Brooklyn Times* a tragic story of a Jewess, Theodora Osnavitsch:

. . . 'That is why I am a Nihilist. Do any of you doubt?' She sprang excitedly from her chair, and in half a minute had bared herself to the waist. The front of her form from neck to belt might have passed as the model for the Venus di Milo. But the back! Ridges, welts, and furrows that crossed and interlaced as if cut out with a red-hot iron . . .[42]

This passage inspired the figure of Anna Klosstock, but presumably in order to make her more attractive to his readers (for anti-semitism was endemic in nineteenth-century England) her Jewish characteristics are toned down: '. . . there was something modern in the beauty of Anna, with her violet eyes, her rich red-gold hair, and her fresh complexion: a beauty more akin to pure Venetian than to that of the Semitic race.'[43] The whole plot relies heavily on the fact that she is exceedingly beautiful and striking.

The novel is constructed in four parts. The first and best describes the destruction of a Jewish community in a south Russian village where for many years the Jews had lived peaceably and the ghetto was little more than a name. A new governor, Petronovitch, arrives, and encourages the villagers to seize the property of the Jews. Anna, the heroine, is raped by Petronovitch when she goes to him to intercede for the life of her fiancé, a young rabbi, who is nevertheless beaten to death. He had considered the wisdom of emigrating with Anna, but had left it too late: '. . . "but sometimes I wonder if it were not wise to leave this land of doubt and fear, and travel further afield, where our people are not everlastingly within the clutch of tyranny and abuse, where indeed they are safe from public persecution and private contumely."'[44] The description of the pogrom is partly based on what Stepniak had written of 'The White Terror' and is well documented and very readable. This 'white terror' 'generally follows on great attempts or detected plots, when searches are made by the hundred, there is hardly a family belonging to the educated classes who, on retiring to rest, do not tremble at the thought that before morning they may be roused from their sleep by the emissaries of the Czar.'[45] Hatton has a peculiar gift of not committing himself too far, bred perhaps of his long experience as a journalist. Just as Anna's Jewishness is toned down in her appearance, so it is toned down in her mind, for she is given the following highly improbable speech — one which is clearly intended to make her more acceptable to his Christian readers, but which would certainly have shocked her fiancé, the rabbi: '"Oh, my dear love!" exclaimed Anna, "I sometimes fear we are not His chosen; that after all we did crucify Him whom we should have accepted!'"[46] That is to say Hatton, while showing the utmost sympathy with the fate of the Jews in Russia, is reminding the reader that they brought it, historically speaking, on themselves, and is exonerating Anna from her part of this responsibility by making her, as it were, repentant.

Much space is given in the novel, especially in the first part, to the cruelty of the regime, particularly toward political dissidents:

> Capital punishment is abolished in Russia, but there are tortures worse than death, and there are deaths from starvation and cruelty in Russian prisons far more numerous than the decapitations in France and the hangings in England. . . . The truth is, according to more than one historian and commentator, strangulation, crucifixion, the gallows, and decapitation were considered too mild for salutary influence on criminals and political offenders.[47]

Nathan Klosstock, Anna's father, is removed to a house of preventive detention in St Petersburg *en route* for what is called administrative exile. Anna herself is first raped, then sentenced to one hundred lashes of the knout and after is carried in a dying state to the hospital, where the reader loses sight of her. Toward the end of part one Hatton sums up in his usual ambiguous way:

> Is it, then, a matter for wonder that so many of the Nihilistic authors of anti-Russian books have been Jews? Is it surprising that the Jews have aided the propaganda against the Russian Government? Under such disabilities, is there anything astonishing in the fact that there is a good deal of wretchedness, knavery, dirt, squalor, and deceit among the commoner class of Jews in Russia?[48]

The reader is left to take this how he will, and to give or withhold his sympathy.

The second part of the book leaves the Russian village for London and introduces a new set of characters, the hero Philip Forsyth, a painter, and his friend Dick Chetwynd a journalist, who may be intended for a sketch of the author himself, for 'Dick was more Radical than Rebel, more Reformer than Republican'. With these new characters a new theme is introduced, the theme of the painter and the picture. Here again Hatton is exploiting a popular motif, for books about painters and sculptors abounded in the last years of the century when the whole question of what art was about (with its side-issue of the representation of the nude) was being thrashed out, and often worn threadbare. This theme extended the field of the middle-class novelist to embrace Bohemia and unconventional behaviour patterns, and it allowed him at the same time to discuss, under cover, his own theories concerning the art of writing, what was suitable material, how far realism should go, and what was the place of symbolism.

Part II opens with the two friends discussing Forsyth's sketch for a new painting, entitled 'Tragedy', to be entered for an Academy award. The subject chosen by Philip is the long trek of a group of condemned exiles on their way to Siberia. The highlight of the picture is the face of a young woman, extremely beautiful, with violet eyes and red-gold hair, who turns against a soldier with a fierce look of hatred in an attempt to save a youth who is fainting by the way in the snow. Philip explains that he had caught a glimpse of this face at the opera, among the audience gathered to hear *Carmen*. Some parts of the discussion between the two friends are of direct interest to us. Philip's mother (like the mother of Oscar Wilde) was a supporter of Irish causes, and he first considers taking as his subject for 'Tragedy' the eviction of Irish peasants, but together with Chetwynd decides that the theme lacks nobility and opts for the more dramatic scene of the Russian exiles. The fact that Hatton saw these two subjects as possible alternatives is significant. One comment of Chetwynd's is also interesting:

'Philip', said Dick, rising and taking him by the hand; 'if you were not a painter to have this outcome for your feelings, or a poet to put them into print, you would be a Nihilist, and possibly a victim of some mad plot to overtake the future by blowing up the Winter Palace, and shouting "Victory" as you fell under the crashing timbers.'

'Do you think so?' . . .

'I do; but this saves you,' pointing to the sketch; 'and it is a greater power than dynamite, a bigger reformer than the knife or the revolver. Put your heroism into your pictures, Philip, and I will forgive you for not being a politician.'[49]

This vision of the artist as contributing actively toward the process of reform, the suggestion that a sketch can be more potent than dynamite draws attention to the whole question of art as a vehicle of propaganda. Art has always been recognised as conveying a message, but Chetwynd warns Philip that this particular message may not go down well with the academicians:

> I think you would have a better chance of the medal if you took a classic subject from Roman History. Moreover, it would give you an opportunity of showing your skill as a student of the figure. Siberia gives you no chance of a careful study of the nude or the semi-nude.'[50]

He is however greatly attracted by his friend's idea, for as a journalist he had covered both the Irish-American and the Russian spheres of action:

> He had exploited the Irish revolt in the American cities, had cabled the earliest declarations of the American-Irish plotters from Mill Street, had written the first interview with Rossa, and had reported one of the secret meetings of the Dynamiters in New York. He had travelled through Russia on a journalistic mission . . .[51]

The owner of the face glimpsed at the opera, the centre of Philip's picture, is identified as the Countess Stravensky, and Philip makes her acquaintance in society, tries to persuade her to sit for him, and falls deeply in love with her, although he has only just proposed to and been accepted by a charming though mercenary and empty-headed English girl, appropriately called Dolly.

The reader then learns what he has been suspecting for some time: the red hair and violet eyes of the Countess are the same as those of Anna. The Countess is leading a double life, moving part of the time in aristocratic and diplomatic circles and partly, as Anna Klosstock, moving among a group of conspirators. She had married Count Stravensky, a secret sympathiser with the Nihilists, on his deathbed, so that his wealth could pass on to the movement. Unfortunately for verisimilitude, Hatton over-embroiders all the romantic aspects of Anna's double existence, and we lose sight of the serious theme in a wealth of ornamental detail, such as the Arabian amulet worn on Anna's left wrist; this was:

> composed of topaz, through which in Arabic was bored in curious

stars the word 'Vengeance'. Mrs Chetwynd's guests only saw the sombre yellow bangle; they little dreamed of the great, solemn, terrible oath that had been sworn upon it.

The Countess was no other than our Queen of the Ghetto, poor Anna Klosstock.[52]

Such romantic clap-trap does not blend with the kind of journalistic realism of which Hatton was capable in his better passages, as when he indicates what was the relation between the British police and the emigré Nihilists domiciled in London. This kind of tacit understanding is something which Hatton's long connection with the press enabled him to appreciate, so that he records a conversation purporting to be held between conspirators in Soho:

'You have seen a detective from Scotland Yard?'

'Yes', said Paul.

'About the visit of the German princes?'

'Yes. We are safe in our asylum here so long as we respect it, that was the police message.'

'All must be free to come and go, eh?'

'That is so. Anything happening to any one of England's guests, and we shall be cleared out.'[53]

This unwritten pact of the terms of police toleration was reflected later in the plot of Conrad's *Secret Agent* and is something that the general reader would know nothing about but of which a journalist would be well aware, and the best things in Hatton's book are these bits of inside knowledge which surface from time to time.

As the plot thickens the romantic 'fictional' elements (fictional in that they bear no relation to facts) become even more central. With Part III the whole scene moves to Venice. The conspirators leave London because they are planning the assassination of General Petronovitch who is in Italy on a diplomatic-mission-cum-honeymoon. The King and Queen of Italy are to be in Venice for the unveiling of a statue and the great Venetian festival is the second high point of the novel, the first being the slaughter of the Jews in the Russian village. Philip, his fiancée and her relatives likewise betake themselves to Venice for a summer holiday. The Countess makes spectacularly dramatic appearances in a red gondola; Philip is more and more in love with her, to the increasing neglect of Dolly. The Countess, though attracted to Philip, is busy seducing Count

Petronovitch who, although on his honeymoon, gives her a secret assignation, his weakness for red hair and violet eyes getting the better of him once again. In an Edgar Allan Poe setting in a Venetian palace she reveals her real identity, and hands Petronovitch over to her fellow conspirators for what is, after all, a very private act of vengeance:

> . . . 'you, first ruining your victim beyond all repair, pronounced the verdict upon his daughter, Anna Klosstock — she now pronounces the verdict upon you — not in her own name, but in the name of the patriotic Brotherhood of the Dawn, who have sworn, as far as in them lies, to rid their beloved Russia, and all the world of such pests as you.'[54]

After which she immediately establishes an alibi by radiantly welcoming the great to a party in her palace, wearing a most remarkable dress which Hatton unaccountably defines as 'plain':

> Her dress was nothing short of an inspiration, so plain was it yet so effective. The general impression it seemed to convey was that of a rich brocade which, despite its splendour, gave to the figure, and fell in pliable and ever-changing folds. With the exception of a rich lace stomacher it was made high to the throat, as were all the Countess's costumes, for reasons which the reader may probably guess. Lest he should be in doubt, let it be at once remarked, by the way, that the stripes of the Russian knout go down to the grave with the victim who bears them.[55]

Part IV takes all the protagonists back to London where Philip is introduced to a meeting of the Brotherhood of the Dawn, Anna's Nihilist friends, one of those secret societies which in novels are never very secret. There is the dramatic scene where Anna turns her naked back in that shadily sadistic striptease that male novelists lose no opportunity of describing:

> 'Let him know why I am a Nihilist of the Nihilists! Let him behold my title to vengeance!'
> As she spoke she tore open her dress, exhibiting a lovely white arm and part of a beautiful bust, turning at the same time with swift rapidity to exhibit her right shoulder and her neck, no farther than is considered correct by ladies of fashion at balls and

in the opera stalls, but sufficient to thrill iron men who had themselves been witnesses of the worst of Russian tortures. Red and blue deep ridges and welts crossed and recrossed each other, with intervals of angry patches of red, and weird daubs of grey that blurred and blotted out all remains and tokens of the beautiful form with which nature had endowed one of its loveliest creatures.[56]

These lacerated shoulders 'sufficient to thrill iron men' seem to me curiously suspect — Victorian pornographers had a penchant for scenes in much the same tone. Even if we absolve Hatton of writing meretriciously in this passage he was certainly writing badly, because he tells us in the same scene that 'a strong gas-light was burning' but that Philip's spirits were chilled by the change to 'the *half-lighted*, dull, prosaic double-locked apartment'.

The scene shifts once again; this time the conspirators with Philip in tow (he has taken the oath of silence, but not of allegiance, a typically Hatton distinction) move to St Petersburg and are about to effect some undisclosed action (either a dynamite attempt or an assassination) which will be the signal for the start of a national revolution, when they are intercepted by the police.

The train was laid. It was the patriotic duty of Ferrari and his confederates to light the match which should bring about that general rising which is the hope and purpose of the great popular movement throughout the Empire.

. . . But everything in St Petersburg is more or less mysterious . . . The police of Russia are as secret as the Revolutionists . . . on this busy sunny day a little troop of police and military, taking very devious routes outside the leading thoroughfares, quietly surrounded a house near the Tavreda Gardens, which had been for four-and-twenty hours under the eye of an astute detective force. The result was one of much greater importance to St Petersburg and the Czar than his officers understood. It prevented the ignition of that train of fire which had been laid with so much skill and patience; and it added to Russia's political prisoners . . . Like so many another revolutionary enterprise in Russia, it was nipped in the bud without exciting any particular attention.[57]

All the conspirators are condemned to exile in Siberia. But Hatton could not close his novel by leaving Philip, a British citizen, in the grip of the Russian bear, so at this point his friend Chetwynd takes action and through diplomatic channels receives an official pardon for Philip from the Czar himself, and sets out to follow the exiles along the route to Siberia, a journey which, if we are to judge from the novelists, was becoming the late nineteenth-century equivalent of the Grand Tour. The conversation between Chetwynd and the official at the Russian embassy is worth quoting; that the author considered it important is shown by the fact that he takes the title of the novel 'By Order of the Czar' from the official's words, the order in question being Philip's pardon, so that the novel ends with an act of imperial clemency. At the same time there is a hint in the passage at the practice of torturing prisoners, showing once more Hatton's rather ambiguous approach:

They had hoped that the young Englishman, the prisoner Forsyth, would have been able to throw some light upon her proceedings and habits. Had he been a Russian subject it was possible that more than ordinary pressure would have been exercised to obtain confessions from him . . . he did not disguise for a moment that he had travelled with her from Venice to Paris . . . thence to St Petersburg. Indeed, there would have been no object in his denying this, because one of the so-called Brotherhood of the Dawn had already confessed it.

'Under pressure?' asked Chetwynd, accepting the cigarette which the Assistant-Minister had politely offered him,.

'Probably,' said the official.

'You have severe measures in this direction, I know,' said Chetwynd, 'and I am deeply grateful for the consideration which has been shown to my friend.'

'You have reason to be so, I think, from all I understand,' said the official. 'We are talking in confidence, but it may help you to a better understanding of my Imperial Master when I tell you that it was by order of the Czar that Forsyth's sentence was commuted to imprisonment; — by order of the Czar, not in response to any diplomatic intervention, but out of consideration for his youth, his evident simplicity, and the fact that he was a young English gentleman.'[58]

The novel ends in Hatton's most romantic vein, very neatly tying together the two main themes: the fate of the political exiles and

Philip's Academy picture. Chetwynd, bearing the pardon, catches up with the exiles (who are journeying on foot) at a highly symbolic location: the 'little opening in the forest where stands this grief-consecrated pillar . . . the boundary post of Siberia, a square pillar, ten or twelve feet in height, of stuccoed or plastered brick, bearing on one side the coat-of-arms of the European province of Perm, and on the other the Asiatic province of Tobolsk.'[59]

In a highly effective though hardly convincing sequence the subject of Philip's painting 'Tragedy' (destined of course to carry off the Academy medal) is played out before Chetwynd's eyes as he overtakes the weary troop of exiles, so that the first sketch is recalled with all the mysteriousness of a scene that has been *déjà vu*:

> 'Thank God!' exclaimed Dick. 'You have a prisoner, Philip Forsyth,' at which moment one of the exiles fell forward from a group, and was caught with difficulty in the arms of a female prisoner, who, turning towards Chetwynd and the officer, disclosed to the English traveller the weird face of the woman in the Gold Medal picture, the scene of which flashed upon Dick with the startling effect of terrible realisation: the winter background of lurid light, the snow, the bearded prisoners, the hooded woman, the mounted guard, the thoughtful student, the woman at bay.[60]

Philip and Chetwynd return home, and the other exiles proceed to Siberia but, as Hatton points out, the Brotherhood 'were always prepared for the martyrdom which they knew they might at any moment be called upon to endure'.

In 1905 Hatton prepared a play with the same title, but with a happy ending for the heroine. The release of a Jewess, a Russian subject who had been at the heart of the conspiracy, makes nonsense of the rigours of the Czar's rule which was the whole point of the story. A curious touch in the play, which is absent in the novel, is a conversation between Chetwynd and Philip's servant, Henshaw:

> *Chetwynd*. You sit for the master now and then, Henshaw?
> *Henshaw*. Why, yes, sir, I sat for 'The Exile of Erin' in his last Academy picture, leastwise for the clothes, when the original Irishman was took up suspicious in connection with the blowing up of the West End Club.

Ferrari. It is not, then, Paris or St Petersburg alone that blow up, as you say? You, too, have your social eruptions.[61]

These few lines serve to link up for the convenience of the audience the three themes of the Russian Nihilists, the Irish evictions and the Fenian explosions in London, reminding us once again that Hatton was, first and foremost, a very competent journalist.

On Peter's Island by A. R. Ropes and Mary E. Ropes was published in 1901 but we are told in the preface that the first idea of the story was formed during the beginning of 1882 at St Petersburg: 'This will account for the prominence given to the Terrorist secret societies, which were at that time active and formidable; it will also account for some descriptions of localities and of customs, which represent the past rather than the present.'[62] The story is set in St Petersburg and concerns the rivalry among oil producers and refiners, Anson (an American) and Kaufmann (a German) against Morózov, a Russian. The anti-hero is a Pole, Stanislaus Lubinski, the moving force of the story together with his sister Sasha. Stanislaus, a charming and dishonest count, is employed as a clerk by Anson, but makes money on the side by accepting pay from the rival Morozov for industrial espionage, reporting his employer's business deals. The basic plot, commercial espionage and arson, together with the love stories of the protagonists, is interwoven with the story of a secret society, known as the Odds and Evens. The principal activity of this society seems to be counter-espionage and the elimination of its own members, bringing the book into line with that stream of novels which tended to belittle plots and plotters. The authorial comment on one of the conspirators' meetings is an indication of the novel's approach to the whole subject:

> . . . some of them would have turned away from the finest opportunity of exploding the Winter Palace, if the plan for the mine had not been duly passed by their engineering sub-committee. It is a law of all deliberative assemblies, however small, that they shall seem to themselves to be marching onward triumphantly, when they have perfected a new method of marking time.[63]

At the end of the novel Smirnoff, the treasurer of the anarchists, makes the following speech:

> 'And so I have felt, as I ruled my books in black and red, and put down roubles and copecks for stupid little items — acids and

cottonwool and glycerine and chlorate of potash, and harmless drugs like that. Nothing came of it all, but my accounts always balanced to the last copeck, and they were a pleasure to look at.'[64]

A curious passage in which the Ropes seem to want to convey that Russian bureaucracy is such that it contaminates even the men who are fighting against it.

One assassination however is shown as being successful, the elimination of the police spy, Major Golovkin, by Stanislaus and his fellow conspirator Grigori, stagemanaged so that he is allowed to read an account of his own death in their secretly printed paper the *Axe* in a rather fantastic though effective scene:

> 'Will you not look at the copy of *The Axe*?' he [Stanislaus] said insinuatingly. 'There is something in it that will interest you.'
>
> 'Very well!' said Golovkin carelessly, as he took up the roughly printed sheet . . . He ran through the outside page of the journal, with a contemptuous growl now and then, at some fervid appeal to the masses, or at some tale, true or false, of cruelty to political prisoners . . . At last Golovkin's eyes rested on something new — a short article with a deep black margin framing it . . .
>
> 'We are glad to announce to our readers the death of Major Simeon Simeonovitch Golovkin, otherwise known as the Centre-bit, aged forty-two' — 'What's this?'
>
> 'Mere bravado,' said a grating voice that Lubinski did not know for his own.
>
> 'Who died suddenly of an overdose of iron on the night of February 3/15 — what the devil does this mean?'
>
> 'It means,' answered the Pole in a loud voice, 'that you are a dead man!'[65]

Golovkin, taken by surprise, is easily assassinated, and the scene ends with a macabre touch: 'Finally, he [Grigori] took up the Nihilist paper, smoothed it out, and laid it on the table in front of the dead man's staring eyes. Then he stood back and viewed his work with a grin of approval.'[66] This was the pose in which the major's colleagues of the third section were later to find him.

The authors' attack on the judicial system in Russia is coupled with an attack on the bureaucracy, and an anecdote recounted, somewhat improbably, by Major Golovkin himself is used to illustrate how a completely innocent victim can become entrapped in the meshes of a system from which there is no right of appeal, an aspect British writers felt very strongly about. Although all these writers show official justice being distorted for the purpose of private revenge (the central plot of *In the Bear's Grip* is a case in point), this anecdote of Golovkin's is one of the best illustrations of how justice can go astray even accidentally in an autocratic regime with no protection of the rights of the subject:

'Do you know what I saw yesterday? I was visiting a prison — I won't tell you where I went, or why — and there was a woman in one of the cells — a political prisoner, they told me. I asked why she was there — she didn't know. I asked the governor of the prison — he did not know either. At last I found out the order for her arrest, and the policeman who had taken her. He was ordered to go to a certain house and arrest the woman who occupied the rooms on the third storey, on the left of the landing as you went up' — Golovkin paused to enjoy his cigar.

'And what happened then?' asked Anson.

'Nothing particular happened. Only he went up a storey too high, and then, when he remembered, came down and knocked at the door on the left — only it was on the left *as he came down*, and the house was so constructed that that made a difference. A mere accident — that was all! And she had been there two years.'

'Gott in Himmel!' ejaculated Franz, staring at the impassive Major; 'and did you get her out?'

'She will be released in a month or two. That is rather indecent haste, but the authorities kindly stretched a point for me. Oh, we have the finest police in Europe, Vladimir Stepanovitch!'[67]

The Odds and Evens are working to overthrow this system: a group of conspirators who meet, bearded and masked, to plan an attempt on the Czar's life. The precise political collocation of the group is never specified, but Arthur and Mary Ropes make the following comment on the treasurer's report:

If the Secretary's minutes sounded uninteresting, the Treasurer's report would have seemed still more so to one who did not know what the various items implied. But the members knew that charges for paper and printer's ink and second-hand type meant the sowing broadcast of a daring revolutionary paper which found its way, by some unknown hand, even to the private cabinet of the

Tsar himself. They knew, too, what was meant by the trivial entries of certain small sums expended on chemicals; yet as Smirnoff's level, passionless voice read the items of the account, and added a few words of explanation as to the articles purchased, it would have been impossible for an outsider to conceive what was the grotesque yet terrible fact — that he might be computing the cost of a Tsar's life. For modern science has placed the luxury of tyrannicide within reach of the poorest.[68]

Why the authors assume that an outsider would find it 'impossible to conceive' the intentions of the group from the treasurer's report of the materials purchased is hard to understand: any newspaper or novel reader of the period would surmise at once what they were up to. Number 13 of the group, Stanislaus Lubinsky, is a more modern type of conspirator than many of the stock bearded figures: he has some of the James Bond characteristics, in that he is physically exceptionally athletic, a phenomenal skater and tobogganer, and he fascinates women: Dunia the red-haired anarchist medical student (who often dresses up as a boy); Constance, the feminine English girl (who took a third in classics, so is not too much of a blue-stocking to be a heroine) and even the great actress Fraülein Wissmann (who 'gave her young knight a flower from her bouquet, with a smile she kept for Grand Dukes').

While the assassination of Major Golovkin is carried through successfully, the assassination of the Czar at the opera (this time a performance of *Faust*) is seen only in the mind's eye as Lubinski waits for Dunia to fire the fatal shot: the red-haired Dunia attired in 'velvet and turquoises, she who could hardly pay for her bare living'. Stanislaus imagines the scene about to be enacted:

> The tall, stalwart figure in its glittering uniform, entering the box; the autocrat sitting down, the centre of all eyes, surveying the crowd of brilliant humanity to whom his will and word were law. Then a girl's figure rising — the quick motion of a lithe white arm — the crash — the shock — the panic; and all this he, Stanislaus Lubinski, must await and see, for he dared not say the word to stop the deed . . . All his faculties seemed to be concentrated on the task of listening for the crash — the screams — that would come muffled through the walls of the theatre.[69]

The Czar, who has received a timely warning, fails to put in an appearance. Stanislaus is so upset when he learns that the Czar is not coming (James Bond's *sang froid* is not among his assets) that he almost gives himself away to the watchful eyes of the secret policeman:

> 'Why, what ails the lad?' for Stanislaus reeled against the wall of the corridor, white and sick with the sudden revulsion from his fear and suspense. Golovkin stared at him curiously. 'Is the fellow fool enough to care a straw what becomes of the Emperor?' he thought, 'or was he the man told off for the job, and did he expect to be killed, whichever side he took?'[70]

The ambiguity in the authors' treatment of Stanislaus Lubinsky's character shows a shift of emphasis as the novel proceeds. At first he is charming though despicable, simply an industrial spy. Later, as his involvement with the conspirators comes more into the foreground, he is treated with more sympathy: 'Must I live a dog's life or else die a dog's death?' he asks, like so many other characters in conspiracy novels who find themselves entrapped by their oaths. Also, when he sets out to kill Golovkin, his reflections come very close to those of Hyacinth in James's *The Princess Casamassima* which the authors may well have read.

> Now that the deed, under whose shadow he had long been living, was close before him, the face of it turned him sick and faint with repulsion. It was not so much that Golovkin had befriended him, had paid him even, out of his own scanty resources: it was the ugliness of the murder that outraged his sense of beauty and fitness. That he, with his fine perceptions, should have to do something so disgusting, was monstrous;[71]

The stress on his 'fine perceptions' and on the ingratitude of the gesture both ring like Jamesian touches, out of keeping with the earlier presentation of Stanislaus as a double-crosser and arsonist.

The authors of *On Peter's Island* have considerable knowledge of the geographical locality and the people, but less, one feels, of dissident movements and their motivation. They seem to have spent some time in St Petersburg but to have frequented there the foreign colony only, living on the margins of the real life of the city. For them the enemy (which is the one with which as foreign residents they had personally to contend) is Russian bureaucracy.

The book ends with a grand cleaning up of the plotters, substantially one feels with the authors' approval, for Chapter 21 bears the title 'Rats in the Wood-Pile'. This wood-pile is the place where the conspirators hold their secret councils (it is hollow because the incorruptible official in charge of this piece of government property had sold most of the wood and left only the outer shell of the pile standing). All are killed or condemned.

Something is said of the conditions in Russian prisons and of the hardships of political exile but the political conspiracy (Nihilist or anarchist?) is only a romantic background to the story of the European oil refiners, who are comfortably paired off with the right girls at the end. Although the whole of their long novel is set in Russia, and considerable space is devoted to the conspirators, only Stanislaus is more than a lay-figure, and he is a common, or perhaps rather uncommon, criminal. Arthur and Mary Ropes remain outside the whole political question fermenting in Russia and seem to have put in the Odds and Evens rather because their readers would expect this kind of local colour in a novel about Russia and not at all because they themselves have anything to say on the subject. Peter's Island is a very long way from Tobolsk.

Reading these novels about Russia we have to bear in mind the interference of international politics in the fictional presentation of dynamite plots. English novels about Ireland, as we have seen in an earlier chapter, show the Fenians as criminals — no sympathy is extended to them and no attempt is made to search for the underlying causes behind their terrorist attacks; America is accused of complicity for harbouring the plotters. In most cases the reverse is true of novels dealing with Russia: sympathy was extended to the Nihilists who were allowed to take refuge in England notwithstanding frequent diplomatic protests from Russia; a sympathy springing not from any support for their socialist ideas (I will discuss in the next chapter how such ideas were treated by novelists when they were found at home) but deriving rather from the fact that Russian interests in Afghanistan conflicted with British interests in the area (border conflicts in the Khyber Pass are to be found in a number of Kipling's poems and tales, and are central in *Kim*). The Nihilists were welcome in so far as they were making life difficult for the Czar, a potential enemy of England and a threat to British India. The novelists of the late nineteenth century who were engaged in writing long, fervid, romantic novels about the Nihilists were in fact helping to influence their readers in favour of British national interests.

Notes

1. Oscar Wilde, *Vera; or, the Nihilists* (privately printed, 1882), end of prologue, p. 14. There is considerable mystery concerning the dating of this play. My own copy from which the passages quoted are taken announces on the frontispiece 'Now first published. Privately printed 1902' and on the page opposite the frontispiece 'Of this work, 200 copies only have been printed, for private circulation. This is No. 150.' The verso of the frontispiece carries the note: 'The play was written in 1881, and is now published from the author's own copy, showing his corrections of and additions to the original text.' An acting copy was however circulated in New York in 1882 when the play was first performed, and where it was a total failure. The performance scheduled for 17 December 1881 at the Adelphi theatre in London was cancelled for political reasons because of the assassination of Czar Alexander II earlier in the year and the fact that the new Czarina was the sister-in-law of the Prince of Wales. It is curious to note that it was Alexander II himself who forbad the performance of *Julius Caesar* at the opening of the Marie theatre, showing that both British and Russian authorities were aware of the power of the media. Regarding the dating of Wilde's *Vera*, I concur with the opinion which dates the first draft as early as 1876.
2. Ibid., Act 2, p. 36.
3. Ibid., Act 4, p. 72.
4. Ouida (Marie Louise de la Ramée), *Princess Napraxine*, three vols. (London, 1884), Vol. 1, pp. 31-3.
5. Ibid., Vol. 1, pp. 33-6.
6. Ibid., Vol. 1, p. 64.
7. Ibid., Vol. 1, pp. 341-2.
8. Ibid., Vol. 2, p. 211.
9. Ibid., Vol. 2, pp. 308-13.
10. Vernon Lee (Violet Paget), *Miss Brown* (London, 1884), Vol. 1, p. 122.
11. Ibid., Vol. 3, p. 317.
12. Ibid., Vol. 2, p. 296.
13. Philip May, *Love, the Reward* three vols. (London, 1885), Vol. 3, p. 18.
14. Ibid., Vol. 2, p. 167.
15. Ibid., Vol. 2, pp. 184-5.
16. The British Library catalogue attributes *Love, the Reward* to the Philip May who edited and wrote in *Ludgate Monthly*, but I find this identification impossible to accept on the grounds of both style and content. The author of *Love, the Reward* was a deeply committed man and one with the courage to break away from the traditional nineteenth-century novel framework. It is hard to imagine how such a man only six years later could produce the insipid third-rate fiction that is to be found in the *Ludgate Monthly* or that a periodical that he was responsible for editing would have remained so undistinguished and colourless.
17. May, *Love, the Reward*, Vol. 1, p. 138.
18. Ibid., Vol. 2, p. 66.
19. Mikhail Nikolaevich Chernychevsky's novel, published in Russian in 1863, was translated into English in 1886 by N. H. Dole and S. S. Skidelsky under the title *A Vital Question; or What Is to Be Done?* This translation is later than the novel by May, so it seems probably that he read the original in Russian. A French translation *Que faire?* signed by A. T. had however appeared as early as 1875.
20. May, *Love, the Reward*, Vol. 2, p. 81.
21. Ibid., Vol. 1, pp. 114-5.
22. Ibid., Vol. 1, p. 76.
23. Ibid., Vol. 2, pp. 218-9.
24. Ibid., Vol. 1, p. 224.

25. Ibid., Vol. 1, pp. 221-2.

26. Ibid., Vol. 1, p. 236.

27. Ibid., Vol. 2, p. 97.

28. Ibid., Vol. 3, pp. 181-2.

29. Ibid., Vol. 3, p. 248.

30. Ibid., Vol. 3, p. 250. This view of America as the natural home of political refugees is echoed by Étienne in Zola's *Germinal*: — 'Vois-tu, si je savais coûter une goutte de sang à un ami, je filerais tout de suite en Amérique!' (p. 247).

31. Charles Henry Eden, *George Donnington, or, In the Bear's Grip* three vols. (London, 1884), Vol. 2, p. 172.

32. Ibid., Vol. 1, pp. 235-6.

33. Ibid., Vol. 1, p. 238.

34. Ibid., Vol. 1, pp. 242-3.

35. Ibid., Vol. 1, pp. 244-5.

36. Ibid., Vol. 1, pp. 247-8.

37. Ibid., Vol. 1, pp. 249-50.

38. Ibid., Vol. 1, pp. 252-3.

39. Ibid., Vol. 1, pp. 253-4.

40. Augustus J. C. Hare, *Studies in Russia* (London, 1885), p. 18.

41. Ibid., p. 309.

42. Joseph Hatton, *By Order of the Czar*, three vols. (London, 1890). See author's note to the Theodora Osnavitsch report at the end of this edition.

43. Ibid., Vol. 1, p. 35.

44. Ibid., Vol. 1, p. 17.

45. Ibid., Vol. 1, p. 56.

46. Ibid., Vol. 1, p. 86.

47. Ibid., from chapter entitled 'The Knout', Vol. 1, pp. 93-4.

48. Ibid., Vol. 1, p. 148.

49. Ibid., Vol. 1, p. 241.

50. Ibid., Vol. 1, pp. 232-3.

51. Ibid., Vol. 1, p. 227. It is more than likely that Hatton is crediting Dick Chetwynd, the observer, with some of his own experiences as a journalist.

52. Ibid., Vol. 2, p. 62.

53. Ibid., Vol. 2, p. 193.

54. Ibid., Vol. 2, pp. 60-1.

55. Ibid., Vol. 3, p. 64.

56. Ibid., Vol. 3, pp. 179-80.

57. Ibid., Vol. 3, pp. 200-3.

58. Ibid., Vol. 3, pp. 216-17.

59. Ibid., Vol. 3, pp. 235-6.

60. Ibid., Vol. 3, p. 240.

61. Joseph Hatton, *By Order of the Czar*. A Drama in Five Acts (London, 1904), p. 71.

62. Ropes, *On Peter's Island*. Preface.

63. Ibid., p. 79.

64. Ibid., p. 305.

65. Ibid., pp. 288-91.

66. Ibid., p. 291.

67. Ibid., p. 12.

68. Ibid., p. 78.

69. Ibid., pp. 140-1.

70. Ibid., p. 142.

71. Ibid., p. 282.

7 DYNAMITE AND DEMOCRACY

The winter of 1885-6 saw a sharp rise in unemployment and London became familiar with demonstrations and hunger marches, culminating in February 1886 in mass meetings in Hyde Park organised by the Social Democratic Federation under the leadership of H. M. Hyndman and attended by no less than 50,000 demonstrators, many of whom had walked vast distances to attend. After these meetings many went quietly home, but the more militant followed their leaders in a march through the centre of London, blocking the traffic, breaking the windows of famous clubs and looting in Trafalgar Square, Piccadilly and St James's Street. The damage done was estimated in the press at £50,000.

The population of London and, it seems, the police, were both unprepared for and appalled by the outbreak of violence which, following as it did on the years of dynamiting, seemed to threaten the stability of the entire Establishment. All the police in the district were told off to protect Buckingham Palace ('What were the Queen's guards for?' asked the indignant citizens whose property lay along the route of the march).

The shock of this new challenge to law and order is clearly reflected in four novels all published in 1886 and all concerned with this new phase of the class struggle: George Gissing's *Demos*, Walter Besant's *Children of Gibeon*, W. H. Mallock's *The Old Order Changes*, and Henry James's *The Princess Casamassima*. None of them are dynamite novels. They have, however, to be taken into consideration because their authors make no distinction between two forms of social protest: the mass demonstrations organised by the socialists and the dynamite of the anarchists and Fenians. Both dynamiters and socialists are seen as creating a climate of fear and mistrust, designed to disestablish the forces of government.

Gissing, when he wrote *Demos*, was already reacting against the more sympathetic attitude that he had shown towards the socialist movement in his first novel *Workers in the Dawn*, published six years earlier. He had at that time, though with little profit, attended socialist meetings, and the hero of this first novel, Arthur, professes some socialist ideas, although his main concern, as in so many of

Gissing's novels, is to escape from his low-class wife and to spend his time in the worship of Helen, socially far above him.

Demos, a bitter novel, shows how a worker, Richard Mutimer, is deflected from his Owenist socialism by an inheritance, in spite of his laudable efforts to use this money by putting his theories into practice, and how he throws over a working-class girl in favour of a wife who is his social superior, thereby giving his enemies scope for personal attack. The élitist aspect of Gissing, which comes out so clearly in his later *The Private Papers of Henry Ryecroft*, is well to the fore, and he fails to identify with Mutimer in the way that he normally does with the central characters of his novels, most of which are to some extent autobiographical. *Demos* was his final and irrevocable refutation of socialism, and from then on he shows more hatred than pity for the oppressed.

When writing *Demos* Gissing was working under great financial pressure. On 4 November 1885 he wrote to his sister Ellen: 'Tomorrow I begin my new book, which is to be called *Demos*. Alas, it must be in *three* volumes. It will deal with Socialism and the working classes, and from a very conservative point of view. I mean to give three months to it, and to make it worth reading and worth having written.'[1] He kept to this exacting schedule, writing again to his sister on 14 March 1886 'I have just sent off the last proofs of *Demos*'. Something of the strain under which he was writing is to be felt in his book. He was also giving time to fieldwork in order to document his subject, writing in another letter to Ellen on 22 November 1885: 'I have finished a third of the first volume of *Demos*, with much toil and endless re-writing. It is more elaborate than anything I have done yet, and the plot has cost me hours of construction, so that I have scarcely done any reading of late. And now I am obliged to go about attending Socialist meetings. Tonight I go to one at the house of the poet Morris in Hammersmith.'[2]

The plot of *Demos* turns, in approved Victorian fashion, round a missing will. The family of a left-wing iron founder, Richard Mutimer, inherit a large fortune from an uncle, an iron-master. This inheritance proves fatal. The mother prophecies this, and is never happy in her new home. The younger son, 'Arry, goes to the bad, and ends up in prison for theft. The daughter Alice is married by a bigamist, Rodman, for her newly inherited wealth, and only at the end returns to her old suitor, an impecunious journalist who has in the meantime learned good manners and been raised to the dignity of editor.

The story centres, however, on the character of Richard, and how he uses the money to finance a socialist scheme, the New Wanley works, based on Robert Owen's New Lanarkshire project. He also throws over his seamstress fiancée, Emma Vine, to marry Adela Walworth, a 'lady' in the Gissing sense of the term. At the end of Volume 2, it is Adela who finds the missing will, leaving almost all the money away from Richard and his family in favour of her old lover, Hubert Eldon. She insists that the will be revealed (Mutimer wishes to destroy it). Eldon's first act is to shut down the New Wanley foundry, throwing all the men out of work. The Mutimers retire to live in comparative poverty, although Richard is financed by an admirer to carry on the work of socialist propaganda in the East End. He creates a money-bank for the workers and in good faith invests their savings in an enterprise set up by his fraudulent (and bigamous) brother-in-law, Rodman. When Rodman bolts with the cash and without Alice, Richard is accused of peculation by the socialists and the old story of how he had thrown over Emma Vine is brought up against him. Adela, who has stood by her husband throughout (though she is in love with Eldon) speaks to a meeting of the workers in his support. This calms the socialists only temporarily — they are now wholly under the influence of Comrade Roodhouse, editor of the *Tocsin* — and Mutimer is compelled to flee for his life, turning into the first open doorway which leads (inevitably) to the house of Emma Vine, where he is killed at the window by a flying stone, and is mourned by both Emma and Adela. Emma, possibly in a reminiscence of Margaret in Mrs Gaskell's *North and South*, is also struck by a blow intended for Mutimer.

A central theme is the split in the socialist party between supporters of Mr Westlake, an intellectual idealist based on the figure of William Morris, and those of Comrade Roodhouse, who incorporates Gissing's version of the ideas of Hyndman and the Social Democratic Federation. Another theme (a constant in Gissing's early novels) is the unbridgeable class difference which makes Mutimer's marriage a failure: 'He was not of her class, not of her world; only by violent wrenching of the laws of nature had they come together.' The reference to 'the laws of nature' sounds familiar to us today in connection with racial intermarriage, but it is not at all unusual to find it used of class intermarriage in the nineteenth century, in an attempt to check the growing trend toward greater class mobility.

A third theme is to be found in the treatment of class warfare, which finds expression particularly in the commentary of Mr Wyvern, the parson, who seems to be speaking for Gissing, and who approves of the actions of the reactionary Hubert Eldon when he closes down the new foundry, throwing the entire workforce into unemployment. Eldon, we should note, also has the author's approval, for he is rewarded at the end of the novel with the prize of Adela, the perfect wife, who is barely shop-soiled having kept Mutimer at a considerable distance during their brief marriage. Eldon states his position unequivocally:

> '. . . in the presence of those fellows [the New Wanley workers] I feel that I am facing enemies . . . They are our enemies, yours as well as mine; they are the enemies of every man who speaks the pure English tongue and does not earn a living with his hands. When they face me I understand what revolution means; some of them look at me as they would if they had muskets in their hands . . . If I had been born one of them I should be the most savage anarchist.'[3]

Significantly it is Hubert Eldon who draws also the Nihilists into the discussion, and who is willing to grant them a nobility of purpose which he totally denies to the English socialists:

> 'Now in the revolutionary societies of the Continent there is something that appeals to the imagination. A Nihilist, with Siberia or death before him, fighting against a damnable tyranny — the best might sacrifice everything for that. But English Socialism! It is infused with the spirit of shop-keeping; it appeals to the vulgarest minds; it keeps one eye on personal safety, the other on the capitalist's strong-box; it is stamped commonplace, like everything originating with the English lower classes. How does it differ from Radicalism, the most contemptible clap-trap of politics, except in wanting to hurry a little the rule of the mob?'[4]

Inspiring words like 'tyranny' and 'sacrifice' are used in this passage only of the foreign Nihilists while the home-born socialists are referred to as 'vulgar', 'commonplace' and as a 'mob'.

Mr Wyvern, the parson in *Demos*, takes refuge also in the old conservative argument with which Gissing seems to sympathise in this novel, although elsewhere he took a different view. Mr Wyvern's sympathies, he declares, are roused by that 'class created by the mania of education . . . it consists of those unhappy men and women whom unspeakable cruelty endows with intellectual needs whilst refusing them the sustenance they are taught to crave.'[5] But then Mr Wyvern possessed some of Gissing's own misanthropy, and assures his hearer that, after all, no one is happy:

> 'One of the pet theories I have developed for myself in recent years is, that happiness is very evenly distributed among all classes and conditions . . . You would urge the sufferings of the criminal class under punishment? I balance against it the misery of the rich under the scourge of their own excesses.'[6]

The socialist press is also censured by Mr Wyvern for stirring up unrest, even the more moderate *Fiery Cross* edited by Mr Westlake (= William Morris):

> 'Papers like the *Fiery Cross*, even though such a man as Westlake edit them, serve the cause of hatred; they preach, by implication at all events, the childish theory of the equality of men, and seek to make discontented a whole class which only needs regular employment on the old conditions to be perfectly satisfied.'[7]

When questioned by Hubert 'Have you any belief in the possibility of this revolution they threaten?' (the sort of question James's upper-class characters are always asking each other in *The Princess Casamassima*) Mr Wyvern is reassuring, and his message seems to be Gissing's own message to the reader: 'None whatever. Changes will come about, but not of these men's making or devising.'

While Mr Wyvern speaks for the moderates, Comrade Roodhouse speaks for the revolutionaries in the words of a lecture which the *Fiery Cross*, the organ of the more moderate socialists, refuses to print. This lecture supports the policy of assassination, and draws a parallel with the activity of the anarchists in Russia.

> In the lecture in question Roodhouse declared his adherence to the principles of assassination; he pronounced them the sole working principles; to deny to Socialists the right of assassination was to rob them of the very sinews of war. Men who affected to be revolutionists, but were in reality nothing more than rose-water romancers, would of course object to anything which looked like business; they liked to sit in their comfortable studies and pen

daintily worded articles, thus earning for themselves a humanitarian reputation at a very cheap rate. That would not do; *à bas* all such penny-a-liner pretence! Blood and iron! that must be the revolutionists' watchword. Was it not by blood and iron that the present damnable system was maintained? To arms, then — secretly of course. Let tyrants be made to tremble upon their thrones in more countries than Russia. Let Capitalists fear to walk in the daylight. This only was the path of progress.[8]

The comrades present at a meeting of the Islington Socialist League to which Gissing devotes considerable space in the first volume are all, with the exception of Mutimer in whom are discerned 'at least the elements of what we call good taste' (which places him at the opposite pole from Henry James's Muniment), shown as being slightly ridiculous:

> Mr Cullen is a short, stout man, very seedily habited, with a great rough head of hair, an aquiline nose, lungs of vast power . . . He [Mr Cowes] is tall, meagre, bald; he wears a very broad black necktie, his hand saws up and down . . . Who will follow? A sound comes from the very back of the room, such a sound that every head turns in astonished search for the source of it. Such voice has the wind in garret-chimneys on a winter night. It is a thin wail, a prelude of lamentation; it troubles the blood. The speaker no-one seems to know; he is a man of yellow visage, with head sunk beneath pointed shoulders, on his crown a mere scalp-lock. He seems to be afflicted with a disease of the muscles; his malformed body quivers, the hand he raises shakes paralytic. His clothes are of the meanest; . . .[9]

How many of the novel's readers are going to take seriously the 'bitter prophecies' of such men as these? Gissing is using the old and most effective technique of discrediting the message by discrediting the speakers who pronounce 'the terrible arraignment of the People.'

The most quoted passage of *Demos* is the dramatic scene where Mutimer's wife Adela bravely goes 'in her lady-like costume of home' to address a socialist meeting and to explain her husband's absence on an occasion when his management of the society's funds is to be called in question:

As she disappeared there again arose the mingled uproar of cheers and groans; it came to her like the bellow of a pursuing monster as she fled along the passage. And in truth Demos was on her track . . . The voice of Demos, not malevolent at the last, but to Adela none the less something to be fled from, something which excited thoughts of horrible possibilities, in its very good humour and praise of her a sound of fear.[10]

The words used, 'pursuing monster', 'horrible possibilities' carry a sexual interpretation and the threat of rape, so that a middle-class woman reading this novel is encouraged to identify with Adela and rejoice at her escape from these men of a different class who are frightening even when 'not malevolent'. Again there is something racist in the whole tone of the passage, in the idea of an unbridgeable gulf. The fact that Adela has actually married a man with the same origins, even though he stands out in so far as he possesses the elements of good taste, is a situation from which it behoves the author to rescue her at the end of the story. The very last sentence of the third volume, as Hubert Eldon draws her to his heart 'with passionate triumph', reflects Gissing's sense of the error of her marriage to Richard Mutimer the iron founder, for 'the untruth of years fell from her like a veil, and she achieved her womanhood'. Whatever Gissing thought that that meant, it was obviously something that would keep her far away from the dangers of socialist meetings.

Walter Besant's *Children of Gibeon*, another three-volume novel of 1886, is concerned, as were both Gissing and Mallock, with the exploration of the question of class in relation to education and heredity. But while for Mallock heredity is everything, and while Gissing fears that mass education will end by producing social misfits, Besant is much more willing to concede the possibility of class mobility. The wholly improbable plot of *Children of Gibeon* turns on two girls, Violet and Valentine, who are brought up together as sisters by Lady Mildred in an aristocratic setting. The purpose of the novel is to illustrate Besant's theory that there will be no difference between two girls so educated, so although the girls are told that one is the daughter of a smith and a washerwoman and the other is an heiress, they are not told which is which, and the novel reveals that no one can distinguish their origins.

Having made this point by placing the two girls in a highly

privileged setting, Besant carries his experiment further by introducing a brother, Claude Monument,[11] likewise the son of the smith
and washerwoman, who has made his way in the world and is now a
barrister and a fellow of Trinity. Besant's introduction of the two
young ladies through their barrister brother to the working-class
family from which one of them has sprung (but which one?) is told
with not a little irony, of the peculiarly dry kind that we associate
today with the works of Ivy Compton Burnett:

> 'Joe is a smith . . . and he works for a builder and decorator. Of
> course he looks like what he is — a working man.'
> 'Things are being brought home to us, Val,' said Violet. 'Go
> on, Claude'.
> 'He is a good-natured man and he has ten children.'
> 'Ten children? They are our nephews and nieces. The world,'
> said Violet, 'is growing wider.'[12]

There is no question but that for Besant education could and did
effect a change of class and social status, nor did the fact of owning to
'low' relations need to cause embarrassment.

> When he [Claude] mentioned the trade of his father and the
> calling of his mother, Violet begged him earnestly not to speak of
> these things if they were painful to him. He declared, however,
> and it seemed strange to her, that it was not in the least painful to
> him to feel that his mother had been a washerwoman.[13]

A comparison between Claude Monument's quiet acceptance of his
origins and the agonies suffered by Godwin Peak in Gissing's *Born
in Exile*, when his uncle proposes opening an eating-house opposite
his college shows the totally different approach of the two authors to
the whole question of class. For Peak 'It would mean that I should
have to leave the college, and give up all my hopes', while
Monument faces the difficulties of his change of class in a much more
rational way, even while acknowledging that these difficulties do in
fact exist:

> 'I have tried to persuade myself,' he said, 'that it makes no
> difference at all what a man's birth may have been. But of course
> I don't quite believe it. I am always measuring my own stature
> with that of my friends, and asking myself if I stand on their level
> as regards — what constitutes a gentleman.'[14]

By discussing the problem on two levels, that of the girls who, unaware of their origins, are wholly free from self-consciousness in this respect, and that of the young man who has climbed on his own merits into the professional class and who is troubled but only because he is aware of the eyes fixed upon every aspect of his behaviour, Besant shows a much more modern approach to the question of class mobility than his contemporaries. If the novel is not so readable as *All Sorts and Conditions of Men* it is because it is too deliberately a pamphlet on the social question, and no pamphlet can stand the strain of extension to the length of three volumes. The World puts in a brief appearance near the beginning of the novel to voice the views against which Besant is campaigning: '"No one will maintain," said the World, "that the daughter of a working man and the daughter of a gentleman can ever stand upon the same level. Education can refine, but it cannot change base metal into gold."'[15]

Though it would seem that Besant is challenging some of the basic assumptions on which society rested, nevertheless he stops short of any intention to abolish class distinctions as such. For this reason he introduces another character, a further brother in the Monument family, Sam, the revolutionary board-school master. The treatment of Sam is satirical: his appearance is unprepossessing for 'his coarse red hair rose from his forehead like a cliff' and 'his legs, if one must speak the truth, were short and curly' but 'never was there a stronger or more determined looking young man'. Besant devotes a whole chapter, called 'How the Band Played' to the enunciation of Sam's socialist doctrines, in which he describes a world in which the state will be the only employer of labour. Sam is preaching a constructive rather than destructive socialism but in the end Besant makes it clear that he considers the whole doctrine purely theoretical and gives the last words in the chapter to Valentine: 'I ask you for advice, and you offer me the chance of a new System. Go away and rail at Competition, while we look after its victims.' Besant, unlike most other novelists of his day, is willing to open the doors of the middle class to members of the lower class who show themselves worthy, but by presenting Sam as ridiculous and his doctrines as futile he is repudiating any suggestion that it is the class system itself which is responsible for the ills of society.

W. H. Mallock's *The Old Order Changes* tells how a group of aristocrats meet in a French château to discuss their role in the modern world. Their number includes a Catholic priest, Lady Chislehurst a bigotted Catholic, Lady Mangotsfield a diehard Tory and the hero Mr Carew and heroine Miss Consuelo Burton whose consciences are troubled by the social question. Mallock, like Gissing, really believed that class boundaries were virtually uncrossable, so that Besant's book, by comparison, is an enlightened exploration of the whole question, and also a good-humoured one, for both Gissing and Mallock are somewhat querulous. In Mallock's book the dubious harmony of this group at the château is shaken by the arrival of a social democratic agitator, Mr Foreman (a punning reference to the leader of the social democrats, H. M. Hyndman) who had been invited by mistake. He is satirised for his bad manners, for although he is described as being 'Fellow of a College at Cambridge' he is shown as unable to handle a cup and saucer, as Lady Chislehurst not very courteously implies: "'The Church was always the best friend of the poor. Mr Foreman, let me give you another cup of tea; and come, I must get rid of that nasty slop in your saucer for you.'"[16]

The irony is unintentional, for never did a book take itself more seriously than this of Mallock's. The slop in the saucer serves the same purpose as the physical defects of the anarchists in *The Angel of the Revolution* and *The Secret Agent* or the agitators in *Demos*: what Foreman says is subtly discredited. But he is snubbed even more conclusively, for when he proceeds to bring Karl Marx and *Das Kapital* into the conversation he is ably put down by Mr Stanley the priest, who is engaged in translating Marx and who challenges the figures on which Foreman bases his examples concerning the nature of profits and interest.

Mallock is unwilling, however, to leave any possible ambiguity in the reader's mind. When Foreman is first mentioned as being on his way to join the group Carew, the hero of the tale, gives him a most uncompromising introduction:

'Do you mean Foreman the agitator? Do you mean the Socialist? Do you mean that lying egotistical scoundrel, half dunce and half madman, who is going about London haranguing the unemployed workmen — poor creatures, whom hunger has made at once savage and credulous — and trying to rouse in them every contemptible quality that can unfit them for any human society — the passions of wild beasts and the hopes of gaping children? Is that really the man you mean?'[17]

In a letter supposedly written by Carew (who is something of a graphomaniac) Mallock sets down the conservative viewpoint more clearly than any of his contemporaries:

> . . . for the same reason I love these old mediaeval towns. I love them because they are to my mind like a mirror in which the past is reflected, when Radicals were not and equality was not dreamed of — the past when men recognized their superiors, and ordered themselves reverently, with no sense of humiliation . . .[18]

And in his own reflections Carew raises a point on which Henry James was constantly, though never so heavy-handedly, to play the changes: "'Yes we *are* different . . . we who can look back through the vistas of centuries, and hear the past speak to us, in our own private language, of our birthright of rule and leadership . . . they make for us, if we only chose to listen to them, a second conscience, an added moral faculty —'"[19] Foreman the agitator, whose leadership depends not on birthright but on popular acclaim, is referred to by Carew not as a man but as an animal: "'My dear fellow,' cried Carew, "for pity's sake come and console me. I've a live Socialist coming here this afternoon — that animal Foreman who spouts revolution in the parks."[20] Foreman's ideas are referred to as dynamite: Carew advises his friends to steer the conversation cautiously: "Social politics might bring us to grief in a moment. He might fire up at a phrase; his eyes would roll and glitter, and we should have him exploding as if he were a packet of dynamite."[21] The bag Foreman carries, though not the black bag of the dynamiter, is seen to be at least potentially as dangerous: '. . . and a servant was sent to Foreman's bedroom for a bag, which seemed when it appeared to be bulging with revolutionary literature.

"Holloa!" exclaimed Harley, "hooray for the dynamite!"[22] Not only do the other members of the house-party equate Foreman and his ideas with dynamite, but the socialist leader himself makes use of the same metaphor when illustrating the effect of Marx's teaching:

> 'Now,' said Foreman, looking up from his paper, 'we are coming to the great theorem of Revolutionary Economics . . . We come to Karl Marx's theorem as to the nature of profits or interest, or — to put the matter plainly — of the entire subsistence of the

leisured and the propertied classes. This is the real dynamite that will shatter our existing civilization — this single economic discovery.'[23]

There is, I believe, a double symbolism in the description of the firework display held at the fête at the Château de Courbon-Loubet on the night before Foreman arrives. This magnificent exhibition, which is witnessed and enjoyed also by the peasants but from a respectful distance some 50 feet *below* the castle walls, is designed to conclude by writing the aristocratic symbols of the crown and the *fleur-de-lys* large across the sky:

> . . . on the ground below and opposite, cascades and wheels of fire began to revolve and glitter. These, though pretty enough, were in themselves not out of the common; but when at last they had come to an end, and there had been a dull interval of a moment or two, fresh sparks simultaneously were struck in a number of places, and, the second after, the whole of the sloping woodland became a glittering garden of white and quivering *fleurs-de-lys* . . . But they were not yet out, or at least only a few of them, when a central glow, brighter than any of its predecessors, gathered to itself the whole attention of everybody. Its shape and meaning were for a few seconds uncertain. Then, clear and shining in each minutest detail, there burst on the spectators the likeness of a colossal crown. It remained for a second only — only long enough to be distinguished by them — and then, as it faded, up from the very same spot a bouquet of rockets rose, so brilliant and numerous that the whole prospect was nothing but a vision of soaring fire.[24]

The evanescence of the fireworks suggests the passing of the splendours of a whole way of life, and the arrival of Foreman the next morning with his bag of revolutionary literature, from which he pulls out 'a limp printed document like an election leaflet' is seen as the beginning of a series of very different kinds of explosion.

It is only in the third volume that we leave the château and the incredible moral problems engendered there for a hero compelled to choose between two young women: Miss Consuelo Burton as the Virgin and Violet as Eve. Not all the 'added moral faculty' deriving from his blue blood can guide Carew between the angel and the temptress. In this predicament he finally tells the whole story to Miss

Consuelo herself, who shows that she possesses all the good sense that he gives her credit for by saying firmly: 'Marry Violet'. Only authorial intervention, revealing that Violet had already contracted a secret marriage, guides him safely to the right choice.

What is more interesting for the reader today is the purportedly first-hand description of the London riots of February 1886, at which Carew is allowed to be present, and which he observes from the vantage point of his club window.[25] The imagery used is indicative of how strongly Mallock felt about the threat of mob violence, and if Gissing's metaphor in *Demos* is sexual, Mallock's here is cloacal: the march of the unemployed workers is seen moving through the streets as 'a great volume of semi-liquid sewage'. The passage is one of the most detailed reports of the march and ensuing riots to be found in fiction, and is a first-rate example of how reporting of news can, while remaining factually correct, select words guaranteed to slant the interpretation which a reader will put upon the information given.

> 'It is the mob — the unemployed,' was the answer. 'They are led by professional agitators. You'll see for yourself in a minute or two . . .' At last he got so far into the bay-window as to be able to see down the street; and what met his eyes was a black advancing mass, moving like a great volume of semi-liquid sewage, on the surface of which certain raised objects seemed to be floating, whilst the edges of it, in one place or another, were perpetually frothing against the sides of the shops and houses. A moment more, and this hoarse and horrible inundation was flowing past the windows at which he himself was standing.[26]

Not only has Carew been transported to London in time to witness the outbreaks, but Foreman is back too, right in the centre of the mêlée, and his actions are totally discredited by the author's use of such words as 'maniac', 'Bedlam' and 'insanity'. He is of course carrying a red flag, and Mallock is making certain that the reader will look askance at the next red flag that he sees:

> 'See', cried another, 'there he is himself — the man in the waggon, with a red flag in his hand' . . . If his satellites looked wild, he looked a great deal wilder; not, indeed, in respect of his dress and hair, for in that way his appearance was quiet and common enough: but he was shouting to those around him like a

maniac loose from Bedlam, and waving the red flag which he held, with corresponding gestures. Sometimes he seemed to use it as a sign of encouragement, sometimes to indicate a particular building. Meanwhile his eyes were starting out of his head; and his whole face was flickering with the livid gleam of insanity. Carew started at the spectacle. This figure was Foreman.[27]

The reaction of Carew to this sight is immediate and predictable: he sits down at once after the demonstration has passed and taking up a sheet of the club notepaper proceeds to pen a letter to the editor of an unidentified newspaper (*The Times*?). The predominant image in the letter is that of dynamite:

Masses of men who, under existing social conditions, suddenly fall from comparative prosperity into privation, and see before them no hope for the future, become dangerous by the laws of social chemistry, as surely as, under chemical treatment, do the harmless materials of dynamite. Like dynamite, too, they are not self-exploding. They remain dumb and impassive till the fuse is applied by the agitator. Then an explosion follows. It is useless to blame the people. The agitator alone is guilty, and there is no guilt in the world of so deep a dye as his. Could he ensure a new order of things by blowing up the old, we might, perhaps, call him a hero; but the only result of his explosion is that the people themselves are crushed under whatever ruin they have caused. The structure of society still remains unchanged, or changed only in being for a short time disjointed.[28]

The whole responsibility is placed firmly on the socialist agitator who is equated with the dynamitard. No mercy will be shown to such men; Carew reflects that he 'would willingly string the lot of them up to a lamp-post'. At the same time he is shown as being less than honest with himself over his immediate reactions to the sight of the demonstrators. The horror and loathing which he registered when standing at the club window have taken on a more seemly guise: '"Blame the people!" he repeated as he put his letter into the box. "Poor devils! Why, as I watched the crowd just now, I was far more inclined to cry over the sight than to be angry at it."'[29] This is not the place to investigate the solution to the social question which Mallock puts forward and which Carew and Miss Burton are going to spend their (joint) lives in elaborating. The whole novel is worth much

more attention than can be given here. But Mr Stanley's outline of
the scheme seems a most appropriate passage with which to take
leave of *The Old Order Changes*:

> 'Her notion, in fact, of a monastery or a convent is a modern
> factory where the hands should be monks or nuns; where the spire
> should rise side by side with the chimney; and the quiet cloister
> should refresh the mind after the rattle of wheels, and looms, and
> belts.'
>
> 'That', said Lord Auden, in a tone of poetic appreciation,
> 'makes a really beautiful picture.'
>
> . . . 'The profits, of course, instead of going to the capitalists,
> the manager, and the specially-gifted few, would be the property
> of the whole body. They would not, however, be divided amongst
> the workers and thus take the form of increased wages. That
> result would stultify the whole scheme.'[30]

Mallock was not the only novelist who was reflecting on the
activities of Mr Hyndman and of the Social Democratic Federation.
Henry James, in a letter to Charles Eliot Norton of 6 December
1886, two months after the termination of the serialisation of *The
Princess Casamassima* in *The Atlantic Monthly* wrote: 'In England
the Huns and Vandals will have to come *up* — from the black depths
of the (in the people) enormous misery, though I don't think the
Attila is quite yet found — in the person of Mr Hyndman. At all
events, much of English life is grossly materialistic and wants blood-
letting.'[31] This then was the conclusion that he had come to at the
end of a period, from September 1885 to October 1886, spent
meditating on contemporary social unrest in England. But it hardly
takes us any further than his reflections at Lyons station in 1882,
subsequently published in 1884 in *A Little Tour in France*, where,
with two left-wing papers in his hands, the *Intransigeant* and the
Rappel, in which he had been reading of a recent dynamite attempt
at Lyons, he comments:

> I wondered as I looked through them whether I was losing all my
> radicalism; and then I wondered whether, after all, I had any to
> lose. Even in so long a wait as that tiresome delay at Lyons I failed
> to settle the question, any more than I made up my mind as to the
> probable future of the militant democracy, or the ultimate form
> of a civilization which should have blown up everything else.[32]

Yet the 'blood-letting' and the 'blowing-up of everything else' play no part in the social novel which James actually wrote, even though in *The Princess Casamassima* James seemed to himself to be plunging very deep into the whole social question. In the long preface which he added many years later he refers to his hero, Hyacinth Robinson, as having 'thrown himself into the more than "shady" underworld of militant socialism', and explains that the scheme of the novel calls for 'the suggested nearness (to all our apparently ordered life) of some sinister anarchic underworld, heaving in its pain, its power and its hate'. We know from his own account in the preface that he set about collecting his material very conscientiously, wishing to fix his impressions of London gathered in long meditative peregrinations about the streets, and that he actually went so far as to visit Millbank prison in order to document his account of Hyacinth's childhood visit to his dying mother in Holloway jail. The opening of the novel, with its descriptions of genteel poverty in Lomax Place, or of Rosa Muniment, the gallant little invalid in the garret, is traced along Dickensian lines, but gradually James's own peculiar genius and peculiar irony take over, so that by the end of the novel the characters are confessing openly to each other that they dislike Rosa and there is a general debunking of the Victorian sentimentality in which the early chapters were steeped.

The two central characters of the novel are Hyacinth, the bastard son of a French prostitute by an English duke, and the Princess, daughter (also outside wedlock) of an American lady and a seedy Italian 'cavaliere': she is also the wife of a great Italian prince. Hyacinth lives on his scanty earnings as a bookbinder (a craft of which he is a master) while the Princess moves in the best society on an allowance from Prince Casamassima from whom she is separated: James never loses sight of the economic background of his characters and of the economic pressures brought to bear on them. These two protagonists are given a very private score to settle with society — although both hold an accepted and respectable place within it, both feel their illegitimacy as a stain. Both come into contact with an anarchist organisation operating on the Continent but tenuously linked with a socialist group (mainly of foreigners) meeting in London at the Sun and Moon. The Princess is in search of new sensations while Hyacinth is moved (particularly at the recollection of his mother's miserable end) by a desire for social justice. In great secrecy Hyacinth takes an oath (of which every other character in the book soon becomes aware) to perform, when called upon, some indefinite action: 'Very likely it would be to shoot someone — some blatant humbug in a high place; but whether the individual should deserve it or shouldn't deserve it was not to be one's affair.'[33]

James himself must have felt that there was a certain vagueness about the details of this central conspiracy, for in his preface, by way of justification, he specifies: '. . . a presentation not of sharp particulars, but of loose appearances, vague motions and sounds and symptoms, just perceptible presences and general looming possibilities.'[34] Loose appearances and looming possibilities are exactly what he in fact gives us when describing the commitment of his characters to socialist or anarchist ideas: the distinction between the two is never kept clear. To this extent James conforms perfectly to the pattern set by most of his contemporaries. Paul Muniment, the chemical worker whom Hyacinth sees as the future prime minister, and who first introduces him to the group of socialists who meet at the Sun and Moon, is also hand in glove with the shadowy European anarchist, Diedrich Hoffendahl, the man who holds all the wires, the equivalent of number one in other conspiracy novels, although James would never stoop to such a definition. For the rest, the characters make the vaguest statements about their political involvement. Hyacinth, for example, declares: '"You didn't know I was advanced? Why, I thought that was the principal thing about me. I think I go about as far as anyone."'[35] while the Princess makes the vague promise: '"You'd find I'd go with you — pretty far"', and later in the novel Hyacinth recalls what the Princess had told him of the manner in which she had already committed herself 'and he remembered with a strange perverse elation that she had gone very far indeed'.

Having found this convenient euphemism, James continues to harp on it. Hyacinth accuses the Princess 'You do go too far', to which she answers, confirming all the reader's worst suspicions: 'Of course I do — that's exactly what I mean. How else does one know one has gone far enough?' Not even the charitable Lady Aurora Langrish is exempt from these vague involvements: 'But it seems to me Lady Aurora, for herself, goes pretty far.'

In an excellent study of contemporary sources (particularly *The Times*) Tilley has pointed out how much James relied on the Establishment press for his political background,[36] and has gone into the probable origins of Diedrich Hoffendahl, the arch-conspirator who visits England in the watches of the night apparently for the sole purpose of making Hyacinth swear his deadly oath. Nothing is said about dynamite — only Madame Grandoni, the ancient duenna of whom James thoroughly approves, makes an appeal to Hyacinth which seems to carry with it the author's own deprecation of violence:

> 'I gathered the other night that you're one of the young men who want everything changed — I believe there are a great many in Italy and also in my own dear old Deutschland, and who even think it useful to throw bombs into innocent crowds and shoot pistols at their rulers or at any one . . . But before you go any further please think a little whether you're right.'[37]

This is exactly what Hyacinth begins to do, and the whole of the second half of the novel is marked by his growing conviction that he is wrong. As he visits the Princess at her country house at Medley, and then even more improbably is transported to Paris and Venice, he grows more and more convinced of the folly of his oath. He even writes a letter to the Princess from Venice which faithfully reproduces the wilful misinterpretation of socialist doctrine to be found so often in the newspapers. This passage is worthy of attention:

> You know how extraordinary I think our Hoffendahl — to speak only of him; but if there's one thing that's more clear about him than another, it's that he wouldn't have the least feeling for this incomparable, abominable old Venice. He would cut up the ceilings of the Veronese into strips, so that every one might have a little piece. I don't want every one to have a little piece of anything and I've a great horror of that kind of invidious jealousy which is at the bottom of the idea of a redistribution.[38]

The argument put in Hyacinth's letter may easily have come from the November issue of *Temple Bar*, a periodical incorporating *Bentley's Miscellany*. In an article entitled 'How Shall I Vote?' which had direct reference to the elections held in England in November 1885, the following statement is made: 'Mr Labouchere does not state his plan for the distribution of the palaces, but I suppose Windsor Park will be cut into small plots . . . Every cherished institution of the land is in the melting-pot. The dissolution of parliament will be followed by the dissolution of the bonds which hold society together.'[39] The vandalism implied in the cutting up of the Veronese ceiling or the division of Windsor Park into small plots is a misrepresentation of the socialist doctrine which taught that, in the interests of the whole population, national art treasures should be maintained by the state: a policy which Hyacinth, one of the dispossessed, might have been expected to appreciate. By making his little bookbinder the mouthpiece of reaction James is seriously sacrificing probability and even credibility, but he would have no difficulty in carrying his contemporary readers with him as they had already assimilated the same arguments from the press.

Hyacinth's Venice letter is only one indication of his change of heart, a change which soon becomes common property, and almost all the other characters find occasion to discuss it with him and with each other. The Princess puts the situation in a nutshell: "'. . . for I can imagine nothing more terrible than to find yourself face to face with your obligation and to feel at the same time the spirit originally prompting it dead within you.'"[40] This is, of course, exactly what happens, bringing *The Princess* into line with a number of other conspiracy novels. The fatal letter arrives summoning Hyacinth to perform his task, and the romantic ending chosen by James is substantially the same as Oscar Wilde's conclusion in *Vera: or, the Nihilists*: Hyacinth points the pistol at his own heart and pulls the trigger.

The insistence on the oath, which is the turning point of the whole novel and occurs right in the middle (up to that moment Hyacinth's revolutionary fervour waxes, immediately after it begins to wane) was a commonplace, as we have seen, of the novels of the period, so there is no need to look for a specific source. I feel tempted nevertheless to quote from an essay by Hippolyte Taine entitled 'Socialism as Government' which was published in the October 1884 issue of the *Contemporary Review*, an issue that James almost certainly read both because he was an admirer of Taine and because it contained an article by F. P. Verney 'The Americans Painted by Themselves' which discussed a number of James's novels and criticised his drawing of female characters. He was habitually residing in London at the time, and his letters and journals betray the interest with which he followed criticism of his own work. Taine's article contains a number of considerations which seem to be reflected in James's novel. Of the revolutionary forces at work Taine says that they were: '. . . shrewd enough to see that brute force is their only weapon, inhuman enough to apply it without scruple or reserve, and to resort to systematic murder on all sides in order to deepen and spread the impression of terror.' But these are generalisations that James could have met with anywhere, and certainly in *The Times*, during 1884-5. What is more to the point is the emphasis Taine puts on the question of the pledge among conspirators: 'No pledge may relieve him of these duties if they are not fulfilled because he has given contrary pledges, he is no less culpable on this account, and besides, he is culpable for having pledged himself; the pledging of himself to crimes was in itself a crime.'

A great deal is made in *The Princess Casamassima* of Hyacinth's pledge or vow, which, as I have pointed out, is taken at the turning point of the novel. James had not far to seek for examples of such pledges: the novels of the 1840s were full of them, and reports of cases where such illegal oaths were taken were rife. Before 1871, when the union of workers was illegal, such movements were driven underground and forced to meet in the open fields on moonless nights, and these were the circumstances in which vows and solemn pledges were exchanged. Such pledges were a far cry from the oaths of the terrorists but their clandestine character and their illegality gave them a romantic aura which fascinated the social protest novelists of the mid-century. In *Mary Barton* (1847) Mrs Gaskell goes further than her contemporaries and describes an isolated act of terrorism, the assassination of the son of a mill owner who was strongly opposed to the unions, and though in no way condoning the act or the secret oath which preceded it, she is unique among the novelists of her time in showing the steps by which men could be driven to such desperate crimes. Other writers showed less comprehension of the pressures to which the workers were subjected: they saw clearly only the fact that the union of workers on a national rather than a local scale was dangerous, and constituted a serious threat to the existing social and economic system. They all, including Mrs Gaskell, deplored the taking of an oath, by which a man pledges his freedom of action in the future, as intrinsically evil, and James, in *The Princess Casamassima*, conforms to the same pattern.

Another article in the *Contemporary Review* which James may have seen was the controversial 'Anarchy, by an Anarchist', an article the editors showed some courage in printing, which puts the whole anarchist case, including a defence of terrorism, very clearly indeed. This article may have suggested the Princess's cry: 'Are we on the eve of great changes, or are we not?' for the author, under the signature of 'Reclus', writes: 'In spirit revolution is ready; it is already thought — it is already willed; it only remains to realize it, and this is not the most difficult part of the work.'[41]

James's doubts as to the strength of his own radicalism which were earlier expressed in *A Little Tour in France* seem not to have been misplaced, if we look closely at *The Princess Casamassima*. It is true that, to use his own idiom, he 'went further' than Gissing in *Demos*, who had stated flatly that 'Changes will come about, but not of these men's making or devising'. Muniment, the strong man in *The Princess Casamassima*, carries conviction when he declares 'I believe . . . in the advent of democracy' and suggests that the process will be far from painless. In Muniment's words: '"It will help the democracy to get possession that the classes that keep them down shall be admonished from time to time that they've a very definite and very determined intention of doing so. An immense deal will depend upon that. Hoffendahl's a jolly admonisher."'[42] What Muniment is describing is class confrontation: the 'admonishing' of the privileged classes by acts of terrorism is one of the steps by which the people are to obtain power. The contorted sentence seems rather designed to conceal than to reveal this message, but James's man of the people, his future prime minister, is here speaking with approval of Hoffendahl's methods. James, that is to say, is making the same socialist = anarchist equation that is to be found in so many of the novels of his contemporaries, an equation which could only encourage his readers to side with the forces of conservatism. James even sacrifices credibility within the economy of the novel in order to put across his own views on the social question, and makes Hyacinth's consciousness the vehicle for the expression of the undercurrent of fear which ran through the privileged classes at the possibility of the overturning of the social order. Tilley has pointed out how the most phlegmatic readers of *The Times* must have been moved by the suggestion that some 'international group' aiming at the overthrow of governments was behind every local attempt, and toward the end of his novel James puts the same message not into Hyacinth's *mouth* (which might have been psychologically acceptable in that he would go to any lengths to win the attention of the Princess) but into his *mind*:

> — the sense, vividly kindled and never quenched, that the forces secretly arrayed against the present social order were pervasive and universal, in the air one breathed, in the ground one trod, in

the hand of an acquaintance that one might touch or the eye of a stranger that might rest a moment on one's own. They were above, below, within, without, in every contact and combination of life; and it was no disproof of them to say it was too odd they should lurk in a particular improbable form. To lurk in improbable forms was precisely their strength . . .[43]

This sense of the ubiquity of the conspiracy, a sense which served above all to obtain public approval for repressive measures, takes on its popular fictional form in the hints at the watch kept by the conspirators upon each other. When Hyacinth receives the fateful letter with instructions for the assassination, he holds the following conversation with Schinkel, the messenger:

'If you hadn't done your job you'd have paid for it.'
   Schinkel mumbled as for accommodation while he lingered, and then as Hyacinth turned away, putting in his door-key, brought out:
   'And if you don't do yours so will you.'[44]

This is the theme-song of all the conspiracy novels.

A social protest novel which James may have known (it was published toward the end of 1884) was Grant Allen's first novel *Philistia* which appeared under the pseudonym Cecil Power, for Allen was anxious to make his name as a scientist and feared, rightly or wrongly, that novel writing would detract from his reputation for serious scholarship. His own account of how he was driven to take 'the downward path that leads to fiction' simply to earn a living 'for Nellie and the boy' hardly explains his choice of subject, for *Philistia* runs counter to accepted opinion on every current question of British international and social policy. While his sympathy with the plight of the Nihilists is in line with advanced contemporary opinion the same cannot be said of his treatment of the oppression of the Irish peasantry to which he devotes a whole chapter. Over and above this, he is the only novelist of the period so far as I know who is seriously critical of British colonial policy in India. This independence of thought can best be explained by the fact that, though he was educated at Oxford and lived and worked principally in England, yet he was of Canadian birth and Franco-Irish extraction.

His first prose publication, in the *Oxford University Magazine and Review*, number 2, December 1869, was a paper on 'The Positive Aspects of Communism', and when he came to write his first novel he unashamedly voiced his own opinions. The novel, needless to say, was not a success. Its failure can scarcely have been due to the faults which are so evident today, ranging from unlikely psychology to therapeutic weeping, for these faults continue through into his many later and more successful novels.

What is refreshingly unusual about *Philistia* is its author's awareness, and examination of the techniques by which public opinion could be, and was being, constantly manipulated. His hero, Ernest, writes for the newspapers to make a living and is shocked and embittered to find how the editor changes the message in his articles by changing their slant, and Allen goes to some pains to illustrate to his readers, through elementary examples, exactly how this is done. The hero of the novel, and mouthpiece of its young author, writes a long and heartfelt defence of his friend the socialist leader Herr Schurz, whom he considers has been unjustly condemned in a trial for seditious libel and incitement to murder: 'He could recollect the very run of every clause and word he had written: "No Englishman can read without a thrill of righteous indignation," it began, "the sentence passed last night upon Max Schurz, the author of that remarkable economic work, 'Gold and the Proletariat'".'[45] Reading over his article as it appears in the press the next morning:

> His eye caught at once the opening key-words . . . 'No Englishman can read without a feeling of the highest approval the sentence passed last night upon Max Schurz, the author of that mis-guided economical work, 'Gold and the Proletariat' . . . It was his own leader, indeed, with the very rhythm and cadence of the sentences accurately preserved, but with all the adjectives and epithets so ingeniously altered that it was turned into a crushing condemnation of Max Schurz, his principles, his conduct, and his ethical theories.[46]

The editor somewhat improbably writes a note of explanation to Ernest to justify his tampering, but the author and his wife solemnly burn the enclosed cheque of eight guineas, though their larder is dramatically empty and they have breakfasted on dry bread and milkless tea. The uselessness of this brave gesture is shown only a few pages later, when Grant Allen goes on to illustrate how honest reporting can be crushed out of a young writer by the 'reasonable-ness' of editorial requirements: 'I hope you didn't mind the way I was obliged to cut them up in some unessential details, so as to suit the policy of the paper . . . You know we are above all things strictly moderate . . .'[47] — a passage where the word 'moderate' has a curiously modern connotation.

Lest the reader should miss the point he wants to make, Grant Allen gives further examples of the editorial changes, whereby 'the whole spirit of the thing had evaporated, or rather had been perverted into the exact opposite . . .' Where Ernest had written 'enthusiasm', Lancaster had simply altered the word to 'fanaticism', where Ernest had spoken of Herr Max's 'single-hearted devotion', Lancaster had merely changed the phrase to 'undisguised revolutionary ardour'.

By burning the cheque, or rather by pressurising his wife into burning it, Ernest had saved some of his self-respect. But Allen is not content to leave it at that: the whole question of freedom of expression is central to this novel. Once again the hero is subjected to the same ordeal when asked to write up the mutiny of a hill-tribe in India. In desperate need of money he writes the required article, on the understanding that the editor shall make whatever alterations he thinks fit to suit the policy of the paper. After consigning the article Ernest is seized with remorse: 'What right had we to conquer the Bodahls? What right had we to hold them in subjection or to punish them for revolting?' The remarkable feature of this chapter is Allen's full consciousness of the power of the writer, and especially of the journalist, to influence public opinion, and at the same time his awareness that there is a control of the media from above, in the interests of the establishment. Ernest struggles with his conscience:

> It was this, then, that he, the disciple of peace-loving Max Schurz, the hater of war and conquest, the foe of unjust British dominion over inferior races — it was this that he had helped to make plausible with his special knowledge and his ready pen! . . . In one moment he thought out a hundred scenes of massacre and pillage — scenes such as he knew only too well always precede and accompany the blessings of British rule in distant dependencies . . .[48]

The story ends in defeat, for though Ernest rushes back to the office in an attempt to stop publication, the type has been set up and the article is in the headlines next morning. In addition this time he does cash the cheque, to provide essential food for his baby daughter who is critically ill. Allen is, right at the outset, studying the difficulties in the path of a writer who wishes openly to express his own views of society, whenever these views run counter to those generally accepted at the time. He notes too how religion, that other powerful opinion maker, is similarly harnessed in defence of the *status quo*: 'Providence is supposed to have ordained the existing order for the time being, whatever it may be, but not the order that is at that exact moment endeavouring to supplant it.'[49]

Allen's own history as a novelist is the sad story of a thinking man driven to accept the rules laid down by editors and publishers, so that of his 41 works of fiction only a handful — the first novel *Philistia* and two which he wrote towards the end of his life, *The British Barbarians* and *The Woman Who Did*, contain anything more than sporadic traces of his real views on the major issues of the day.

Only in *Philistia* does Allen dare to introduce an international group of social agitators, very like those who meet at The Sun and Moon in James's *The Princess Casamassima*, or to allow his hero to raise the controversial Irish question at an earl's table in the presence of an absentee landlord, Lord Connemara, or again to present the Nihilist point of view through the words of Borodinsky who outlines the history of Romanoff repression, so that a listener who has attended the meeting for the first time comments: 'it never struck me to think what they might have to say for themselves from their own side of the question'. *Philistia* received few reviews and those few were unfavourable. Mr Chatto, exercising the temporal right of publishers, had already requested and obtained a happy ending, though Grant Allen protested that he did not well see how he could keep Ernest alive.

After the failure of *Philistia* Grant Allen was soon forced into an admission of total defeat: 'I am trying with each new novel to go a step lower to catch the market'; and Richard Le Gallienne tells us how Allen's friends were all obliged to make one promise: 'Never, under whatsoever temptation, to read one of his "commercial" novels'. One day I intend to show how Allen's ideas and ideals, variously disguised, seeped through even into these many pot-boilers: but that will be a long story. What is relevant here is that Allen never lost his awareness of the possibility of alternative points of view. In *Philistia* Ernest is speaking for his author when he assures his friend, who has attended a meeting of international socialists '"You may not agree with all you hear, but at least you learn to see others as they see themselves; whereas if you mix always in English society, and read only English papers, you will see them only as the English see them."'[50]

Conrad's short story 'The Anarchist' published in *A Set of Six* in 1908, but dated 1905-6 by Lawrence Graver,[51] turns entirely on the situation of a man who is hiding away from an anarchist group with which he has been connected. He has taken refuge on an island in the estuary of a great river in South America, where he works without wages, because it is the only place where he feels safe from his early associates, a group of housebreakers and bank robbers with political leanings. The whole story is told in retrospect. His troubles began when one evening he shouted *'Vive l'anarchie!'* which led to his imprisonment and subsequent involvement with a group of 'compagnons'. He is captured by the authorities during the first bank robbery in which he takes part, but seems throughout to be more afraid of the other members of the group than of the police. His own report runs:

> 'My beginner's part would be to keep watch in the street at the back and to take care of a black bag with the bomb inside until it was wanted. After the meeting at which the affair was arranged a trusty comrade did not leave me an inch. I had not dared to protest; I was afraid of being done away with quietly in that room.'[52]

The tale of his subsequent escape from a convict settlement and his enslavement to the man running a cattle ranch ends with his refusal to return to civilisation and freedom: 'I shall die here,' he says. Then adds moodily, 'Away from *them*.' Conrad is here simply echoing James and other conspiracy novelists in his picture of the terror which such groups exert over their own members, an element which was central in the dynamite romances.

Conrad's other tale dealing with an anarchist group, 'The Informer', was published in the same volume, and, according to Lawrence Graver, was written in December 1905. This tale recounts the watch kept on an anarchist group in Hermione Street, London, by the organisational headquarters in Brussels, in order to trace the source of a leak. The supergrass is caught by means of a faked police raid. But besides the spies spying on each other we meet once again in this story the figure of the professor, absurd yet ominous, whom the investigators find in his laboratory on the top floor of Hermione Street:

> There, surrounded by tins of Stone's Dried Soup, a comrade, nick-named the Professor (he was an ex-science student) was engaged in perfecting some new detonators. He was an abstracted, self-confident, sallow little man, armed with large round spectacles, and we were afraid that under a mistaken impression he would blow himself up and wreck the house about our ears. I rushed upstairs and found him already at the door, on the alert, listening, as he said, to 'suspicious noises down below . . .' His was the true spirit of an extreme revolutionist. Explosives were his faith, his hope, his weapon, and his shield. He perished a couple of years afterwards in a secret laboratory through the premature explosion of one of his improved detonators.[53]

With this version of 'the Professor' we have a return to the chemist Mezzeroff, the 'far more dangerous man', first presented to the British public with his collection of designs of infernal machines in 1885 by a correspondent from New York.

There is, however, no explosion in 'The Informer', and in fact I have found only one British naturalistic social novel (as opposed to dramatic romances and tales of science fiction) where an explosion actually occurs. This is Richard Whiteing's *No. 5 John Street* (1899), and the explosion with which the story ends is the work of a single anarchist and not of a conspiracy. The tale is set in the year of Queen Victoria's diamond jubilee (1897). The narrator undertakes to act as agent general and representative to this jubilee for a small Pacific island, and to write a report on the condition of England for the Governor. The purpose of the book is to illustrate the defects of the existing socio-economic structure simply by describing life as it is lived, for the edification of the islanders, whose experience is limited to their own primitive form of communism under the benevolent dictatorship of the island's Governor. The narrator, who moves in the best society and has £10,000 per year, conscientiously sets out to see for himself what life is like among the London poor, so that he may be able to send a reliable and circumstantial report:

> I had been invited to join a University settlement at the East

End. I went down to look at it, but it proved to be a mere peep-hole into the life I wanted to see, with the Peeping Tom still a little too much on the safe side. The inmate did not live the life. He observed it merely from the standpoint of all the comforts of home. And if he sometimes plunged into the waters of tribula-tion, it was only in corks.

Now the essence of my plan was that I should, for a certain time of probation, get my own living with my own hands. I not only wished to report with knowledge, but I was most eager to see what I was worth in the market. I, therefore, put myself under heavy bonds to Honour to find a job, and to make it keep me — say for six weeks. During that period, no matter what the hardship, or what the temptation, I would make my own earnings serve . . .[54]

Number five John Street is the address of his lodgings during this period, and he is befriended by such characters as Low Covey, Tilda the Amazonian flower-girl, Nance who dies of poisoning from her work in Sir Marmaduke's rubber factory, an old '48, who introduces himself: "'I'm a Social Democratic Federation, that's what I am, and a Anarshist after that.'"[55] yet another example of the by now familiar hybrid.

The character who brings the book alive is Tilda, one of the sisterhood to which Millicent Hennings, Eliza Doolittle and Liza of Lambeth belong, and whose warm-heartedness and generosity win the approval of the narrator whose solution for economic problems has hardly advanced beyond that of Dickens or Mrs Gaskell: 'Tilda scorns to bid for a place at the board, being under the impression that, the less eaten by those who can do without it, the more will there be left for those who cannot. This only shows that her political economy is scarcely in even the rudimentary stage.'[56] His satire is here directed not at Tilda's reasoning but at the principles which underlie the theories of political economy.

The flavour of the book comes from the contrast between the two spheres in which the narrator moves. In high society he listens to opinions like those of Sinclair: "'Circulate the wealth; you can't go wrong there. Can you now? Whenever I go to church for a charity sermon, and hear about poor people starving for want of money to buy a penny roll, I wish I had six stomachs, to hold as many meals.'"[57] and in John Street he listens to Tilda's comment when taken for an outing in the country: "'It's like a symetry,'" she murmurs, as though to mark her sense of the perfect peace.'[58] This picture of the country as a place for a day's outing is only one of the many Dickensian touches, and Whiteing's attack on the lethal working conditions in Sir Marmaduke's factory takes us back to the social protest novels of the mid-nineteenth century. The description of the stink of rubber from the factory which pollutes the surrounding dwellings is dealt with in the same facetious tone sometimes used by Dickens in his ecological sallies:

> For, to tell the truth, as to odours, our offence is somewhat rank, and what we may happen to lack in ozone we make up for in the vapour of naptha. The naptha begins a quarter of a mile away from my gate, and within that range the hardiest flowers have a desperate struggle for existence. There is not a flea in the factory — I say it with pride. The mephitic air grows thicker as you near the buildings, and within them it is a vapour that leaves no cranny unvisited as it mounts storey by storey to the roof. On the topmost floor we have another and a special infusion of carbon bi-sulphide, which is given off by the processes that involve some danger to life. As the whole combination rises to the sky, it is enough to make the angels hold their noses; and it must cause frequent false alarms there in its persistent suggestion of a leakage in the roof of hell.[59]

In the novels of the 1880s and 1890s social protest found its outlet in violence: either the secret violence of conspiracies involving only a small group of militants or the violence of class confrontation starting with the protest march and demonstration. The crowds are present in Whiteing for the jubilee, but they are the good-humoured crowds of a royal occasion, ready with their gibes at the nobs but ready too with 'Ooh, isn't she lovely' exclamations of awe and wonder. Tilda's conversation with the Princess of Wales, engaged in charity work, while the committee stand by helpless to intervene but 'to all appearances . . . engaged in mental prayer', shows that Whiteing, far from desiring the overturning of the *status quo*, was really only pleading for improved working conditions, and maybe higher wages, in the offensive factory.

The novel ends with a dynamite bomb attempt on Sir Marmaduke's mansion, the work of Azrael, a Russian exile. Of Azrael we are told little: '"They say he is a first-rater — college professor in his own country — but had to bolt, because they wanted to send him to Siberia. That's where they send most of 'em, I believe.'"[60] The narrator divines his purpose, no very difficult task, for when they burst into his room: 'The laboratory table is enough, with its litter of fulminates and acids and miscellaneous gear of the arsenal of Anarchy. His luggage is a bomb.'[61] Tilda however has been even quicker, and gallantly gives her life to save that of Sir Marmaduke and his friends, although she has just returned from the funeral of Nance, her closest friend, a victim of the factory fumes. The narrator arrives on the spot a moment too late:

> But before I reach it, a loud report rends the air, and I stop at last, only to see this — Tilda stretched dead and warm, and with the martyr's smile on her white face turned to the sky.
>
> Beside her, about her, lie the fragments of the murderer, with a rent in his side big enough to sink a ship. There is another rent in the low wall that separates the garden from the street. A conservatory beyond, which almost touches the wall, is a smoking ruin; and glimpsed through the smoke is a dining-room in hideous confusion, as host and guests stand petrified in the attitudes in which they have risen to their feet.
>
> The scene tells its own tale. The wretch tried to scale the wall so as to plant his charge against the house. The girl closed with him and dragged him back. But in the struggle the bomb exploded and did its work, alike on the guilty and the innocent.
>
> . . . This, then, was the dark decree. Tilda was to die with Nance — both victims, the one to the curse of the disease, the other to the curse of the remedy.[62]

By sacrificing the one great-hearted character of *No. 5* in the explosion Whiteing directs the sympathies of the reader, even supposing they were that way inclined, firmly away from Azrael and his 'remedy'. His socialists fare little better than his anarchist, for the spontaneous protest meeting that follows Nance's funeral is described as the 'Council of Pandemonium' which reveals 'the hate of the sections against one another as well as their hate of society': 'The Blacks of Anarchy scream their rage against the Reds of Social Democracy as sneaking poltroons who have gone the mile or twain, but shrink from the journey's end.'[63] The quarrel between socialists and anarchists, 'the delirium of plague-stricken wretches tearing each other on their beds of pain', degenerating into an open fight for the platform, almost certainly owed something to contemporary press reports of the in-fighting at international meetings where the delegates of different movements struggled for dominance. Whiteing believed in the old formula of goodness-at-heart for setting things to rights, and implies that protest meetings in themselves are deleterious.

Notwithstanding all the trouble that the narrator has put himself to in order to obtain first-hand information for the Islanders we are hardly surprised when they refuse to believe him, and when they totally reject his version of the 'condition of England' question.

Nor are the socialists treated any better in Charles Gleig's *When All Men Starve*, 1897, another jubilee novel. The socialist = anarchist equation is never questioned here, and the last chapter of the book, entitled 'Anarchy', narrates the rising of the masses and the sacking and burning of Buckingham Palace:

> To-night, at least, there is no Government, no Parliament, no police. Each man has become a law unto himself, and the Have Nots prey unrestrained upon the goods of the defenceless, emasculated owners of property . . . King Anarchy assumes the purple robe of government and holds high revel.[64]

The stress is all on destruction, there is no hint at an alternative economic system or a planned society. The 'student of Socialist newspapers' described as a 'burly ruffian' thinks that 'it would be well to make a bonfire of this royal domain as a sort of public protest against the principles of government'. Works of art are wantonly destroyed: 'The pictures they care not for, and slash and destroy as they hurry from room to room.'[65] In a reminiscence of the end of Disraeli's *Sybil*, a few of the rioters, muddled with drink and blinded by smoke, perish fearfully in the leaping flames. The last words of the novel are a repetition of the kind of anti-socialist propaganda which had been so effective in fiction throughout the century, the picture of a dawn which holds no hope:

> The mob dances its mad dance of anarchy, revelling in the downfall of the Respectabilities, forgetting in this brief hour of its triumph the curse of Labour, the squalid wretchedness of vanished years.
> So they dance on, till the grey dawn steals up from the east and

the burnt palace looms black and haggard in the cold light of morning.[66]

Only one novel before the end of the century really overturned accepted values, and this was *An Unsocial Socialist* by George Bernard Shaw, published in 1884. Agatha, the heroine, slides into the story down the banisters, but the novelty of Shaw's approach goes beyond this gesture in the face of convention. Reading a volume of clinical lectures and feeling discouraged because her own sensations were exactly like those described in the book as the symptoms of the direst diseases, Agatha puts it by in alarm to take up a novel: '. . . which was free from the fault she had found in the lectures, inasmuch as none of the emotions it described in the least resembled any she had ever experienced.'[67] Shaw's rebellion against the norms of the social novel is no less fundamental than is his attack on the psychology of the novels of the nineteenth century. Through the character of Sidney Trefusis, *alias* Smilash, Shaw questions the validity of the entire system both of the family and of society. Trefusis, a professional agitator, has no time for the man who wants to heave a brick, let alone a dynamite bomb. Speaking of a bargeman, he comments:

'This man is one of my converts,' said Trefusis apart to Henrietta. 'He told me the other day that since I set him thinking he never sees a gentleman without feeling inclined to heave a brick at him. I find that socialism is often misunderstood by its least intelligent supporters and opponents to mean simply unrestrained indulgence in our natural propensity to heave bricks at respectable persons.'[68]

That this misunderstanding of socialism 'by its least intelligent supporters and *opponents*' was extremely widespread can be seen from the survey of the 1886 novels in this chapter, all written just after Shaw's criticism and reflecting views which the young Shaw, an unorthodox Marxist, was calling in question. His technique was the use of shock tactics, as when he debunks Victorian sentimentality by suspending a love scene to give space to an ecological discourse against the pollution of the English waterways. It was at least two centuries since the *carpe diem* theme had been put across so trenchantly: '"Why do you stare at that cursed canal, blindly dragging its load of filth from place to place until it pitches it into the sea — just as a crowded street pitches its load into the cemetery? Stare at *me*, and give me a kiss.'"[69] The passage is perhaps even more startling in that the girl Trefusis is speaking to happens to be his wife.

Unfortunately Shaw's novel gets completely out of hand: the plot grows more and more farcical and Trefusis's chosen vehicle, the diatribe, grows wearying. But both the tone and the message belong to the future, whereas the most striking thing about most of the novels that I have been considering is that, however up-to-date in content, their tone and message belong to the past. In some ways the social novels of the 1880s and 1890s seem more out of touch with reality than those of the 1840s and 1850s. Dynamite found its way into fiction but did little to disrupt either the form of the novel or the social *mores* with which it was dealing. The last chapters of almost all the novels I have examined in this book distribute rewards and punishments on the same basis as they had been doing throughout the century, nor has the nature of those rewards and punishments altered. Security may be tottering, but money, social position and a 'good' wife are the status symbols awarded to those who stand firm against the attacks on society, while the dynamitard, as often as not, is hoist with his own petard.

Notes

1. *Letters of George Gissing to Members of his Family*, A. & E. Gissing (eds.) (London, 1927).

2. Ibid.

3. George Gissing, *Demos: A Story of English Socialism*, three vols. (London, 1886). Quotations are taken from the 1972 photographic reproduction of the 1897 edition; Vol. 3, p. 102.

4. Ibid., Vol. 3, p. 113.

5. Ibid., Vol. 3, p. 118.

6. Ibid., Vol. 3, p. 116.

7. Ibid., Vol. 3, p. 121.

8. Ibid., Vol. 2, p. 115.

9. Ibid., Vol. 1, p. 118.

10. Ibid., Vol. 3, p. 235.

11. The choice of name for the man of the people in these 1886 novels, in Gissing *Mutimer*, in Besant *Monument* and in James *Muniment* can hardly be a coincidence, and deserves further study. He appears in James's notebooks in an entry for 9 July 1884 together with other possible names for use in *The Princess Casamassima* 'Langrish, Pynsent, Muniment'. Gissing had already used his form of the name in a short story 'Mutimer's Choice' dated by Coustillas June or early July 1884, so James may have had this in mind. Besant insists on the name: 'Violet considered the name for a moment. "Monument". It might have been worse. Fancy being a monument.'

12. Walter Besant, *Children of Gibeon*, three vols. (London, 1886), Vol. 1, p. 75.

13. Ibid., Vol. 1, p. 68.

14. Ibid., Vol. 1, p. 72.

15. Ibid., Vol. 1, p. 45.

16. W. H. Mallock, *The Old Order Changes*, three vols. (London, 1886), Vol. 1, p. 306.

17. Ibid., Vol. 1, pp. 49-50.

18. Ibid., Vol. 1, pp. 163-4.

19. Ibid., Vol. 1, p. 130.

20. Ibid., Vol. 1, p. 284.

21. Ibid., Vol. 1, p. 299.

22. Ibid., Vol. 2, p. 50.

23. Ibid., Vol. 2, p. 63.

24. Ibid., Vol. 1, p. 214.

25. See note 14 to Chapter 4 above.

26. Mallock, *The Old Order Changes*, Vol. 3, pp. 31-2.

27. Ibid., Vol. 3, pp. 34-5.

28. Ibid., Vol. 3, p. 47.

29. Ibid., Vol. 3, p. 49.

30. Ibid., Vol. 3, p. 215.

31. Henry James, *Letters*, Léon Edel (ed.), Vol. 3, 1883-1895 (London, 1981), p. 146.

32. Henry James, *A Little Tour in France* (Boston, 1884). Quotations from Tauchnitz edition (Stuttgart, 1954), p. 279.

33. James, *The Princess Casamassima*, p. 279.

34. Ibid., preface.

35. Ibid., p. 100.

36. Basing himself on *The Times*, W. H. Tilley in *The Background of 'The Princess Casamassima'* (Florida, 1961) makes out a very convincing case for the Rupsch-Reinsdorf connection. I have included some of the current press reports of their trial in Chapter 2 above. Lionel Trilling in *The Liberal Imagination* (New York, 1950) suggests that Mikhail Bakunin or Johann Most (who was a bookbinder by profession) are the likeliest historical sources. There seems to be no reason why James should not have incorporated suggestions from a number of contemporary figures. See my essay 'Democrazia e decoro: Princess Casamassima' in *Il gusto di Henry James*, Barbara and Giorgio Melchiori (Turin, 1974) for further discussion of the sources of *The Princess*.

37. James, *The Princess Casamassima*, p. 196.

38. Ibid., pp. 334-5.

39. *Temple Bar*, November 1885, p. 316.

40. James, *The Princess Casamassima*, p. 493.

41. Elisée Reclus, 'Anarchy by an Anarchist', *Contemporary Review* (May, 1884).

42. James, *The Princess Casamassima*, pp. 377-8.

43. Ibid., p. 415.

44. Ibid., p. 482.

45. Charles Grant Blairfindie Allen (pseudonym Cecil Power), *Philistia*, three vols. (London, 1884), Vol. 3, p. 81.

46. Ibid., Vol. 3, p. 82.

47. Ibid., Vol. 3, p. 91.

48. Ibid., Vol. 3, p. 128.

49. Ibid., Vol. 1, p. 92.

50. Ibid., Vol. 1, p. 29.

51. Lawrence Graver, *Conrad's Short Fiction* (Berkeley, Cal., 1969).

52. Joseph Conrad 'The Anarchist' in *A Set of Six*, 1908. Both this story and 'The Informer' are thought by Graver and by Daleski to have been completed before Conrad began work on *The Secret Agent*. All quotations from *A Set of Six* in Conrad's

Collected Works (London, 1921-7) p. 149.

53. Joseph Conrad, 'The Informer' in *A Set of Six*, p. 88.
54. Richard Whiteing, *No. 5, John Street* (London, 1899), p. 11.
55. Ibid., p. 87.
56. Ibid., p. 257.
57. Ibid., p. 167.
58. Ibid., p. 285.
59. Ibid., p. 224.
60. Ibid., p. 181.
61. Ibid., p. 321.
62. Ibid., pp. 321-2.
63. Ibid., p. 319.
64. Charles Gleig, *When All Men Starve* (London and New York, 1897), p. 187.
65. Ibid., p. 190.
66. Ibid., p. 192.
67. George Bernard Shaw, *An Unsocial Socialist* (London, 1887. First published in *Today*, 1884). Quotations are taken from the Virago edition (London, 1980), p. 139. This observation of the psychological effect of reading a medical encyclopedia was exploited with great success a few years later by J. K. Jerome in *Three Men in a Boat* (Bristol, 1889).
68. Ibid., pp. 78-9.
69. Ibid., p. 66.

DYNAMITE ROMANCES

Most of the novels that I have been writing about are, to a greater or lesser extent, committed novels: they carry a conscious message from author to reader in however muddled or even contradictory a form. But there are many other dynamite and conspiracy novels where the author is taking no conscious political or social stance, in which we find some or all of the elements already discussed: the secret society, the figure of the chemist, assassination as an end in itself.

It would be a mistake to think that these novels carry no message. Reading them today, at another time and in another place, it is easy to pick out the shared assumptions between author and contemporary reader which serve to reinforce traditional accepted moral, social and political principles. It is only when an author is contradicting the expectations of his readers that he needs to pause and explain, to give examples and to prove his points. The bulk of nineteenth-century novels, however, rest firmly on a basis of given and unquestioned patterns of social behaviour, censoring any deviation from this norm by making the last chapter a prize day on which there are never any surprises. The plots can be up-dated with the introduction of topical events and even the discussion of new ideas, but in the end everything must be put back into its place in the social order.

What I have called dynamite romances are for the most part a hotch-potch of elements borrowed from the more serious novelists, jumbled together to make a readable tale, and structured with the elaborate plot development of a modern photo-romance. Quite a number of these ran as serials in the weekly and monthly magazines which abound in the 1880s, a good example being Miss Betham-Edwards's *The Flower of Doom* which came out in *All the Year Round* from March to May 1885. While the more serious novelists try to give their stories a credible social and geographical setting, these romancers prefer to avoid the task of research by keeping everything vague. The hero and heroine of *The Flower of Doom* belong to an unidentified country where 'an outlandish jargon' is spoken. The hero, or anti-hero, is a conspirator and dynamiter, and the lady pleads with him to turn over a new leaf: 'Is there not misery enough in the world that you must heap up the sum? And in these black plots and fiendish intrigues, it is ever the innocent who suffer for the guilty.'[1] The temptation to reform a villain is one of the strongest impulses to which Victorian heroines are subjected, and Bernarda cannot at first resist his pleas: '"I, the arch conspirator, cannot live alone. We dynamiters, as they call us, need sympathy as well as ordinary men."'[2] Doubts as to his nationality assail the reader when he declares: '". . . yet were I called upon in this sacred, this awful cause, to connive at the destruction of an entire city — aye, were it London itself, I should say, not the vindictiveness of man but the indignation of Heaven has spoken!"'[3] Could the 'outlandish jargon' that Miss Betham-Edwards has in mind conceivably be Irish? His name, after all, is Edgeworth. Later in the story we find confirmation of this, for 'The ring with its impearled shamrock glittered on her finger. The fragile china cup she now handed to him had a shamrock too.'[4]

From the conspiracy novels (it seems legitimate to assume that she never read the newspapers) the author has taken over the idea of the watch kept by the conspirators over each other, so that Edgeworth argues that he is trapped in the conspiracy and cannot escape, yet at the same time holds forth on the nobility of the Cause: '"Should I from choice, think you, league myself with midnight assassins and contrivers of wholesale murder — join the fellowship of desperadoes who would give me my death-stab tomorrow if I betrayed them? . . . Thus ignominiously to die for our people were, in my eyes, a holy martyrdom."'[5] Bernarda marries the conspirator sacrificing herself in the noble attempt to wean him from his evil ways. Then she realises that she is too late, and it comes to her that: 'He had all along pledged himself to take part in some dreadful deed, and was now finally called upon to fulfil his word, or perhaps some horrid lot had fallen to his name, and he was singled out by chance of all his confederates to be the perpetrator of some unparalleled crime.'[6]

This was exactly the situation in which Henry James's Hyacinth was soon to find himself — James started publishing *The Princess Casamassima* only a few months after these words appeared in the 25 April issue of *All the Year Round*. Rather than a direct influence I think that both writers were dipping in their very different ways into the bran tub of conspiracy and fishing out whatever suited their stories. Miss Betham-Edwards's heroine wins through in the end, after much preaching: '"You cannot disarm conscience. And you are one of the leaders. Your defection on moral grounds would be as an inner voice speaking to many.'"[7] But it is only when she receives the secret message in the form of the flower of doom (the conspirators, it seems, have begun to consider her interference as an unwarranted threat to their designs), and is mysteriously murdered, that Edgeworth is convinced at last of the error of his ways, so that the tale ends with his unconditional surrender of his views:

> From that day, Edgeworth, the anarchist, the dynamiter, the revolutionary, disappeared from the scenes . . . The plotter now plotted against his followers, his former creeds. Whenever some revolutionary enterprise miscarried, or some deep-laid scheme was revealed, he was said to be at the bottom of the disclosure. The arch-conspirator of former days now lived but to frustrate conspiracies. For the sake of his murdered wife, who had endeavoured to change his purpose, he had become the deadliest enemy of his old associates.[8]

The scheme of this tale is thoroughly traditional: instead of reforming a drunkard or a gamester the heroine is called upon to reform a dynamiter, and is so far successful that if the economy of the plot cannot allow her to live (her death being the mechanism which sprung the reform) at least she is seen to die happily ever after. That the life of a heroine should be sacrificed to the redemption of a hero was considered a fair exchange in the accepted social economics of the novel.

Vagueness was not the prerogative of Miss Betham-Edwards. When E. Lynn Linton, again in 1885, wishes to discredit Kirkland's wife in *The Autobiography of Christopher Kirkland* so that her hero can be justified in separating from her, she involves her in an intrigue with a young Pole who was said to have escaped from prison. He is brought to Kirkland's house by one of his wife's political friends and is given asylum. Kirkland explains: 'Who he was, what he was, what he had done there or was doing here, I did not know then and I do not know now. That he was the centre of some movement and held the strings of some plot was evident: but in what direction and to what end, were kept from me.'[9] Holding the strings of some plot has exactly the same vague yet menacing sound here that it has in James's *The Princess Casamassima*, where the same thing is said of Hoffendahl. The plot in *Christopher Kirkland* includes 'experiments in chemistry', so that the experienced reader will at once jump to the conclusion that dynamite is involved; and the fact that the refugee and Kirkland's wife conduct their experiments in an upper room from which the husband is rigidly excluded convey if not proof positive, sufficient innuendo to condemn the lady out of hand.

In Grant Allen's *For Maimie's Sake* (1886) the chemist theme is central, and once more the chemist is a Pole, Benyowski, who seems to be well versed in the experiments of Mezzeroff. The author of *Philistia* by now had his finger very much on the pulse of the times, ten years later he produced *The Woman Who Did* which enjoyed such a *succès de scandal*, so it is hardly surprising to find him trying his hand at the dynamite novel. It is a tangled tale, but is worth a closer look.

The hero is Sydney Chevenix, a gentleman and an amateur scientist who dabbles in dynamite: he is attempting to invent a silent explosive. His paid assistant, Benyowski, is strictly a professional. He refers to an occasion when at St Petersburg an attempt was made to remove unobtrusively the chief of the Investigation Bureau in the Police Department:

> 'The charge exploded with very little detonation, comparatively
> . . . I believe, indeed, with careful experimentation, it might be
> made, almost, if not quite, completely noiseless . . . It blew up
> vertically, exerting hardly any lateral pressure . . . It blew up the
> — well, the objects above it, straight into the air; and when I last
> saw it, it had knocked — h'm — the objects in question — slap
> against the ceiling. But I didn't wait to see much of the explosion.
> The circumstances were unfavourable to scientific observation
> . . . it exploded beautifully, and the Chief of the Investigation
> Bureau executed an upward movement of extraordinary rapidity
> towards the offices of the Third Section, just overhead. For
> myself, though present only in the quality of spectator (I need
> hardly say) I judged it prudent not to await the moment of his
> subsidence.'[10]

Grant Allen, in a friendly discussion between these two men, the gentleman amateur and the Nihilist, puts the case for the alternative uses of dynamite, and naturally sides with the gentleman amateur.

> 'A good easy explosive for blasting rock with — a new power to
> cheapen the construction of railway tunnels, of canals, of docks,

of harbours — a material that will enable us to do away at once with the Alps and the Pyrenees, with Panama and Caucasus, with the Himalayas and the Hindu Kush — that would be a thousand times more practically valuable to the world in the end than all your beautiful Utopian plans for the ultimate regeneration of human society by blowing up the Czar or the Chief of the Third Section.'[11]

The author has no doubts that his readers will agree with him over the value of dynamite in the development of civil engineering. What is more surprising for a reader today is the way in which Sydney Chevenix continues his argument:

'Just picture to yourself the use of such an explosive in war, for example! You're fighting a lot of uncivilized enemies, and you set out your sharp-shooters under cover somewhere, and they pick off the enemy, one by one, noiselessly, silently, unseen, unsuspected; and the unsophisticated savages don't even know they're being shot, or where the firing comes from, but merely find their men dropping all around them like magic by the dozen, as if an invisible fire from heaven had suddenly smitten them . . . There's an engine of civilization for you.'[12]

Allen's contemporaries may be forgiven for failing to suspect that he wrote this passage with his tongue in his cheek, for Chevenix is described as 'rubbing his hands briskly with all an inventor's enthusiasm'. Yet by contrasting the British and Polish scientists' views as to the proposed application of dynamite in practical politics, Allen is tacitly inviting his readers to pause and think. Benyowski suggests that it should be used in a Nihilist assassination:

'You're fighting a lot of enemies of the human kind — emperors and bureaucrats and such-like vermin — and you stick a little bit of the new explosive under the chief criminal's bed, and it goes off pop in the middle of the night, noiselessly, silently, unheard, unnoticed, and nobody even so much as suspects the miscreant's dead, till some flunkey or other goes in in the morning and finds the creature's remains lying in little fragments scattered all about promiscuously over the bed and carpet — here a leg, and there an arm, and yonder a rib or two! Ha! Ha! that would be just magnificent, wouldn't it? That would, indeed, be developing the resources of civilization!'[13]

The resultant mess, whether the raw material of the experiment was emperor or savages, can be presumed to be qualitatively much the same and quantitatively much less in the case of the emperor, as Allen was well aware, but by describing in horrific terms the result of the Nihilist's explosion as opposed to the tidy 'picking off' and 'dropping' of the enemies in the war against the savages, the author is tipping the scales of reader-sympathy in favour of Chevenix's application. That is to say Allen is here using the technique of the weighted word, of which he had so bitterly complained in *Philistia*, in the interests of the British as opposed to the Polish scientists, and in support of the exploiters rather than the exploited. Only by exaggerating the utterances of Benyowski so that his dynamite explosion is seen in terms of comic effect, and only by presenting the Pole as a stage villain ('and Stanislas Benyowski laughed silently the suppressed laugh of a professional plotter') can Allen salvage some rags of self-respect when writing what his readers expect to be told, in the way they expect to be told it.

That Allen himself felt that he had salvaged something from the wreck of his self-esteem is suggested by the fact that Richard Le Gallienne, when he reports how Grant Allen's friends were forbidden to read his commercial novels, adds 'And indeed, I must not forget Grant Allen made one exception: *For Maimie's Sake.*' So presumably Allen felt that his own friends would be able to read the passages quoted as ironical. The novel is indeed a curious one.

Chevenix is presented, in contrast to Benyowski the plotter, as the disinterested scientist, at work on the perfect explosive: 'It'll be a splendid thing, if only we can develop it. I shall work day and night at the investigation myself till I've got it perfect.' Although this is his intention Maimie intervenes, and she interrupts an experiment at a critical point rather than keep her waiting. Maimie falls into the 'Eve' category of Victorian heroines and in the end, when Chevenix has chivalrously disappeared for her sake so as to leave the road clear for his friend Adrian whom Maimie obviously prefers, she marries Adrian.

In order to disappear Chevenix disguises himself as his dead assistant and finds himself at the heart of a Nihilist dynamite conspiracy. Fortunately Vera Trotsky, the leader of the conspirators, falls in love with him and protects him against the suspicions of the other plotters. What a suspicious crowd they are: much of the novel is concerned with their elaborate plans to eliminate each other, bringing the story into line with other dynamite novels. Vera

Trotsky also conforms to type in that she moves on two levels, she is to be met in good society and she takes command at the secret meetings of the conspirators. Chevenix is allowed by the author to be attracted to her, for 'A woman's sympathy is always grateful to a man in adversity, even though the woman herself who gives it be an adamantine communist.' She never succeeds in converting Sydney, though his views on social justice undergo a certain modification when he finds himself compelled to live on his assistant's salary after he has taken the dead man's place: '. . . for the first time in his life Sydney Chevenix began to reflect to himself that a hundred a year had been really a very beggarly salary to offer an accomplished chemist like Stanislas Benyowski.'[14] Fortunately, being a gentleman, he can fall back on article writing for the journals to round off his £100 per year.

The conspirators run true to type in the energy they expend on impeaching and eliminating each other, which allows at least for the practical experimentation of new dynamite techniques. One is removed by Benyowski with an explosive cigar, which should have left no trace, in defiance of 'the clumsy English policemen'. Grant Allen comes down on the side of law and order, and his superintendent (one of a long line to follow in fiction) is too clever to be taken in:

> 'It's very fortunate', the superintendent murmured reflectively, 'that we happened to dredge up that end of cigar stuck into the mouth. If he hadn't been smoking it, so, in a holder, and if the holder hadn't been driven right through the palate in the way it was, we shouldn't have had anything tangible to go upon to show it was anything more than an ordinary boating accident. Of course, the circumstances would have been very suspicious — very suspicious; but there'd have been nothing really damaging or convincing to go to a jury.'[15]

And it is a policeman who sums up the predicament of the conspirators, all more afraid of each other than of the law and its representatives:

> 'It's clear,' the inspector said, shaking his head with an air of profound but baffled wisdom, 'he's afraid to tell us what he knows about the matter. He's terrorized by the others, that's the long and the short of it. It's always the way with these foreigner

communist people. Even if you shoot them, they won't peach upon one another. He thinks if he tells nothing now, they may let him off this time with just a bullet through his breast by way of a warning; but if he confesses how it all happened, they'll kill him before long, as safe as houses. And upon my word, if I were in his place, I don't know but that I'd do as he does. It's a deuced awkward thing to have a pack of these lawless communist people down upon you in a regular body.'[16]

Grant Allen is here subscribing to the traditional fictional view, which was to some extent substantiated by the facts published in the press, that the conspirator's worst enemies were his fellow conspirators and that the fear of defection or infiltration set in motion a process of impeachment and auto-elimination that effectively blocked the activities for which the group had originally been formed, a view in which novel readers no doubt took some comfort, especially as it was conveyed to them in the trustworthy form of the utterances of a police inspector.

Hugh Conway, whose real name was Frederick John Fargus, was a bestseller writer, and his *Called Back*, first published in 1884, ran into a new edition the following year. To a modern reader it is a highly melodramatic rigmarole which stretches credibility to the utmost. Gilbert Vaughan, the hero, goes blind at the beginning of the story, and setting out alone for a walk by night lets himself into the wrong house and stumbles into a room where a murder is taking place. His life is spared because his blindness prevents him from identifying the criminals, who turn out much later in the novel to be Italian patriots, Macari and Dr Ceneri, engaged in a conspiracy involving the assassination of the Czar. If this seems an unlikely occupation for an Italian patriot we can find at least one other example in fiction, in Hatton's *By Order of the Czar* in which Ferrari (in the stage version Ferari) plays a not insignificant part in Russian affairs.

Having witnessed, or having not witnessed, the murder, the narrator's sight is restored through surgery, and travelling with a friend in Italy he falls in love with a girl glimpsed outside a church, only to lose trace of her. Meeting her soon after in Regent Street, London, he discreetly follows her home and takes lodgings in the same house. She is closely guarded by a watch-dog in the form of an old Italian maid, Teresa. The narrator buys Teresa's support and seeks an introduction to the girl's guardian and uncle. He also learns that she is called Pauline. He soon satisfies the guardian, Dr Ceneri, of his respectability and sound financial position and arranges to marry Pauline if she will accept him. The marriage is fixed for the next day, Dr Ceneri answering for Pauline's acquiesence. The narrator quickly learns that he has married a girl who has lost her memory, who obeys every order but has no mind or will of her own. Entrusting Pauline once more to Teresa he rushes back to Italy to confront the guardian, and learns that the injury to his wife's mind was traumatic.

The title refers to the process by which her mind is called back to the moment when she had witnessed the murder of a youth: the narrator, by leading her to the spot (which is the same house that he had entered by mistake as a blind man) recreates the situation in which she suffered the shock, and (after a near-fatal attack of brain-fever) her memory is restored. *But* the time for a happy ending is not yet.

Before claiming his rights as a husband, the narrator is determined to learn the identity of the murdered youth who had meant so much to Pauline. From this point onwards the novel is concerned with the narrator's quest for this information, which takes him half-way across the world. Why, one wonders today, did he not simply ask his wife, now that her memory was restored. But no, there were certain questions that a gentleman could not put to a lady, and besides he has not revealed to her that she is his wife until he can learn more about her past (her memory has been restored only up to the moment of the murder).

The narrator returns once more to Italy where he learns that Dr Ceneri has been arrested in St Petersburg under charge of conspiracy against the life of the Czar. Macari, a confederate, who had been in love with Pauline himself, lies to the narrator, telling him that the murdered youth had been Pauline's lover. The narrator is greatly upset, but does not wholly trust Macari, and determines to make the long journey to St Petersburg to ascertain the truth from Dr Ceneri himself. The conversation between the narrator and Macari on this occasion gives an idea of how very generic were the details of the conspiracy. The narrator is the interrogator:

'How long do you stay?'
'Until I am called abroad again. Things have gone very wrong with us there. I must wait until the atmosphere has quieted down.'

I looked at him enquiringly.

'I fancied you knew my trade,' he said.

'I suppose you are a conspirator — I don't use the word offensively, it is the only one I can think of.'

'Yes. Conspirator — regenerator — apostle of freedom, whatever you like.'

'But your country has been free for some years.'

'Other countries are not free. I work for them. Our poor friend Ceneri did the same, but his last day's work is done.'

'Is he dead?' I asked, startled.

'Dead to all of us. I cannot give you particulars, but a few weeks after you left Geneva he was arrested at St Petersburgh. He lay in prison for months awaiting his trial. It has come off, I hear.'

'Well, what has happened to him?'

'What always happens — our poor friend is at this moment on his way to Siberia, condemned to twenty years' hard labour at the mines.'

Although I bore no particular love to Ceneri, I shuddered as I heard his fate.[17]

Arriving in St Petersburg the narrator finds that Ceneri has already been despatched on the long trek to Siberia. Before setting off in pursuit Vaughan is granted an interview with the Russian chief of police, and the activities of the revolutionaries are discussed:

I learned from the suave, obliging Russian chief of police that a few weeks after I had seen him in Geneva, Ceneri had been arrested in St Petersburgh. A deeply laid plot, involving the assassination of the Czar and several members of the government, had been revealed through the treachery of a confederate. The police, fully cognisant of everything, had waited until the pear was nearly ripe, and then struck with dire results to the plotters. Scarcely one of the principals escaped, and Ceneri, one of the most deeply implicated, was shown scant mercy. He certainly had few claims on their consideration. He was no Russian groaning under oppression and despotic government. Although he called himself Italian, he was, in truth, cosmopolitan. One of those restless spirits who wish to overturn all forms of government, save that of republican. He had plotted and schemed — even fought like a man — for Italian freedom. He had been one of Garibaldi's most trusted workmen; but had turned fiercely against his master when he found Italy was to be a Kingdom, not the ideal republic of his dreams. Latterly he had directed his attention to Russia, and the plot he was engaged in having been betrayed, his career, in all human probability, was ended.[18]

Armed with diplomatic permits granting him an interview with Ceneri, if he can find him, the narrator crosses thousands of *versts*, by rail and by tarantass, until he catches up with the exile who is reduced to a pitiable state. The conditions in the Russian prison are described as being appalling, but once again Conway relies on vagueness — the only detail to which he pays much attention being the noisome smell:

> 'This is the prisoner I am looking for,' I said, turning to the officer who stood at my side, mitigating to some extent the noxiousness of the atmosphere by the cigarette he puffed vigorously.
>
> 'I am glad you have found him,' he said politely. 'Now the sooner we get outside the better; the air here is unhealthy.'
>
> Unhealthy! It was foetid! I was filled with wonder, as I looked at the bland French-speaking captain at my side, at the state of mind to which a man must bring himself before he could calmly stand in the middle of his fellow-creatures and see such misery unconcernedly — could even think he was but doing his duty.[19]

After communicating the precious information that the murdered youth was not Pauline's lover but her brother, Ceneri is regaled on bread and meat by the narrator and registers his own protest against Russian prisons, but again there is no documentation, only an unsubstantiated reference to 'horrors'.

> 'I swear to you, sir,' he continued with more fire and animation than he had yet displayed, 'that if the civilized nations of Europe knew one-tenth part of the horrors and deeds in a Russian prison, they would say, "Guilty or innocent, no human beings should be tormented like this," and for the sake of common humanity would sweep the whole accursed government from the face of the earth.'[20]

Conway, that is to say, has picked up the anti-Russian message which was in the air (and in the newspapers) at the time, and is passing it on without going to any trouble to absorb it and make it his own. His political confusion can be seen in his authorial comment on Ceneri's patriotism: 'Let us be for years and years at the mercy of a foreigner, and we may understand what patriotism, in Ceneri's sense, means.' The relevance of this comment to Ceneri's support of Garibaldi and to the freeing of Italy from Austrian domination is clear, but it is difficult to see how it can be applied to his subsequent activity among the Nihilists. There is a lot of muddled thinking, as well as muddled storytelling, in the book, but as it was more widely read than much better books we cannot afford to overlook its relevance.

Two other conspiracy novels concerning Italian patriots are worthy of attention, George Fleming's *Vestigia*, 1884, and F. Marion Crawford's *Marzio's Crucifix*, 1887. They are pre-dynamite historical novels (though one of them mentions the Orsini bomb) concerned with the unification of Italy, but as they were being written in the 1880s they contain implicit comment also on contemporary events. *Vestigia* may also have influenced James's *The Princess Casamassima*. The plot of this novel is refreshingly simple. Told off to assassinate the King of Italy, in Piazza Indipendenza in Rome, after he has taken a mysterious pledge at the Circolo Barsanti, Bernardino de Rossi (Dino) manages to let nearly as many people know about his predicament as Hyacinth Robinson was to do. And, as in Hyacinth's case, everyone is very anxious to save him from the results of his pledge. His future father-in-law, Andrea, offers his savings to buy him off. Italia, his fiancée, insists that his little sister Palmira shall accompany him to Rome to provide him with an alibi, and Valdez, who had involved him in the conspiracy, fires the shot instead of handing the pistol to Dino as had been planned. Valdez is imprisoned (the shot had missed the king and wounded a marchese) and Dino returns home to marry Italia.

The arch-conspirator, like Hoffendahl in James's novel, is a stranger, a German, who 'had the power of assuming at will an indescribable air of ease and authority'; he was a man 'accustomed to undisputed command'. His hand is marked by an ugly scar, 'the red mark of an old wound'. Dino falls under his spell and places himself unconditionally at the service of the movement, as Hyacinth was to do.

'What is there to be done, sir? I'm ready', he said quietly.

The German looked at him grimly for a moment, and then for the first time his face relaxed into its wonderful child-like smile.

'*Schön*', he said approvingly.[21]

Like Hyacinth too, Dino at once starts to repent of his rash pledge:

He stood up suddenly in his place, and stared at the three impassive faces before him. They were all watching him.

'My God!' he said in a broken whisper; 'great God! *you want me to assassinate the King!*'[22]

And throughout the novel he continues to reflect more and more regretfully on what he will be called upon to do: 'It had seemed so easy a thing then to pledge away his future. He had done it without consulting Valdez — suddenly, madly, on the desperate impulse of the moment. He had done it in a moment of mental crisis; because he believed in the cause, heart and soul, because he had been a fool.'[23] A Russian countess takes a passing interest in Dino, and although her role in the story is only marginal, yet the tone in which she questions him is surprisingly like the tone used by the Princess to Hyacinth in James's novel:

'. . . he says you are one of the discontented people, — a radical, a red republican, *que sais-je — moi*? Is it true?' she asked calmly, fixing her large disdainful eyes upon the young man's face.

He bowed gravely. 'Since the Signora Contessa does me the honour to inquire. I am a radical; that is my belief.'

'Really? And you think we are all equal? We are all equally discontented, 'tis true enough; *mais après*?'[24]

In the second volume the full meaning of his sacrifice dawns on Dino, who is shocked not only by the act which he will be called upon to perform, but also slowly realises that he has signed his own death warrant:

That he was to forfeit his life in the proposed attempt was so much a foregone conclusion he did not even think of it. He could have sworn that he had never thought of it once since that first branding instant of revelation; but the conviction of it had eaten its way into him until it had become a part of his slightest, most involuntary action.[25]

In the end Valdez performs much the same service for Dino as the Princess performs for Hyacinth: he undertakes to free him from any further undertaking in the future. Valdez declares:

> 'I've been to see the head man of the committee since I came up here, and I've settled one thing for you, — after tomorrow your name gets struck off the books . . . It was I who brought you into this thing at the beginning. And I made a mistake. You're not fit for it. But you've never reproached me with what it costs you, my lad; never once.'[26]

The story, unlike James's *Princess*, ends happily, for the pistol is never handed to Dino, so that he is in no way involved in the investigation which follows the failure of the plot, and can return home to live happily ever after. There are certainly a number of parallels between the situations in which Dino and Hyacinth find themselves but James's subtlety of treatment is altogether lacking in Fleming. The central theme of both novels, as of a number of others, is the evil which follows an unconditional pledge to a subversive movement, however generously given. James may have read *Vestigia* in the year following its publication and before setting to work on his own conspiracy novel, but it is quite possible that the two authors, having decided independently on the pledge theme, developed it autonomously along the same lines, the lines which had been laid down for them by earlier novels, and which press reports of actual plots and of the behaviour of actual plotters reinforced. Fleming, like James, may have been influenced by reports of the Rupsch-Reinsdorf attempt on the life of the German Emperor, although James, writing after the trial of the conspirators, had more material from which to document his work.

Yet another novel concerned with Italian plotters is F. Marion Crawford's *Marzio's Crucifix*. This also is set in Rome and is the story of Maestro Marzio Pandolfi, a skilled metal worker and member of an anarchist group. Most of the plot is concerned with the vicissitudes of the courtship of Marzio's daughter by Giambattista, the virtuous apprentice. Marzio favours another lover. The plotting that goes on in the novel is mostly of an amorous nature, but

Marzio's teaching is clearly subversive: "'You must begin by knocking down, boy, if you want to build up. You must knock down everything, raze the existing system to the ground, and upon the place where it stood shall rise the mighty temple of immortal liberty.'"[27] Naturally such a man looks favourably upon Gasparo Carnesecchi as suitor for his daughter's hand. Of Gasparo we are told (but the words are those of a priest, so we must allow for bias) that he 'represented the devil in person', and the priest goes on to meditate:

> He was known to be an advanced freethinker, a radical, and, perhaps, worse than a radical — a socialist. He was certainly not very rich, and Lucia's dowry would be an object to him; he would doubtless spend the last copper of the money in attempting to be elected to the Chambers. If he succeeded, he would represent another unit in that ill-guided minority which has for its sole end the subversion of the existing state of things.[28]

The author also pauses to reflect on the meaning of the term 'socialist' and his conclusions confirm the socialist = anarchist = dynamiter equation to be met with so often:

> In Germany it [socialist] means an ingenious individual of restricted financial resources, who generally fails to blow up some important personage with wet dynamite. In Italy a socialist is an anarchist pure and simple, who wishes to destroy everything existing for the sake of dividing a wealth which does not exist at all.[29]

It is significant that the image of the dynamiter which presents itself to Crawford's mind is that of a German chemist, the manipulator of a peccant engine.

In *Mademoiselle Ixe* Lanoe Falconer introduces another stock figure, the sympathetic Nihilist. Mademoiselle Ixe is employed as a governess by the Merrington family, and if the story has a moral it must surely point to the wisdom of doublechecking all governesses' references. For Mademoiselle Ixe not only shoots a guest of her employer's, a mysterious count; she also uses bible stories for the purpose of propaganda when teaching the children:

[Evelyn] 'I hate Jael.'
   'Why do you hate her?' asked Mlle Ixe.
   'Because she killed Sisera in such a mean way.'
   'Perhaps it was the only way in which she could kill him.'
   'Why should she kill him at all?'
   'Because he was the enemy of her people.'[30]

The governess's appearance reflects, as so often in these novels, the ambiguity of the author's approach to his subject. At first sight we are presented with 'a very dark and repellent face, in which various types were blended — a face with long Eastern eyes and a protruding animal jaw . . .' This is the same animal element which Fawcett stressed in *Hartmann the Anarchist* and Mallock in *The Old Order Changes*. Yet just before Mlle Ixe goes down to commit the murder Evelyn observes her looking at baby Winifred '. . . and she sees Mlle Ixe's changeful face as she best loves to remember it, with a downward gaze, mild and benignant as that of a Madonna'. These two impressions of the same woman (and we have to bear in mind that the madonna image is invariably used of the *good* woman in romantic and Victorian literature) show, better than any amount of comment could do, how the author is hesitating between two interpretations of the Nihilist — hatred of her crime but sympathy with her cause. After the shooting, which fails to kill the Count, Mlle Ixe attempts to justify her action to her employer:

'. . . he is the enemy of my people, and of humanity, too. Ah! if you knew all that he has inflicted on innocent men, and even women, you would shudder to eat at the same table with him. He has been tried and judged by his fellow-creatures; I would have been his executioner.'
   'This is all very fine,' said Mr Merrington. 'But in England, Mademoiselle, we call this sort of thing murder, and we hang people for it.'
   'In England you are quite right,' said Mlle Ixe, composedly. 'In England you have a law which protects and avenges you. In our country it is not so. Our law is the will of our tyrants, we must avenge ourselves.'[31]

It is only at the end of the story that we learn that Mlle Ixe is a native of Russia. Evelyn, the eldest of her pupils, has helped her to escape after the shooting, but the sympathy of Lanoe Falconer, while saving her from the English gallows, cannot stretch so far as to let her crime go unpunished, so the tale ends with a letter received by Evelyn from a Russian prison. In this letter Mlle Ixe tells her story, revealing that she was a Russian aristocrat who became a Nihilist to help the oppressed. The whole novel, which is very short and simple, is remarkable for its lack of corroborative detail: what comes across to the reader is only a general impression, but it is an impression that is significant, and is to be found in this tale in its most elementary form — an impression that Nihilists may do very shocking things, such as shooting your guests in your own house, but that they are driven to it by terrible injustices way back home in Russia.

Compton Reade's *Who Was then the Gentleman?* (1885) is a long novel with a very mixed-up plot involving two distinct dynamite explosions, one in America staged by the Irish miners, the material of which is derived from reports of the activities of the Molly McGuires, and one in England for a question of personal revenge, described as a 'Hibernian *vendetta*'. The dynamiters are Irish, Conolly and Frayney, and the reader is constantly reminded of the fact because their dialogue is transcribed as a broad brogue. For example when Conolly suggests to Frayney to blow up the mine at a moment when all the Yankee miners are working down it, Frayney replies: '"They'll niver expect us to have the owdacity to blaze the whole caboose wid the hands about her. Bee the holy Moses, Mick, but the mother as bore you must have been a foine woman intoirely.'[32] The villains are Errol, a younger son of Sir Robert Marmyon, who dabbles in vivisection, and a trade union leader, Flaymar, who dabbles in dynamite. They are assisted by Dr Lembic, a scientist, and by the Irish dynamiters who had operated so success-fully in America. The very far-fetched plot turns on the substitution of two babies and the question of who is the legitimate heir to the Marmyon estates.

The real heir, Robert Hodge, the victim of the exchange, is brought up as a country labourer, and listens to the doctrines of Flaymar, the secretary of the union. Comic names are used here for the purpose of discrediting the activists: the leader is Hercules Flaymar, of the Central Democratic Leverage Union, and he is assisted by a solicitor Mr Ferretman, articled in the office of Bugglins and Flease. Robert for a while militates in this movement, and even speaks out at a union meeting on the rights of labourers, denouncing landlords and clamouring for political rights. The author's comment is explicit:

. . . unless the political agitators chose to employ dynamite, there was not much chance of the repose of the Court being disturbed. Nevertheless, the autocratic baronet felt himself considerably aggrieved by a meeting of this character being held within the limits of his demesne, and he was particularly annoyed to learn that this outbreak of the communistic spirit, as he euphemistically put it, followed so fast on the heels of Father l'Isle's mission . . . 'They came here to excite my people against me, to preach local sedition, to disrupt the sacred bonds which bind society together and safeguard the rights of property.'[33]

In the third volume the hero is converted from radicalism to ritualism: '"As Father l'Isle puts it, time was when I desired the greatest happiness of the greatest number in this life. Now, I add to that desire the still more earnest wish for the greatest happiness of the greatest number in the next."'[34]

A final chapter called 'Epilogue' settles the whole social question to the author's complete satisfaction. The idea of redistribution, which is seen in terms of the *Temple Bar* article from which I quote in Chapter seven, is rejected in favour of paternalistic liberalism. Robert Hodge, now acknowledged as Robert Marmyon, turns his village from 'one of the saddest to the very happiest and most prosperous in the shire':

A year ago, if he had inherited then, and with the ideas he then held as articles of belief, he would have simply cut up the estate into so many portions, and divided them equally among the labouring men. Experience, practical and religious, had toned down that idea, while it had elevated his own appreciation of the responsibility of ownership. But, while he had ceased to be a Communist, he was none the less a Liberal of Liberals. Every cottage on the estate was enlarged or improved . . .[35]

The dynamite explosions, though considerable space is given to them, are not really essential to the economy of the novel. The whole American episode serves to fill up one of the three volumes, but gets us no nearer solving the question of the inheritance. It allows the author, however, to hold forth directly to the reader on the way in which the Irish should be treated, and he comes down in favour of 'the law of Judge Lynch':

Those who on this side of the ocean contend that the Irish, on account of their excellence of disposition and conspicuous virtues should be condoned such temporary ebullitions of temper as may result in assassination, incendiarism, or any other form of outrage, including the reckless abuse of the potentiality placed at the disposal of every scoundrel in Europe by the invention of nitro-glycerine, would not meet with many sympathizers in the United States. Our American cousins, for their own reasons, utilize readily enough Hibernian malice when it happens to be directed against England and the English; but when that same ugly quality affects their own lives and limbs they never pause to parley.[36]

Compton Reade is here picking up newspaper criticism of America for harbouring the enemies of England, and he shows that the Yankees were very intolerant of such dynamite activity on their own soil:

. . . Such a roar went up to high heaven as seemed to proclaim the dissolution of this planet, while the crashing glass in the windows told its own tale; indeed the very tumblers they had been drinking out of fell to pieces spontaneously, while the din caused the drums of their ears to whizz, and almost stunned them.
'In the name of horror,' cried Dolopy . . . 'That's not the noise of revolvers!'
'It is not, Sir,' groaned the judge, his face deadly pale. 'It is not, sir. That, sir, is the sound of mater'l called dynamite. Those darned Irish have blown up the mine . . .'
. . . 'They have blown up the mine,' replied Dolopy, 'and we're off to enjoy the spectacle of the Irish being exterminated.'[37]

Lest any of his readers should miss his anti-Irish message Compton Reade dots his i's very decidedly in the third volume:

. . . This is a digression, but the purpose of this narrative would fail, if its moral were in any item obscured. The Irish ought to be forced by the public opinion of the civilized world to own the justice, and the tender regard for individual life and liberty, of the people whom they hate, revile, slander, and crave to injure.[38]

These words suggest that Reade believed that he was writing a committed novel, yet it is impossible to take seriously the mixture of themes and motives which he jumbles together so inextricably. His villains, whether dynamiters or vivisectors (and Errol is both) are granted no saving graces. No gleam of patriotism inspires his Irish plotters, who kill for the sake of killing: 'Beedad no; and d'ye think now that we'd be arbithrated upon? Not h'woile there's a bull't or a knoife to be handled . . . Give yer own vordict, man, in your own case, and ye'll never be in the wrong.'[39]

The vivisectors likewise take a grisly satisfaction in their work, their interest being sensual rather than scientific. This seems to be the message conveyed in the following passage, though the author contradicts himself (not for the first or the last time):

> Both relished cruelty, and were endowed with that extra lust which impelled them to enjoy their bent to the utmost . . . He [Dr Lembic] was, indeed, rather a philosopher and a student than a sensualist, and his sublimest pleasure was the low moan of a gagged dog as the knife first lay bare its quivering flesh. He cherished an ambition, however, of a yet keener gratification, when he should be able — he knew not how, to dissect little by little, and without anaesthetics, some members of the human species.[40]

This is an odd definition of a scholar and student, but Reade is paving the way, however clumsily, for Wells's *The Island of Doctor Moreau* ten years later. The perversion motif is used humorously in a comment on one of the female characters: 'Miss Ida is as lovely a piece of goods as I've seen for many a long year; in fact, I should like to vivisect her', and seriously in a comment by the vivisector on hospital experimentation:

> 'Of course, in the hospitals we have virtually *carte blanche*, and use it to the utmost of our ability; but here, as elsewhere, we are bound by the cords of prejudice. For instance, a man is brought in, some one of those tough labouring men, that make excellent subjects for experiments. Well, we've got him there, and if it wasn't for a set of nursing sisters, and people who are half-hearted, we might use him as you and I use a dog. Instead of that, we are perforce compelled to confine our experiments to the part affected — whatever it may be, and to effect a perfectly unnecessary cure.'[41]

The press campaign which publicised the Oxford anti-vivisection movement in the spring of 1885 probably gave the author the idea of Dr Lembic, but the combination in the same novel of vivisector and dynamiter, two forms of de-humanised scientific experimenter, is indicative of a growing tendency to ask where applied science was leading.

The second dynamite outrage, which takes place in the penultimate chapter of the third volume, serves no practical purpose except to show that the villains are villains indeed, and to entertain the reader with details of the explosion at Marmyon Court. It is a wonderful piece of bad writing, the work of an author hurrying to the end of a novel which he, like the reader, feels to be too long. In the same passage we learn that 'their calculation was erroneous' and that the infernal machine 'was timed too accurately to deal destruction at a certain fixed minute with unerring punctuality'; its sound 'tick-tick-tick' reminds the hearer of a watch that had *not* been wound up; the heir, when dragged out of the wreckage, is 'one mass of contusions and *scars*' but is also described as 'streaming with blood from flesh wounds', and the noise of the explosion is truly extraordinary: 'a crash, as it were, of the Archangels' trump which awoke every sleeper with an electric shock, seismic in its intensity'. Most of the novels I have been referring to in this book are remarkably well written, considering the speed of composition required from the author of a popular book. But this lengthy screed of Compton Reade's errs not so much in grammar as in logic, a flaw which seriously affects not only the single paragraph but the structure of the plot.

Perhaps the palm for unreadability should go to the three volumes of *The New Antigone* (1887) published anonymously but attributed to W. F. Barry, where the plot structure is equally unsatisfactory, but where the reader is borne down at the same time under a weight of pedantic classical quotations, for *The New Antigone* sets out to be a very serious novel indeed. The names of the characters are also discouraging: Ivor Mardol, Rupert Glenville and Hippolyta Valence are hardly the people one would expect to find mixed up with dynamiters.

An anarchist society, run by a duke, is motivated by no patriotic or idealistic purpose — the members, having savoured all the most refined pleasures of this world, have nothing more to hope for and are trying to get a last kick out of life. One wonders whether the eminently respectable author (the extent of classical quotation suggests a clergyman or schoolmaster) was aware that this was one of the basic motivations underlying the plot-structures of contemporary pornographic novels. In both cases the absurdities soon become apparent. Why a group of serious working men should sit and listen to Colonel Valence, the dynamitard and associate of the Duke of Abdullum who had 'sounded the most unfathomable depths of refined and cultured vice', is a mystery, but the author meretriciously tried to lend credibility to these aristocratic dynamiters by implying that the Duke and the Colonel were directly concerned in the assassination of the Czar, using a historical event which had taken place six years earlier to nobilitate fictitious characters. He also places some of the guilt for this assassination on a moderate socialist, Ivor Mardol, insofar as he is given a foreknowledge of the plot:

> [Ivor speaking] 'They have done it at last.'
> 'Done what?' said the artist.
> At that moment he caught the announcement distinctly which was filling the air, and he heard the words, again and again,
> 'Assassination of the Emperor of Russia.'
> He started in his seat, and tried in the gloom to make out his companion's face, but could not.
> 'Ivor, Ivor', he cried, 'did you know this was going to happen? Tell me, for God's sake.'
> 'Don't ask me what I know,' returned Ivor; 'it is unspeakable, appalling.'[42]

Rupert Glenville, the artist hero who spends the last volume searching for Hippolyta his lost love and the daughter of an anarchist leader, is interrogated by the Duke in a chapter entitled 'Anarchy in Purple' to learn his reasons for wishing to join the conspirators, and is told: '"There is, or has been, in the life of each one here — and of those outside who belong to us — a personal reason why he should despair of the society that has made him what he is."'[43] This is linked with the usual warning of the irrevocability of membership: '"You must now realise that our band is not so easily put on, and that it never can be taken off."' There may be a recollection of Henry James's Hyacinth in the scene where Rupert, the hero, imagines himself a suicide:

> He saw himself lying on the floor of his dressing-room, shot through the heart, a pistol lying at his right hand. There was a

gloomy fascination in imagining the look of deadly calm on his face, the attitude of his limbs as he lay where he had fallen, the disorder in the room, and the silence brooding over it.[44]

Instead Barry's plot calls for a much less credible unravelling. All the leading characters remove from England to a Spanish convent where Hippolyta is to be found. After some extremely melodramatic recognition scenes and an attempted suicide, Mardol is drowned, Hippolyta takes the veil and her father is persuaded to drop his anti-social activities.

There is much talk of dynamite among the anarchists, but apart from the assassination of the Czar, which only an extremely unsophisticated reader would be inclined to credit them with, it all comes to nothing. The argument against violence is entrusted to Mardol, the moderate socialist, who pleads in favour of propaganda as more potent than explosions:

'Do you believe that Voltaire or Goethe would have countenanced regicide while the printing-press remained? Would Rousseau have taught Émile the Gospel of dynamite? Is Victor Hugo a mere and sheer anarchist? . . . You decree the destruction of the innocent, the blowing-up of cities, the plunder of the poor by your howling rabble . . . The Revolution means liberty and light. It means equality in the best things, the only things worth having — love and justice and truth. It means reason, not dynamite.'[45]

The case for the opposition, the dynamite party, is put by Colonel Valence, but we should not lose sight of the fact that it is he who is converted at the end of the novel:

'I thought the struggle was for light. I see it is for bread. Look out in the streets tonight and consider the faces that pass. Beyond these walls,' his voice sank lower, but it was wonderfully clear throughout, 'lies the anarchy of London. Rags, hunger, nakedness, tears, filth, incest, squalor, decay, disease, the human lazarhouse, the black death eating its victims piecemeal, that is threefourths of the London lying at these doors. Whose care is it? Nay, who cares for it? The piles of the royal palace are laid deep in a lake of blood. And you will leave it standing? You talk of light; you prefer sentiment to dynamite and assassination!'[46]

As is usually the case in dynamite novels, anarchist meetings are attended by a number of foreigners, and it is one of these who delivers 'a sermon, in well-chosen language and with apposite illustrations, on the text of dynamite. A stern gospel, which the fanatic standing before them clearly believed in'. The passages just quoted, both for vocabulary — 'sermon', 'gospel', 'lazar-house', 'nay' — and style, with the piling up of rhetorical questions, deepen the impression that the author must have been a clergyman. Although he is writing a dramatic romance rather than a dynamite novel proper, Barry has picked up enough of the debate on the social question to involve his artist marginally in a conspiracy. Valence's argument in favour of the use of dynamite is the oppression of the poor, and this brings Barry's basic reasoning (setting aside the decadent duke and his intimates as merely trimmings) into line with the Establishment press, confusing social protest with dynamite outrages.

The opening paragraph of Marie Corelli's *The Sorrows of Satan*, which probably sold more copies in its day than all the other novels mentioned in this book added together, makes exactly the same point:

> Do you know what it is to be poor? . . . This is the grinding curse that keeps down noble aspiration under a load of ignoble care; this is the moral cancer that eats into the heart of an otherwise well-intentioned human creature and makes him envious and malignant, and inclined to the use of dynamite.[47]

This message, written right at the end of the century by the most popular of popular novelists, seems to me to be an appropriate conclusion, summing up as it does the development and the limitations of the Victorian social conscience by presenting the reader once more with the familiar equation that social protest and terrorism were synonymous. This book may, I hope, exemplify the mechanisms by which such an equation came in the nineteenth century to be so generally accepted, and may even lead us to question the basis of some of the assumptions held and upheld with like conviction today.

Notes

1. Matilda Betham-Edwards *The Flower of Doom or The Conspirator*, *All the Year Round* (March-May 1885), p. 26.

2. Ibid., p. 29.

3. Ibid., p. 50.

4. Ibid., p. 52.

5. Ibid., p. 50.

6. Ibid., p. 122.

7. Ibid., p. 123.

8. Ibid,.., p. 149.

9. E. Lynn Linton, *The Autobiography of Christopher Kirkland*, three vols. (London, 1885), Vol. 3, p. 46.

10. Grant Allen, *For Maimie's Sake: A Tale of Love and Dynamite* (London, 1886), p. 24.

11. Ibid., p. 25.

12. Ibid.

13. Ibid.

14. Ibid., p. 234.

15. Ibid., p. 251. Sergeant Cuff in Wilkie Collins's *The Moonstone* (1868) was a forerunner with whom Grant Allen, though no great reader, may well have been familiar.

16. Ibid., p. 215.

17. Hugh Conway (pseudonym of Frederick John Fargus), *Called Back* (Bristol, 1884), p. 130.

18. Ibid., pp. 187-8.

19. Ibid., pp. 209-10.

20. Ibid., pp. 257-8.

21. George Fleming, *Vestigia*, two vols. (London, Edinburgh, 1884), Vol. 1, p. 129.

22. Ibid., Vol. 1, p. 132.

23. Ibid., Vol. 1, p. 176.

24. Ibid., Vol. 1, p. 193.

25. Ibid., Vol. 2, p. 71-2.

26. Ibid., Vol. 2, pp. 227-8.

27. F. Marion Crawford, *Marzio's Crucifix*, two vols. (London, 1887), Vol. 1, p. 24.

28. Ibid., Vol. 1, pp. 218-19.

29. Ibid., Vol. 1, p. 219.

30. Lanoe Falconer (pseudonym of Marie Elizabeth Hawker), *Mademoiselle Ixe* (London, 1891), p. 127.

31. Ibid., p. 161.

32. Compton Reade, *Who Was then the Gentleman?*, three vols. (London, 1885), Vol. 3, p. 65.

33. Ibid., Vol. 1, p. 120.

34. Ibid., Vol. 3, p. 246.

35. Ibid., Vol. 3, p. 324.

36. Ibid., Vol. 3, p. 101.

37. Ibid., Vol. 3, p. 97.

38. Ibid., Vol. 3, p. 103.

39. Ibid., Vol. 3, p. 11.

40. Ibid., Vol. 1, p. 146.

41. Ibid., Vol. 1, p. 147. The same vivisector = dynamitard equation was made

some years later by George Bernard Shaw when in 1900 he delivered a lecture to the London Anti-vivisection Society entitled 'The Dynamitards of Science'.

42. W. F. Barry, *The New Antigone*, three vols. (London, 1887), Vol. 3, p. 158.
43. Ibid., Vol. 3, p. 145.
44. Ibid., Vol. 3, p. 165.
45. Ibid., Vol. 3, pp. 172-4.
46. Ibid., Vol. 3, p. 176.
47. Marie Corelli, *The Sorrows of Satan* (London, 1895), p. 1.

SELECT BIBLIOGRAPHY

Allen, Grant *For Maimie's Sake: A Tale of Love and Dynamite* (Chatto & Windus, London, 1886)
—— (pseud. Cecil Power) *Philistia*, 3 vols (Chatto & Windus, London, 1884)
Barlas, John E. *Holy of Holies. Confessions of an Anarchist* (J.H. Clarke, Chelmsford, 1887)
—— *Phantasmagoria* (J.H. Clarke, Chelmsford, 1887)
Barry, W.F. *The New Antigone*, 3 vols (Macmillan, London, 1887)
Bellamy, Edward *Looking Backward — if Socialism comes. 2000–1887* (Ticknor, Boston, 1888)
Besant, Walter *Children of Gibeon*, 3 vols. (Chatto & Windus, London, 1886)
Betham-Edwards, Matilda 'The Flower of Doom or The Conspirator', *All the Year Round*, March–May 1885
Buchanan, Robert William *The Coming Terror: A dialogue between Alienatus, a Provincial and Urbanus, a Cockney* (Heinemann, London, 1891)
Burnaby, Fred *Our Radicals: a tale of love and politics*. Edited, with preface, by J. Percival Hughes. 2 vols. (R. Bentley & Son, London, 1886)
Conrad, Joseph *The Secret Agent, A simple tale* (Methuen, London, 1907)
—— *A Set of Six* including 'The Anarchist' and 'The Informer' (Methuen, London, 1908)
Conway, Hugh (Fargus, Frederick John) *Called Back* (J.W. Arrowsmith, Bristol, 1884)
Corelli, Marie *The Sorrows of Satan or the Strange experience of one Geoffrey Tempest, millionaire. A romance* (Methuen, London, 1895)
Crawford F. Marion *Marzio's Crucifix*, 2 vols. (Macmillan, London, 1887)
Doyle, Arthur Conan *A Study in Scarlet* (Ward Lock & Co., London, 1888); first appeared in *Beeton's Christmas Annual*, 1887
Eden, Charles Henry *George Donnington, or In the Bear's Grip*, 3 vols. (Chapman & Hall, London, 1885)
Ex-M.P. *A Radical Nightmare, or England Forty Years Hence* (Field & Tuer, London, 1885)
Falconer, Lanoe (Hawker, Marie Elizabeth), *Mademoiselle Ixe* (T. Fisher Unwin, London, 1891)
Fawcett, E. Douglas *Hartmann the Anarchist; or, the doom of the great city* (E. Arnold, London, 1893)
Fleming, George *Vestigia*, 2 vols (Macmillan, London & Edinburgh, 1884)
Gissing, George *Demos: a story of English Socialism*, 3 vols (Smith, Elder & Co., London, 1886)
Gleig, Charles *When All Men Starve* (J. Lane, London & New York, 1897)
Greer, Tom *A Modern Daedalus* (Griffith & Co., London & Edinburgh, 1886)
Griffith, George Chetwynd *The Angel of the Revolution: a tale of the coming terror* (Tower, London, 1893)
Hatton, Joseph *By Order of the Czar. The tragic story of Anna Klosstock, Queen of the Ghetto*, 3 vols (Hutchinson, London, 1890)
—— *By Order of the Czar*. A Drama in Five Acts (Hutchinson, London, 1904)
James, Henry *A Little Tour in France* (J.R. Osgood, Boston, 1884)
—— *The Princess Casamassima*, 3 vols (Macmillan, London & New York, 1886)
Jenkins, Edward *A Week of Passion*, 3 vols (Remington & Co., London, 1884)

Select Bibliography

Lee, Thomas *Falsivir's Travels. The remarkable adventures of J. Falsivir . . . at the North Pole and in the interior of the Earth* (pr. pub, London, 1886)

Lee, Vernon (Paget, Violet) *Miss Brown*, 3 vols (W. Blackwood & Sons, Edinburgh & London, 1884)

Lynn Linton, Eliza *The Autobiography of Christopher Kirkland*, 3 vols (Bentley & Son, London, 1885)

MacKay, Donald *The Dynamite Ship* (Page, Pratt & Turner, London & New York, 1888)

Mallock, William Hurrell *The Old Order Changes*, 3 vols (Bentley & Son, London, 1886)

May, Philip *Love, the Reward*, 3 vols (Remington & Co., London, 1885)

Minto, William *The Crack of Doom*, 3 vols (W. Blackwood & Sons, Edinburgh & London, 1886)

Moore, George *A Drama in Muslin* (Vizetelly & Co., London, 1886)

Ouida (de la Ramée, Marie Louise) *Princess Napraxine*, 3 vols (Chatto & Windus, London, 1884)

Reade, Compton *Who was then the Gentleman?*, 3 vols (J. & R. Maxwell, London, 1885)

Ropes, Arthur Reed & Mary Emily *On Peter's Island* (John Murray, London, 1901)

Shaw, George Bernard *The Impossibilities of Anarchism* (Fabian Tracts no. 45, London, 1893)

—— *The Irrational Knot* (Constable, London, 1905); first appeared in *Our Corner*, 1885–7

—— *An Unsocial Socialist* (Swan, Sonnenschein & Co., London, 1887); first appeared in *Today*, 1884

Stevenson, Robert Louis & Fanny Van de Grift Stevenson *More New Arabian Nights. The Dynamiter* (Longmans, London, 1885)

Trollope, Anthony *The Land leaguerers*, 3 vols (Chatto & Windus, London, 1883)

Victoria (Queen) *The Letters of Queen Victoria*. Second series . . . Edited by George Earle Buckle (John Murray, London, 1926)

Whiteing, Richard *Number 5 John Street* (Grant Richards, London, 1899)

Wilde, Oscar *Vera: or, the Nihilists* (privately printed, 1882)

INDEX